HOUSING CRISIS U.S.A.

Joseph P. Fried was born and raised in New York. While still a student at Columbia University, he began working for *The New York Times*. His first assignment as a *Times* reporter was in the real estate news department in the late 1960's, a job he calls "an intensive and invaluable course in one of the basic failures of American society." In addition to *Housing Crisis U.S.A.*, Mr. Fried has written articles on urban affairs and other subjects for popular and historical magazines. His wife, Randy, is a school teacher in New York, and he has a daughter, Susan.

Joseph P. Fried

HOUSING CRISIS U.S.A.

Foreword by John V. Lindsay

Penguin Books Inc
Baltimore · Maryland

Penguin Books Inc
7110 Ambassador Road
Baltimore, Maryland 21207, U.S.A.

First published by Praeger Publishers, Inc. 1971
Published in Penguin Books 1972

Copyright © Praeger Publishers, Inc., 1971

Printed in the United States of America by
Kingsport Press, Inc., Kingsport, Tennessee 37662

To

SUZY AND RANDY

Contents

Foreword

A common game among children when I was a child was to select a familiar word or phrase and rapidly repeat it over and over until it lost all meaning and was reduced to a hilarious cacophony of syllables.

And so it is with the nation's "housing crisis." We've been talking about it for so long that some of us now fail to grasp its meaning. Unlike the children's game, however, the results aren't a bit amusing.

What does the failure comprise? A lot of things, and there has perhaps never been a more vivid and comprehensive catalogue of the sorry tale than what Joe Fried presents in this book:

- The failure of government at the national level to place decent housing high on its priority list
- The failure of state and local government to create atmospheres conducive to speedy new construction
- A social climate in some areas that seeks to perpetuate segregated housing patterns
- Soaring construction costs, placing the bulk of new private housing beyond the grasp of most Americans

All of these factors are chronicled here with almost depressing precision. In New York, we've done better than many on some problems, and we find ourselves struggling unsuccessfully with others.

Last year, we set a record by starting construction on close to eighteen thousand units of city-assisted low- and middle-income housing; yet our housing vacancy rate continues to struggle to get above the 1 per cent level.

We have one of the largest, most efficient public housing authorities in the world; yet our public housing stock, even if 100 per cent vacant, could not accommodate all of the eligible families waiting to move out of deteriorating or temporary housing.

We have systems of rent control and rent stabilization to keep rentals within the reach of the middle class, but relentless forces continue their campaign to leave tenants once again at the mercy of market rentals—in a market where vacancies are virtually nonexistent.

We have spent millions of dollars to rehabilitate deteriorating structures in many of our declining neighborhoods; yet more owners than we can possibly help are walking away from their properties because much of our housing is simply becoming too expensive for the private sector to maintain unassisted.

The list is endless. What is the answer? A complex and elusive one, of course, to a highly complex and elusive problem. But it is clear that the principal cure rests not in the cities across the nation fighting for fiscal survival, nor even with the state governments fighting among themselves for adequate shares of federal revenue. The resources to combat the problem of housing shortage and blight are available only to the federal government.

Fitfully recognizing this responsibility, Congress and the appropriate federal agencies have developed, piecemeal, a bewildering and internally inconsistent series of laws, rules, and regulations, which often appear to have little purpose other than to inhibit states and localities from taking advantage of federal help. The combination of construction-cost limitations on each unit built, income limitations on eligible tenants, and percentage limitations on families eligible for subsidies has often succeeded in thwarting each of those programs. To simplify and coordinate federal housing programs should be among Washington's most immediate tasks.

But the most pressing problem of all—financing—has seen by far the greatest abdication of federal responsibility. One of the most consistent examples has been the failure of Congress to authorize sufficient mortgage interest subsidy funds—funds that, as Mr. Fried points out, spell the difference between housing for the affluent and housing for lower- and middle-income families. Aggravating this insensitivity has been the failure of Washington to fully utilize even those meager sums.

Thus, at this writing, the Administration has refused to request one-sixth of the total amount of the mortgage interest subsidies authorized by Congress. And New York City, which has the sites selected, the relocation plans ready, and the developers and sponsors chosen, could eat up all of this subsidy money itself. Added to the pressing needs of Chicago, Saint Louis, Boston, Los Angeles, and other urban centers across the nation, our plight serves to highlight Mr. Fried's "national failure."

The cities' long, lonely fight for fiscal survival is a sad story. And even sadder is the fact that it must be told again. Surely, the pressing need for new housing within the reach of the nation's poor and middle classes has been amply established. Surely, those who have been pointing out the facts of life concerning the state of housing in this country have made their case. Joe Fried has felt the need to make that case again. And, of course, he's right.

Too many Americans, paying too high a price for housing that is inadequate for their needs, await Washington's answer.

MAYOR JOHN V. LINDSAY
New York City, 1971

HOUSING CRISIS U.S.A.

This nation now has an overwhelming moral responsibility to achieve within the reasonably near future a decent home and a suitable living environment for every American family which it pledged itself to achieve 20 years ago.

—The National Commission on
Urban Problems *(1968)*

Despite all our fancy rhetoric we never have been really concerned about the problems of the poor. We've always permitted enormous suffering amidst affluence. It was true in the time of slavery, and it's true today.

—ARTHUR NAFTALIN, retiring
Mayor of Minneapolis *(1969)*

The housing shortage is an ugly rumor—circulated by people who have no place to live.

—HENRY MORGAN, comedian

1. Introduction to the Crisis

An Outing in Brownsville

On a muggy June day in 1968, a group of politicians, civic leaders, and newsmen picked their way through the garbage-littered streets of the squalid Brownsville section of Brooklyn. They were on a tour designed to provide a firsthand look at the wretched conditions of the area, one of the worst slums of New York City. Their particular concern that day was abandoned apartment buildings, the vacant and vandalized hulks that abounded in Brownsville, and some of the city's other black and Puerto Rican slums, lying like vulture-nibbled carcasses amid a herd of diseased and starving cattle. On the theory that not all the local residents would appreciate the concern manifested by the visit, the group was escorted by a contingent from the local police precinct.

As the visitors crunched over smashed glass on the sidewalk and squeezed between shells of abandoned and stripped automobiles at the curb, a city councilman decided it was time to begin publicizing the foulness around him—and, of course, his own presence on the tour. Positioning himself so that an especially decrepit building formed the backdrop for the television cameras, he began commenting on the surrounding scene with the kind of declamatory indignation guaranteed to get the cameras rolling and the microphones thrust into one's face on such outings. As the newsmen clustered about, he vowed to seek a full-scale, no-holds-barred city council investigation into the causes and cures of slum-building abandonment. The words, the tone, even the stance he assumed while delivering the promise were almost exactly the same as when the same councilman had vowed to seek the same kind of investigation during the same kind of tour two months before in the equally decayed South Bronx. When I noted this (I had been the only newspaper reporter to cover both trips) and asked why he was still promising to seek what he had promised to seek two months before, he muttered something about "the press of council business" and moved on.

By then the visitors had been confronted by a local militant who, with more than a little vehemence, was providing his view of the reasons for abandoned buildings and all the other scars of deprivation that had become synonymous with Brownsville in the 1960's.

"You want to know what caused this?" the black man asked the predominantly white group. "Ask the goddam landlords who cut down maintenance and services as soon as the first blacks and Puerto Ricans moved into the neighborhood. Ask the owners who let their buildings go to hell while putting every penny of the rent money into their pockets or the stock market. Ask the city officials who didn't give a shit, who let the owners collect their rents and milk the buildings till there was nothing left to squeeze out of them, and then it was goodby Brownsville. Ask *them,* man. Don't come around now, when it's too late."

As microphones and scrawling pencils recorded his words, a white official of a landlords' group who was accompanying the tour decided he had to speak up. "That's right, put it all on the landlord," he shouted at the local man. "Never mind that rent control in this city doesn't give landlords enough income to keep up their buildings. Never mind that some of these families break the place up and you have to go through hell and high water to evict them—and meanwhile you're getting hit with violations because of the damage they do. Never mind that you can drop dead begging and you still won't get a bank loan to fix up a building in a neighborhood like this. My friend, you don't *begin* to know why these buildings have been abandoned."

"Bullshit," the local man replied. While the two continued their unscheduled debate amid the filth of Strauss Street—one dressed in the rumpled T-shirt and dungarees he had been wearing when he had rushed out of his nearby apartment, the other in a well-tailored gray suit uncreased by the air-conditioned bus trip that had brought him to Brownsville—the other visitors began returning to the chartered buses. Several civic group officials and clergymen from more prosperous areas of the city were talking over what they had seen, and their tones clearly indicated that they were appalled by the extent of the squalor around them. "People are actually *living* in that building," one of them said, pointing to a tenement where a woman and a small child gazed with mild curiosity from a curtained window on the second floor. Most of the other windows in the crumbling four-story structure were smashed out, and the apartments behind them appeared scarred and vacant. In what had once been a store on the first floor, garbage was heaped in the display window as if shoveled in between the jagged edges of the shattered plate glass.

By this time a dozen or so neighborhood teenagers were trailing the group (whether they would have been doing more if there had been no police escort is uncertain) and making no secret of their belief that nothing would come of the visit. "They came to see the animals in the zoo and now they're going home," one youth sneered as the visitors boarded the buses and began opening box lunches to be eaten on the ride back to Manhattan.

That evening, with familiar feelings of depression and futility, I sat at my desk writing a story about the tour for my newspaper, *The New York Times.* In a year of writing about real estate and housing I had made many trips to Brownsville and the other slums of the nation's largest city. I had read government reports and academic studies making it clear that the wretched housing to be found in New York was amply repeated throughout the country: in the moldering, rat-ridden tenements of Chicago's Woodlawn and the rickety cabins and cottages in the dried-up gullies and coves of Appalachia, in the slum shanties of San Antonio and San Francisco, in the freezing hovels of the Oglala Sioux on their South

Dakota reservation and in the suffocating shacks of the migrant farm workers on the sun-baked flatlands of Collier County, Florida—in hundreds of cities and hamlets where dilapidated and deteriorated housing pocks the landscape of space-age America like craters on the moon.

And in still another year of covering real estate and housing news, I would make more trips to the slums and read more reports and studies, and I would learn that the posturing and empty promises of the local councilman before the cameras in Brownsville and the South Bronx were abundantly reflected at higher levels of government; that the debate between the slum-area militant and the landlords' spokesman, in shedding far more heat than light on the subject, was typical of much of the discussion of the plight and problems of housing in America; that the consternation over miserable housing felt by some of the visitors to Brownsville was shared by many decently housed Americans throughout the country, but that these appalled Americans were in a minority, while the majority of their countrymen were not appalled, or at any rate not enough to overcome the hostilities and fears that prevented the nation from doing what had to be done to solve its housing problems.

I would learn all this, and sometimes I would accept it as a fact of current life, to be greeted with the same hope of better days ahead as is a driving rainstorm on the afternoon of a long-planned picnic. But most of the time, as on the day of the trip to Brownsville, hope was washed aside by depression and a sense of futility.

A Reporter Learns

A year before that trip, when I had told a friend that my first assignment as a reporter would be in the real estate news department at the *Times*, he had shrugged his shoulders sympathetically and said, "Well, if nothing else, you'll be the first to hear about all the great apartment bargains."

His response was understandable. Real estate news was something less of a prospect than the Paris bureau or a beat at the White House. On the other hand, it was a reporting job in New York City—about as easy to come by in the late 1960's as an attractive and spacious Manhattan apartment at less than sky-high rent—and one took his opportunities where he found them.

As it turned out, two years on this beat were more than a first reporting job. They were an intensive and invaluable course in one of the basic failures of American society: the failure to provide for so fundamental a human need as decent shelter for millions of citizens in a nation that thumps its chest at having achieved "the greatest standard of living ever known to man." (So far as the "great apartment bargains" were concerned, the nation's housing crisis reached one of its most acute stages in New York City in the late 1960's, and if I was the first to hear about anything, it was the latest explanation for the conspicuous *rarity* of apartment bargains, great or otherwise.)

Actually, like many Americans, I had experienced some of the causes and effects of America's housing tribulations long before reaching working age. But at the time I had hardly comprehended these experiences for what they were—as is the case with most people.

For example, I grew up in the 1940's and 1950's in a neighborhood that was then on the fringe—but today is in the heart—of the Bedford-Stuyvesant section of Brooklyn. This is an area whose name, like Harlem, has become synonymous with massive concentrations of poor and ill-housed New York blacks, a section that, like many such districts throughout urban America, has expanded its boundaries in recent decades as suburban-bound whites have been extensively replaced in America's big cities by blacks, Puerto Ricans, and Mexican-Americans migrating from the nation's rural areas and its Caribbean possession.

Before beginning the change from all-white to all-black in the 1950's, my own block and the blocks immediately around were populated largely by Jewish, Italian, and Irish families, headed for the most part by blue-collar and low-level white-collar workers. They owned brownstones that had been built in the last years of the nineteenth century or occupied small apartment buildings dating from the early decades of the twentieth. As they were replaced by black and a few Puerto Rican families (the process began slowly, about 1953, and accelerated so that most of the transformation was complete by 1957), my block slowly but perceptibly deteriorated. Some of the buildings—the apartment houses like the one I lived in far more than the privately owned brownstones—became rundown. Garbage always seemed to pile higher than I had previously recalled before the sanitation trucks came around to swallow it up.

At the time, I had no other explanation for this than the one prevailing among the departing whites, teenagers like myself and their parents: The "coloreds" ("niggers") were responsible. When one asked why this was so, the answer, given sometimes bitterly, sometimes with resignation, was "because they're animals" or "because that's what *always* happens to the neighborhoods they move into." Some of the whites were willing to concede that "not all of them are like that," that the first black families that moved onto a white block were usually "of a better class." But they were inevitably followed in by "the lower-class ones," the argument went, and so any white had best start thinking of packing up and getting out when the moving van containing the furniture of the first black family pulled up. (The same applied to Puerto Ricans.)

It did not seem like a complete explanation, and it did not seem fair, but, as I noted, it was the only explanation I had at the time. It would be several years before I would learn why it was not complete and why it was not fair, something most of the kids I grew up with probably never learned and none of their parents ever learned.

And how do you put it to them? How do you convince people, who have closed their minds to all but their own narrow perspective, about such things as the self-fulfilling prophecies of landlords and mortgage lenders: how uncertainty over the future of racially and ethnically changing neighborhoods motivates apartment-house owners and bankers to cut back on the money they put into properties in these neighborhoods, thereby contributing as much to the decline they fear as do the living patterns of any new racial and ethnic groups? How do you convince my former neighbors that their old block and their old neighborhood were victims of a glaring distortion of national priorities that made, and still makes, American society unable to cope with social and economic needs stemming from profound technological and demographic changes—a distortion that has deprived poverty-stricken rural areas of resources for dealing with a decline in agricultural jobs that for a quarter of a century has sent masses of poor immigrants to the cities, a distortion that has also deprived the fiscally overwhelmed cities of resources with which to meet the needs of these newcomers while trying to maintain a decent level of such traditional services as garbage collection?

How do you, in short, convince my old neighbors that the political, economic, and sociopsychological realities of American life have a profound impact on the nation's housing, and on its neighborhoods, and that these realities provide a far more complete and much fairer explanation of why our old neighborhood deteriorated than the explanation that my former neighbors adamantly embrace?

In 1959, while a college student, I had another firsthand encounter with an aspect of America's housing problems whose full significance at first escaped me. I was employed as a relocation-needs interviewer in the first phase of one of the nation's major urban redevelopment efforts conceived in the 1950's, the West Side urban renewal project in Manhattan, designed to transform twenty badly blighted blocks into a new community of modern high-rise apartments and gracious brownstone living.

As I climbed the reeking stairways of the doomed, dank tenements on Columbus and Amsterdam avenues and squeezed into the cramped, dingy rooms of deteriorated "SRO's" (brownstones converted for single-room occupancy by entire families, sometimes with four or five people in a room); as I watched armies of cockroaches skitter past babies playing on splintered floors and float in stopped-up sinks and toilets, I had no doubt that the impending renewal was the best thing that could be happening to the people in these places, because anything they were relocated into would be a major improvement. The other interviewers, college students working part time like myself and young housewives from Greenwich Village, were of the same conviction. We all agreed that the only opposition to government-sponsored urban renewal in America could come from slumlords who grew fat on the profits they squeezed from hapless tenants such as these.

It would be several years before I would learn that there was good reason for nonslumlords to oppose urban renewal, or at least urban renewal as practiced under governmental sanction in this country for many years. As a newspaper reporter in the 1960's, I from time to time ran into families living in East Harlem, the South Bronx, and other New York slums who had been relocated there from the West Side urban renewal area. Only by the widest stretch of the imagination could their new surroundings be considered a meaningful improvement over their old ones, whatever some government bureaucrat might proclaim from the comfort of a well-upholstered office downtown.

Perspectives on urban renewal and on the relationships between housing and race, housing and fiscal patterns, and housing and a dozen other subjects were not the only things gained in my first reporting assignment. Among other lessons, I learned that although the United States Government has placed the number of inadequate housing units in the nation at the widely quoted figure of 6 million, the number is actually more like 11 million, or one out of every six housing units in the nation—and that even this is a crude and conservative estimate at best, because the society whose computerized technology has rocketed man to the lunar surface has been unable thus far to measure the quality of its housing in any but the most rudimentary way.*

I learned that, at a time when "the urban crisis" has become a sociological and journalistic catch phrase, there is a tendency among those preoccupied with big-city slums to forget that housing squalor lurks no less abundantly amid the magnolias and sycamores of what is supposed to be a purer America, with half and possibly more of the nation's substandard housing in rural areas.

I learned that the inability to afford decent housing is a greater affliction for the nation's blacks, Mexican-Americans, Puerto Ricans, and American Indians when measured in terms of their proportions of the American population, but that the majority of so-called "house-poor" families in the United States are still white families that are not of Latin-American origin.

* A housing unit is a single-family home, an apartment in a multifamily building, or a furnished room in a boarding house.

And I learned that although the poor and near-poor suffer most from the nation's shortcomings in housing, the effects of these shortcomings are hardly limited to these segments of the population. Growing numbers of middle-income Americans are also encountering difficulty in some areas in finding new housing acceptable by middle-class standards at prices within middle-class means.

But I was getting paid not simply to learn, but to pass along to the readers of my newspaper the information I was picking up. As a reporter assigned to a specific subject area, I had a good deal of freedom in choosing the stories I wrote. There were, of course, events and developments involving real estate and housing that the editors wanted covered for the next morning's paper (the Brownsville tour is an example), but at least half my time was spent on articles that I initiated myself—articles about aspects of the subject that were brought to my attention by individuals and groups active in housing affairs or by readers in letters and telephone calls, and articles about aspects that I simply was curious to learn more about.

An example of the latter: In 1966, before I had become a reporter, a bevy of city officials had been quick to express indignation and vow to seek reform when the plight became known of a dozen Puerto Rican families whose new homes were sinking into the Bronx bog on which they had been built. The families had bought the houses after having struggled and saved for years to escape from slum areas. Within months, the descent into the bog had begun and giant cracks had developed in the brick walls. In 1966 the structures were declared unsafe by the city and ordered demolished. An inquiry by the city's buildings department had found that the piles on which the foundations had rested had not been driven deeply enough and that the engineer hired by the builder to supervise the pile-driving had left much of the responsibility to a twenty-two-year-old assistant. The homeowners had won a court judgment against the builder, but by then he had gone bankrupt. Suits charging the buildings department with negligence in inspecting the construction had been dismissed by the court. Thus the families had lost all the hard-earned money they had put into the houses.

When their situation was publicized in 1966, a shower of rhetoric about the callous victimization of minority groups streamed from political and bureaucratic mouths, accompanied by promises to seek legislation and more buildings department manpower to prevent the same thing from happening again. The matter then disappeared from the news pages.

I had read about this at the time, and two years later was reminded of it as I came across the 1966 articles while doing research on another story. What in fact *had* come of the indignation and proposals for reform of two years before? I wondered. Several phone calls established that nothing had. There were still no city or state requirements for builders' warranties or other forms of surety to cover losses to homeowners caused by defective construction. The procedure under which the competence of engineers and architects was policed by the state was as snail-paced and complex as ever; in fact, charges against the engineer in the Bronx case were "still pending." Proposals for increasing the undermanned plan-examining and field-inspection ranks of the buildings department had also fallen by the wayside, squashed by the usual budgetary squeeze, thus negating the effect of some of the procedural changes ordered by the department as a result of the Bronx experience.

It was a case where no news was *the* news, an example of the kind of news that is pursued much less frequently than it should be by the nation's newsmen (myself included; lest I seem self-righteous, I should note that I have been as guilty as anyone of "following up" stories far more in intention than in actuality). The quiet interment of all the proposals for reform was recounted under the headline, "Aftermath of Sinking Homes in Bronx: Preventive Measures Bog Down, Too."

The story is illustrative for another reason: It stimulated a sizable volume of mail. When one regularly writes for a large-circulation newspaper about such a bread-and-butter subject as housing, he quickly finds himself the recipient of a steady flow of letters from readers. When, as with housing, the subject is closely bound up with matters of race, and when the locale is New York City, where tenants and landlords are locked in what at times appears to be full-scale warfare, the flow not infrequently crests in a wave.

Occasionally the letters offer praise for bringing to public attention an issue that the letter-writer has long been bothered by or wondering about. More often the communications are critical; sometimes rationally so, sometimes with reason accompanied by a good dose of heartfelt emotion, and once in a while with such an outpouring of venom that one can only shiver. In the last category I would include the eight pages of single-spaced typewritten ranting I received from an anonymous advocate of a final solution for New York's welfare problems: resettlement of the city's welfare recipients "and all those likely to go on welfare" in Antarctica. This advice was offered, along with a batch of other heated commentary on both sides of the issue, in response to a 1968 article about an unsuccessful campaign by civil rights and community action groups in New York to gain city and state legislation that would have made it illegal to refuse to rent apartments to families because they were on welfare.

The daily mail also brought (as it usually does to a reporter specializing in a subject) an abundance of news releases from government agencies and nongovernmental organizations. In my case the "handouts" were from federal, state, and city housing and renewal agencies, from associations representing builders, landlords, and tenants, from civil rights groups advancing the interests of specific minorities, and from civic-betterment organizations advancing what they professed to be the total public interest. Although the bulk of each day's handouts was readily discarded chaff, there was always something of news value—either immediately so ("hard news" items such as announcements by public agencies of new programs or policies and announcements by private groups of campaigns or court actions) or germinally so (items of little importance by themselves but indicating larger developments or trends worthy of public attention and of the time and effort needed to investigate and write about them).

At this point, a word about handouts—and about "contacts," the people a reporter regularly deals with and comes to know as he writes about a subject on a steady basis. Notwithstanding the groans evoked by each batch of press releases to be plowed through between sips of the morning coffee, news releases generally are the most efficient way for an organization to get its viewpoints and news of its activities to the media and for the latter to keep tabs on what various groups are up to. Contacts can be all-important in determining whether a reporter covers his beat well; sometimes they will put him on the trail of stories of public importance that he might otherwise never come across, and they can provide him with a pool of ideas and outlooks that he can draw on, often at a moment's notice, for perspective in writing a particular article.

On the other hand, there is always the danger that a reporter will slip into the habit of doing little more than rewriting handouts or serving as a mouthpiece for certain of his contacts. To avoid this, the good reporter, at least as I see him, keeps constantly in mind that his purpose and those of the people and parties he writes about are entirely disparate. Theirs is to promote the well-being and outlook of the interests and principles they represent, while his is to shed as much light as possible on the activity he is covering, with as much fairness as possible to the often contending individuals and groups involved but without inhibitions stemming from fears of offending them or "making them look bad."

Thus, when the New York City Housing Authority announced in 1968 that it was liberalizing its procedures for admission to low-income public housing because of "changing values and changing goals," I felt it my function as a newspaper reporter not only to report the changes and the stated reason but also to point out that the agency had been under pressure from civil rights groups to re-examine its admissions procedures because these groups had felt the procedures to be unfairly stringent. When landlords' groups declared in 1968 that New York City could not pass a proposed local law regulating rent increases in certain types of apartments without first obtaining state approval in the form of state enabling legislation, it seemed my job as a reporter to point out too that, whatever the merits or demerits of the proposed law, city and state officials agreed that the state, though in a different context, had already given the city the necessary authority several years before. When spokesmen for tenants' groups blamed statutory weaknesses for the negligible use being made of a new law permitting nonpayment of rent to compel landlords to remove long-standing violations, it seemed my function to note as well the feeling of city officials that the law had not really had a chance to prove itself yet because of protracted court suits brought by landlords to challenge it.

Perhaps one test of how well a reporter is covering a controversial subject like housing would be a peek into his telephone book or the index-card file in which he keeps the phone numbers used in his work. If the great majority of the numbers belong to officials of government agencies, or to any other single category of sources, chances are that readers of this reporter are not being well served.

Sometimes in a complex and many-sided subject such as housing, a newspaperman's attempts to put things in perspective are frustrating and futile. This is often the case, for example, in the numbers game that politicians are wont to play with housing, especially at campaign time. A city administration (it could be anywhere) claims that it has built more public housing in a certain year than the previous administration did in its most productive year. In support, it cites a dozen more groundbreakings. "Lies and distortions!" cry opponents of the incumbent administration and members of the previous one, charging that the groundbreakings were intentionally premature to swell the statistics for the year. In fact, they note, a number of the groundbreakings took place on sites that had not even been cleared of all their old structures. "So who says you have to hold off excavating for a large new building on a large site until every one of the small old buildings has been razed?" the incumbent administration's housing spokesman retorts, with enough reasonableness in his words to make the temptation to disbelieve him dissolve in uncertainty.

The reporter has no choice but to give equal play to the claims and counterclaims, knowing that the truth they befog is beyond his reach. To get at it would require something like visiting every disputed construction site with lie detector equipment and demanding that the job superintendent swear that only in his purely technical and apolitical wisdom was the order to begin digging given.

Perhaps the foes of the incumbent administration also contend that it is claiming credit with its groundbreaking statistics for projects that don't even belong to it, projects that were actually "put into the pipeline"—conceived and planned—by the previous administration. The incumbents dismiss this with the response that when they took office the plans for these projects were half-baked or dormant and that it was the new administration that gave them the shape and breath needed for life. Even if a reporter has the time and fortitude to trace the tortuous history of a dozen projects through the labyrinthine production pipeline of governmental housing bureaucracy, how is he to decide between the subjective claim that at a given point the design for a housing development was as good and finished as it had to be and the equally subjective claim that at the same point it was of poor quality and required virtually complete reworking?

But such frustrations were minor compared with the major frustration experienced while writing about real estate and housing for two years in the late 1960's. This was the frustration of knowing that the majority of the American people not only know and care little about the processes that provide the walls around them and the roofs over their heads, but are just as unconcerned that the society that first propelled explorers to another world and sheltered them safely from the unknown perils of such a venture has failed to provide decent shelter for at least 30 million of its people in the familiar atmosphere of earth.

Two Presidential Studies

In 1968, two major governmental reports were issued that extensively documented the dire housing situation facing the American people. These were the report of the National Commission on Urban Problems, headed by former Senator Paul Douglas of Illinois, and the report of the President's Committee on Urban Housing, headed by the industrialist Edgar Kaiser. Both groups had been named by President Lyndon B. Johnson to examine various aspects of the nation's housing picture to determine the nature and extent of America's housing needs and the barriers to meeting these needs.

The Douglas commission concentrated on such matters as state and local building and zoning laws and the extent to which these impeded the production of housing; the effect that federal, state, and local tax policies had on the quality of existing housing and on the construction of new housing; and the accomplishments and failures of the federal government's efforts since the Depression to help remedy the nation's shortcomings in housing. The Kaiser committee focused on the opportunities that had to be created and the obstacles removed if the private sector of the economy were to play a meaningful role in helping to overcome the nation's housing deficiencies—or, as President Johnson put it, on "the way to harness the productive power of America, which has proved it can master space and create unmatched abundance in the market place, to the most pressing unfilled need of our society: [providing] the basic necessities of a decent home and healthy surroundings for every poor American family now imprisoned in the squalor of the slum."

In their reports, and in the more than two dozen research studies on which their findings were based, the two federal study groups presented a picture of unfulfilled housing needs—and of pervasive social, economic, political, and institutional obstacles to meeting these needs—that hardly allows for the kind of national self-congratulations with which the Middle America of Richard Nixon and Spiro Agnew is spinning its saccharine philosophical frosting for the nation's 200th-birthday cake in 1976. Both government groups communicated a sense of deep urgency about the nation's housing deficiencies and made clear that a massive commitment of national resources—governmental and nongovernmental—and a monumental effort in national cooperation would be needed if these deficiencies were to be overcome in the forseeable future.

When the reports were first issued, they received due coverage in the nation's serious press and then, as with most government commission studies, quickly dropped from view, except among those professionally or academically concerned with their material. For the influential policy-makers of the Nixon Administration, the reports appear never to have been *in* view, despite the fact that one of them (the Kaiser committee report) was the product of a group in which presidents and board chairmen of corporations and banks were in a two-thirds majority.

It is understandable why the reports did not have much circulation among the general public. Like most governmental studies, they were highly detailed and technical, beyond the scope and patience of the intelligent layman, no matter how interested he might be in knowing more about the state of the nation's housing. It is understandable, too, why the reports have been disregarded by the policy-makers in Richard Nixon's White House. Like the 1968 report of the National Advisory Commission on Civil Disorders and the 1969 report of the National Commission on the Causes and Prevention of Violence, the Douglas and Kaiser studies expose some major warts on the American body beautiful, and the constituency that brought the Nixon Administration to power is hardly receptive to the news that these disfigurements are surface scars of deeply rooted national malignancies that require expensive and intensive treatment, not minor blemishes easily remedied by a few red, white, and blue bandages.

But whether their technical material or their unwanted message is to blame, consignment to oblivion should not be the fate of these thoroughgoing examinations of so important a matter as America's shortcomings in shelter. One hope in writing this book has been that it will help focus more attention on the major findings of these significant governmental studies.

The Overview

At this point some perspective is undoubtedly called for. The United States is certainly not the only developed country with severe housing difficulties, and the shortcomings in American housing, as serious as they are, are fewer today than in the past.

The truth of the first statement will be borne out by any working-class or middle-income resident of London or Tokyo who recently has had occasion to search for a decent apartment within his means. It will be vigorously testified to by any Parisian who has had to pay an exorbitant amount in "key money" to succeed to a relatively desirable apartment that has become vacant. Swedes, residents of a society that epitomizes the welfare state and knows no slums as America knows them, can tell nevertheless of the badly overcrowded conditions in which many live and of long waits, as much as five years, to get into government-subsidized housing. In Moscow, the process of getting into decent housing also remains painfully slow despite a large-scale apartment construction effort that began in the 1950's, at least twenty years behind the massive population influx to the large cities that accompanied the intensive industrialization drive begun in the Soviet Union in the 1930's. Many Muscovites continue to share cramped and dingy communal flats, often with an entire family in one room.

In short, most developed countries (and from London's Notting Hill to the *bidonvilles* ringing Paris, the worst slums America has to offer are easily rivaled in such highly industrialized European nations as Britain and France) have little to boast of when comparing their own housing situations with that of the United States. Moreover, in regard to some housing amenities America is well ahead of the rest of the world or among the leaders, according to statistics of the Organization for Economic Cooperation and Development. Nine out of ten American homes have bathrooms, for example, a far higher percentage than found in any other country, while the 99.8 per cent of American dwellings with electricity in the 1960's ranked second only to Switzerland's 100 per cent, and the 92.9 per cent of homes in the United States with inside running water was third behind Switzerland's 98.8 per cent and West Germany's 96.7 per cent.

So far as the housing situation in the developing countries of Asia, Africa, and Latin America is concerned, the only word that can possibly describe it is catastrophic. United Nations Secretary-General U Thant, in a 1969 analysis prepared for the U.N. Economic and Social Council's Committee on Housing, Building, and Planning, declared that exploding populations, compounded by large-scale urbanization, made it imperative that the existing stock of housing in the developing nations be doubled during the 1970's and 1980's just to provide sufficient shelter for the increase in population—a necessity over and above replacing the countless millions of hovels that now serve as homes in these countries. The likelihood that this need will be fulfilled is, of course, nil.

But the housing inadequacies of other societies, as widespread as they are, are not the standard against which America's showing in shelter must be measured. Rather, the state of American housing must be measured against what this country has proved it can do, and what it has done, technologically and industrially. It must be measured against such feats as being the first nation to land men on another world and bring them safely back. And when it is measured against such a display of national ingenuity and determination, and against the capacity for national accomplishment that this feat illustrates, then America's achievement level in fulfilling the very basic need of all its citizens for decent shelter must be regarded as wretchedly inadequate.

Nor is there any consolation in the thought that the state of American housing today, whatever its demerits, represents a significant improvement over the past. As recently as forty years ago, roughly one-third of American families were said to be living in good homes, one-third in "fair" homes ("more or less lacking in conveniences, but not unwholesome"), and a big one-third in housing that was "definitely subnormal by any decent standard." Yet today, it is argued, despite an intervening Great Depression that for some years caused the proportion of substandard homes to rise even beyond the one-third of four decades ago, only one-sixth of American housing (assuming one puts aside the federal government's rosier one-eleventh figure) is of substandard quality. Moreover, one often hears, even the worst housing today is better than the slums of the past, especially in urban areas, where housing and building codes requiring at least minimal standards of safe and healthful construction and maintenance are common today, whereas in the last century they were virtually nonexistent, so that the slum buildings of that era routinely had one privy for 200 or more people, apartments without any windows, and yards ankle deep in the overflow from stopped-up privies and water closets.

Just how much the proportion of bad housing has been reduced over the past forty years, assuming that the broad estimates of that day were an approximation of reality, is highly uncertain at best, as has already been indicated, and will be fully explained in Chapter 7. As for the matter of whether the worst slum today is better than the worst slum yesterday, I recall that issues such as this often fueled vehement late-night bull sessions in the freshman wing of my college dormitory. (Few of those partial to today's slums, it invariably turned out, had ever had firsthand experiences with one.) Unquestionably space-age slums have more toilets and windows per capita than those of the horse-and-buggy era—after all, this has been a century of unparalleled scientific achievement. Unquestionably too, many of today's slum dwellers even have television to take their minds off the decay around them and to show them the blessings of mainstream America that they are forgoing by being foolish enough to remain slum dwellers.

But the relative merits of the decrepit dwellings of today as opposed to those of yesterday is not the point, any more than the issue is America's shortcomings in housing compared with those elsewhere on the planet. The point is that at a time when the United States has had the will and resources to blaze man's way onto the lunar surface—and, for that matter, when nearly 2 million families in the world's richest nation are well off enough to possess second homes for vacation use and nearly a million and a half to have three cars—one American family out of six, and more likely a higher proportion (the uncertainty is itself a damning indication of American society's concern with the matter) does not even have a decent first home.

And the sad probability is that Americans will be walking on Mars and more distant worlds before the situation changes significantly for the better.

2. Local Government and the Crisis

ROMNEY'S RIDES

On a July night in 1970 George Romney, Secretary of Housing and Urban Development in the Administration of President Richard M. Nixon, took an automobile ride that vividly dramatized for him, and the nation, a major aspect of the American housing crisis in the second half of the twentieth century. It occurred in the Detroit suburb of Warren, where the former governor of Michigan had gone for a session with officials of that community and the other suburbs around the Motor City. There had been reports out of Washington that Detroit's suburbs, starting with Warren, had been selected as the first target of a drive by the Nixon Administration to "open up" the nation's overwhelmingly white suburbs to black Americans by cracking through the barrier of local attitudes and zoning laws frequently hemming nonwhites into problem-plagued central cities, of which Detroit, more than 40 per cent black in population, was a foremost example. The suburban officials had wanted an opportunity to make clear to Romney that they had no desire whatever for the distinction reportedly in store for them. It was obvious that they were hardly reassured by the Cabinet officer's repeated statements that he was seeking not "forced integration" but only "affirmative action" toward desegregation as the price of Warren's receiving federal urban renewal money.

As he was leaving the rather inconclusive session, Romney was subjected to unmistakable evidence that the office-holders' views were only a faithful reflection of their constituents' feelings. Hundreds of shouting, sign-waving white suburbanites converged on the secretary's car as it pulled away from the high school where the meeting had been held. Shaking their fists, pounding on the hood, and shouting curses and jeers, they left no doubt that, so far as they were concerned, the small handful of black families then living in Detroit's suburbs were already more than enough. Not until the police cleared a path for the vehicle was the nation's top housing official liberated from the crowd's anger.

Three summers before, George Romney had taken another police-protected automobile ride to witness a different aspect of the relationship between local government and the nation's housing problems. With a policeman literally riding shotgun beside him, the then governor of Michigan had been driven through the streets of Detroit's black ghettos for a firsthand look at the devastation freshly inflicted by the costliest black riot of the 1960's. Forty-three persons had died and whole blocks had been reduced to ashes and charred beams in the Detroit eruption of 1967, the culmination of social ferment and unfulfilled needs that successive municipal administrations of the Motor City, like those of nearly every other major American city, had proved increasingly unable to cope with—and at times had exacerbated.

Among the most critical of the unmet needs was housing. Despite steadily spreading blight, no new government-financed public housing had been built in Detroit since the middle 1950's. All together, a total of some 3,300 public housing units had been built since 1949—less than one-third the number of old housing units demolished in the same period to make way for urban renewal alone. To nobody's surprise, most of the 11,000 apartments bulldozed on renewal sites had been occupied by low-income and working-class blacks. Jerome Cavanagh, the youthful mayor who presided over Detroit from 1962 to 1969, conceded: "I think housing has been one of the obvious lacks of success in our administration." Five years before the riot, Cavanagh's administration had been born in a blaze of liberal activism and soaring optimism. After the outburst, it limped out of office with the housing problem even more severe than a decade before.

The failure of Detroit's government to cope with the city's housing needs, and the bitter opposition to providing housing opportunities for black families in the surrounding suburbs, reflect two sides of the same prominent coin involving the relationship between local government and the nation's housing difficulties in the middle years of the twentieth century. Whatever local factors give one city's housing problems a somewhat different cast from those of another city, and however many suburban areas can be cited in which black families may be found in appreciable numbers, the basic facts are the same throughout the country. America's large cities—partly because of economic and social forces beyond their control, partly because of their own missteps and inadequacies—are incapable of coping with their housing troubles. Meanwhile, the suburbs ringing them are for the most part refusing to lend a helping hand—or, to be more accurate, are refusing to remove a strangling hand.

Choking Cities

The economic forces beyond municipal control that are preventing cities from dealing adequately with their housing needs stem from the fiscal arrangements of American government. Of the total taxes collected in the United States since World War II, only about 15 per cent has been collected by local government. About 65 per cent has been collected by the federal government and the rest by the states. Thus the amount of revenue available to municipal governments beyond the small portion they have directly collected has depended on disbursements from the other levels of government, which have reflected spending priorities set outside the city, most importantly in Washington because of the great proportion of the tax yield taken in by the federal government. And the priorities chosen in the nation's capital have hardly been of a kind to secure a sound night's sleep for a money-pinched big-city mayor struggling simply to keep his schools and subways running, let alone hoping to replace hundreds of blocks of wretched slums with decent housing. Most big cities can't even budget sufficient funds to enforce the maintenance codes governing minimum standards in existing housing.

Just as important as the limited amount of revenue directly collected by local government have been limitations on where this revenue can come from—which not only have constricted local resources to meet the vast and ever more expensive needs of a big city, but have also dealt housing an additional severe blow in that the major source of revenue permitted to local government is the property tax.

As creatures of their states, the nation's cities, counties, and towns have no powers, including that of taxation, that are not granted them by the states. And the states have so restricted the tax-levying authority of their local jurisdictions that most locally raised revenue has come from taxes on the value of property. One government-sponsored study reported that two-thirds of all locally raised general revenue in the United States in the 1950's and 1960's arose from property taxes. There were sharp variations from this over-all figure: Some cities, including Boston, were dependent on the property tax for more than 80 per cent of their locally raised revenue. In metropolitan areas on the whole, about half of the property-tax base was estimated to consist of housing.

Forced to rely to such a great extent on the property tax, and facing a constant demand for additional, improved, and increasingly expensive municipal services, cities have often had no alternative to pushing their property-tax rates up to levels that many housing analysts feel place a disproportionate and unfair burden on housing. One researcher for the National Commission on Urban Problems found:

> As percentages of actual cash outlays for housing [property taxes in metropolitan areas] range—excluding the South—from sales-tax-equivalent rates of 18 per cent for large apartment houses outside New York City to 30 per cent or more for single-family houses in the Northeast, and multi-family properties in New York City. *In*

> *general, the upper end of this range applies to most of the nation's large cities outside the South. . . .* These very high tax rates are greatly in excess of the rates applicable to other forms of consumer expenditure, with the exception of taxes on liquor, tobacco, and gasoline.

The implications of the property tax as a steep levy on housing consumption are as severe for the nation's cities as they often are for its citizens, and involve a vicious-circle irony.

Where a struggling homeowner has to scrimp to meet his tax bill, he will often cut back on other expenses, including those for maintenance. Where the owner of rental housing cannot pass his tax costs on to the tenant as a component of the rent, because to do so would make a given apartment unmarketable (or because he is prevented from doing so by too-rigid rent control regulations), his alternative, to protect his profit, often is again to cut costs, including those for maintenance. Where high property taxes cause widespread unmarketability of housing, construction of new housing may decline, especially in the lower- and middle-income rent ranges (more affluent families more easily absorb increases in housing costs flowing from a given rise in a city's property tax). So far as rehabilitation is concerned, the likelihood of higher assessed values on renovated housing tends to discourage improvement, because the resulting tax increase frequently is far out of proportion to the increase in rental income resulting from the improvements.

All of these factors, housing economists generally agree, work toward the spread of residential blight. And it is here that the vicious circle spins around the cities. On the one hand, the existence of slums invariably entails a stepped-up need for municipal services affecting health and sanitation, police protection and fire-fighting, and efforts to arrest housing decay itself. On the other hand, the major source of revenue that financially pressed cities are forced to rely on to pay for such services *itself* contributes to the spread of slums when tapped too hard.

A second major ramification of mandated reliance on property taxes for the preponderance of locally raised revenue has been the effect it has had on shaping the course of urban renewal. To preserve the strong property-tax base so important to municipal fiscal health, city governments have felt pressed to plan renewal projects with the aim of achieving the greatest possible property-tax yield from the renewed sites. Hence the heavy emphasis for so many years on lucrative commercial and high-rent residential construction in renewal areas, and the dearth, until recently, of public and publicly aided housing, whose tax yields are pittances in comparison. With this in mind, many urban experts argue that municipal governments cannot be held entirely to blame for the "push-out-the-poor" aspect of government-sponsored renewal that for so many years drew bitter criticism to the urban renewal program.

At this point, it should be emphasized that big-city governments are not the only local jurisdictions hindered in meeting the housing needs of their constituents by fiscal forces beyond local control. Rural and suburban governments are no more capable of making up their areas' housing deficits—and slums in the older suburbs are far from uncommon—without massive federal and state aid than are the central cities. But it is in America's large cities, where the dry powder of economics is packed with the burning fuse of social discontent, that the fiscal inadequacies of local government have their most explosive implications, as the 1960's clearly demonstrated. And it was no doubt with the vision of more burning Detroits and Newarks in mind that John Gardner, then chairman of the Urban Coalition and former Secretary of Health, Education, and Welfare, declared in 1969:

> Our greatest cities have lost command of themselves and their futures and they lie helpless as the multiple waves of crisis roll over them. . . . They have reached the end of their rope. Until we institute a thorough examination of our patterns of taxation and allocation of resources across federal, state, and local levels, we shall never save our cities.

The economic forces beyond municipal control are bound up with, and have been intensified by, equally fundamental and pervasive social forces: the massive country-to-city and city-to-suburbs migrations, that have resulted since World War II in the replacement of millions of middle-class whites in the central cities with rural black and Spanish-speaking poor whose needs have entailed vast increases in municipal expenditures for poverty and welfare programs; intensifying racial antagonisms (exacerbated by the rural-to-urban migration) that have severely hindered the construction of government-aided low-rent housing within the central cities as well as outside of them; and, more recently, the surge of sentiment among the minority poor for "a voice" in the programs affecting them, a demand that, whatever its merits, has not been one to facilitate the swiftest implementation of housing programs.

But as significant as these social and economic factors have been, the buck cannot be passed entirely to them: Big-city governments have made prodigious contributions of their own to their housing agonies. Bureaucratic blundering and red tape, as much a part of the nation's city halls as the masonry and mortar that form them, have added incalculably to central-city housing woes. In city after city across the country, public planning and development proceed at an agonizing snail's pace, and developers of both private and government-assisted housing chant a litany of complaints over the delays and frustrations encountered in obtaining necessary permits and approvals from municipal bureaucracies. The results go beyond inconvenience to sponsors, builders, and architects. In the highly inflationary construction industry, increased time means increased costs. And where projects of a large scale are involved, the wheezing wheels of the bureaucratic machinery can mean hardship and inconvenience to residents as well.

This certainly was the case in New York City with the construction of Co-op City, a 15,000-apartment, $300-million project—the nation's largest apartment development—being built in the early 1970's on 300 acres of largely undeveloped land in the distant reaches of the Bronx. The first occupants of Co-op City, who began moving in late in 1968, found themselves without adequate utilities, roads, and schools largely because of the city's "failure to coordinate its planning and budgeting procedures with construction progress at the project," according to Charles Urstadt, New York State Commissioner of Housing and Community Renewal, whose agency supervised the development of Co-op City. An official of the nonprofit group sponsoring the state-assisted project, the United Housing Foundation, while guiding me amid the maze of masonry towers and massive excavation pits that marked the Co-op City site in 1968, was more specific in his grievance. "The city was committed in 1965 to do its part, but it didn't begin moving until last year, when it appointed a coordinator to speed things up with the thirty agencies we have had to work with," he recalled.

The ineptitude of municipal bureaucracy often extends as well to finishing off projects. Where cities are involved in paying construction costs or in approving such payments, contractors and subcontractors frequently find themselves waiting several years before being fully compensated for their efforts. The head of the subcontractors' association in one major Eastern city summed up the consequences of this for many cities when he described the worsening situation in his own area: "This cost of negotiating, litigating, and waiting to be paid must be charged back to the city in future bids. Thus the cost of building goes up unnecessarily. Furthermore, some of the best building contractors and subcontractors now absolutely refuse to work for the city, because they can't put up with the shenanigans. With fewer bidders on housing contracts, quality must suffer and prices must go up."

Still another aspect of municipal self-injury on the housing scene lies in the abundance of outmoded and excessively restrictive provisions found in many cities' building codes. The obstacles presented by such provisions are not, of course, solely a big-city problem. Of the 8,300 local building codes counted across the country by the National Commission on Urban Problems as the 1960's ended, some 3,800 were in effect outside of metropolitan areas. Most of the 4,500 within metropolitan areas were in suburban jurisdictions or small cities. Outside as much as inside the large central cities, overly rigid and antiquated provisions have long been hallmarks of local building ordinances—the results of a combination of legislative laziness, ignorance of technological advances, and intense pressures from manufacturing and labor-union interests opposed to new materials and methods of construction that might reduce the market for their own products and labor.

But to note that unnecessarily restrictive and antiquated construction laws characterize local governments of all sizes in no way mitigates the importance of such ordinances as major self-created contributions to the housing problems of big-city governments. The cities suffer keenly from two aspects of the building code barrier. First, the maze of inconsistent and often conflicting requirements formed by more than 8,000 local codes is a major element working against establishment of a cost-lowering, mass production housing industry, a development that would aid cities immeasurably by enabling governmental housing programs to produce more for their money and by helping make private construction of low-rent and moderate-rent housing more feasible.

Second, and more specifically, within many cities building code restrictions often prevent the use of many of the cheaper materials and methods of construction that have been developed in recent decades. During the past thirty years, an international revolution has occurred in structure and style—though one would hardly know it from reading many big-city building codes. As the President's Committee on Urban Housing noted in its 1968 report, "many codes were either written, or based upon those that were written, fifty years ago or more."

This was the case, until 1968, in the nation's largest city. Until it adopted a new and modern building code that year, New York, historically the most progressive city with respect to local action to provide government-aided housing, had been operating under a construction ordinance written in the 1890's and last substantially revised in the 1930's. As a result, such perfectly safe materials as reinforced brick, reinforced gypsum concrete, prestressed concrete, and structural plywood could not be used, precluding the possibility of cost-cutting competition with materials that were permitted, nor could chemical methods of strengthening marginal land be employed that were less expensive than the piling operations required under the old code.

The old New York restrictions remain typical of restrictions still abundant in the building codes of the nation's large cities generally in the 1970's. The National Commission on Urban Problems, for example, in a survey of forty-eight of the fifty-two largest cities, found that the building codes of nearly three-quarters of the sample prohibited the use of plastic pipe in drainage systems, even though, as the commission reported, use of such pipe in one- and two-story homes "is now allowed, at least technically, by most of the major model building codes or their plumbing code counterparts." Nineteen of the forty-eight cities prohibited the use of preassembled electrical wiring units, and thirteen forbade the use of preassembled combination drain, waste, and vent bathroom plumbing systems, despite the fact, as the commission observed, that "among the more important methods of reducing building costs is the prefabrication or offsite assembly of plumbing or electrical units."

Given the consistently drained, too often wasted (precisely because of hurdles like excessively restrictive building codes), and always vented resources of government housing programs, this is hardly a comforting finding.

Adding to the difficulties posed by restrictive construction laws is the fact that many cities have electrical and plumbing codes administered separately from their building codes. What this array of legal requirements can mean to a city's efforts to plug its housing gap was vividly illustrated in Atlanta. A builder of prefabricated homes working in the Thomasville urban renewal area used factory-installed plumbing and wiring systems that he thought acceptable, inasmuch as his over-all construction plans had been approved by the city's building department, which had issued him a permit. But the city's plumbing and electrical inspectors denied their permits to the completed houses, and the builder was forced to rip out the plumbing and wiring in the units already completed and ship the remaining units without the plumbing and electrical systems. He responded by raising the price of each house $500.

Just how much more expensive private and government-aided housing construction has been in the nation's cities over all because of excessively restrictive and outmoded construction requirements is difficult to estimate. However, when New York's building code was revised in 1968, estimates were made of the savings that might result from use of the cheaper materials and methods permitted under the new regulations. These estimates included savings of from 5 to 10 per cent on the framing and foundation costs involved in the construction of single-family or two-family houses; savings of about 5 per cent on the cost of a concrete framework for a twenty-eight-story apartment building, and savings of as much as 20 per cent on the foundation costs for such a structure.

The National Commission on Urban Problems, in a highly informative survey, assembled a list of twenty-one "excessive code requirements"—those exceeding the requirements found in national model building codes and exceeding the Federal Housing Administration's minimum property standards—most frequently encountered by prefabricated-home manufacturers in twenty states. The excessive restrictions had to do with items such as foundation footings, sheathing, plumbing, and electrical components. The commission concluded that if a home manufacturer were required to incorporate all twenty-one items in a unit that would cost $12,000 to build under the model code or FHA standards, the construction cost would rise by $1,838, or 15 per cent.

Nearly all housing experts agree that the most up-to-date building codes would not, by themselves, bring costs down to where a vast increase in the production of low-rent and moderate-rent housing would be facilitated. The costs of land, financing, and maintenance and operation, including property taxes, would have to be drastically lowered as well. At the same time, there is little disagreement that reducing these costs would be pointless if the resultant savings go to pay for technologically needless and excessive construction expenses entailed by anachronistic building requirements.

Yet another area in which city governments are contributing to their own housing miseries is the property tax itself. Although, as previously noted, the basic reliance on this tax for most locally raised revenue is beyond local control, and although some of the rules in levying the tax that are injurious to housing are also state-imposed and thus beyond local control, still other features of the levy with a significantly harmful impact on housing *are* within the means of municipal governments to remedy.

Among the most prominent of these features is the prevailing local government practice of assessing vacant land at a much lower percentage of market value than built-up property, and assessing underutilized sites at a lower percentage of market value than properties improved to or near their fullest potential. The reasoning often offered in justification of this practice is that it would be unfair to tax a property owner out of proportion to what he can pay from his earnings on a holding.

On its face, this argument appears eminently fair. But critics respond that the notion of the property tax as an income tax is fallacious and often screens a practice that enriches landowners at the expense of a city's over-all housing needs: the speculative holding of vacant or underutilized land in the hope that future development of surrounding sites will cause the value of the land to rise sharply, in which case it may be sold at a fat profit. Speculation-inflated land prices are an important element in the high cost of housing production in many areas, and by contributing to the protective fiscal screen around such speculation, the cities can certainly be accused of helping to worsen their own housing situations.

In an argument long advanced by many urban experts, the suggestion is made that the property tax be consciously and vigorously wielded to discourage such land speculation. The cities could contribute to this approach by assessing idle and underused land at levels reflecting their market value. Then owners of such land—whether vacant lots or land underlying parking lots or slum buildings—would be under financial pressure to put their properties to "higher uses" (in order to be able to pay the higher taxes) instead of being permitted, as under the prevailing system, to sit back and wait for the development of surrounding sites to send the value of their own properties soaring.

A second major benefit is also predicted from this suggested reversal of property tax assessment policies: As the proportion of a city's property tax take from the land component of the tax base is increased, the proportion from the so-called "improvements" component (structures, including housing) could be decreased, lessening the tax pressures that so often prove stifling to residential construction and renovation.

Besides the prediction of such practical benefits, a philosophical argument is offered by those who would have assessments of idle and underused land reflect actual market value. They point out that the value of such land has often been increased as a result of public expenditures to develop the surrounding area—expenditures for utilities and for transit, educational, and recreational facilities —rather than because of any expenditures that the landowners might have made to improve their sites. Thus it is only fair, the argument continues, that owners of land benefiting from public investment pay back, in the form of sizable taxes, a decent portion of the public expenditure that raised the value of their holdings and permitted them their handsome gains.

While agreeing with the arguments of equity and economy in behalf of reversing the underassessment of vacant or underutilized land, some housing experts nevertheless urge care in any move to have assessments reflect market values. They observe that, although the long-term effects of such a move would no doubt be favorable to housing over all by striking a blow against speculation-inflated land prices and softening the tax bite on housing, the short-term effects could sometimes be disastrous for existing desirable housing.

The hazard would occur where areas of old but solid, well-maintained low-rent or moderate-rent housing became popular with builders of commercial structures or luxury apartments. As the market value of the land in such areas increased, as it would with new activity and builders' desires in the areas, assessments reflecting the higher values could lead to taxes that would make continued operation of the old but solid housing just as uneconomical as continued operation of parking lots or slum buildings in these areas. Thus city tax policies would be helping to strike a blow against decent low- or moderate-rent housing, already in too short supply in most cities.

From the standpoint of housing needs, there is good reason to doubt the wisdom of any change in tax policy that makes no distinction between old but good housing and slum housing or parking lots. (From a sheer economic view—land utilization in relation to market value—all three categories could be lumped together as "underuse" of land.) Thus any reform toward having assessments of idle or underused land reflect market values, fundamentally desirable in itself, should be arranged so as not to harm existing desirable housing.

One possible way to do this would be to abate higher taxes resulting from a switch to assessments reflecting market values where the property is good-quality housing. Such abatement may not affect an owner's intention to sell such housing to a man planning a more lucrative office building on the site. But at least it would keep the reformed tax policies from contributing to the economic pressures on the owner to sell, and thus from contributing to the reduction of the all-too-scarce supply of solid low-rent and moderate-rent housing.

Property taxes, building codes, and bureaucracy are not the only ways the governments of the nation's cities have contributed to perpetuating or worsening their housing difficulties, as one learns while delving into the intricate world of real estate. New York City is a conspicuous example, with a rent control system that (until a major effort at revision was made in 1970) too often encouraged indifferent or shoddy maintenance while discouraging or encumbering high-level maintenance, and a zoning law that has helped add to the financial straitjacket squeezing the housing-construction process.

Just how significantly rent control has contributed to the drastic housing plight* of the nation's largest city has long been the subject of endless, emotional, and ever conflicting contentions by

* How drastic New York City's housing plight is in the early 1970's is vividly illustrated by the following: A joint study by the U.S. Department of Housing and Urban Development and the New York City Planning Commission as the 1960's ended found that the city needed 780,000 new or rehabilitated units to make up for the more than 500,000 units that were dilapidated or deteriorating (according to the Census Bureau's rudimentary standards), to relieve overcrowding in sound units, and to provide a decent vacancy rate (the rental-apartment vacancy rate was less than 1 per cent in 1971, with the market as constricted for middle-income families as for the poor). By contrast, permits were obtained in 1969 for construction of fewer than 9,000 nonluxury units under all public and publicly aided federal, state, and local housing programs going in the city. The number was under 13,000 units in 1970. Non-publicly-aided private housing was even more depressed, with permits for building 8,800 units obtained in 1969 and only 6,800 in 1970. In the case of apartments planned among these privately financed units, most if not all were to be in the high-rent class; in the case of single-family homes among them, all would be beyond the means of lower-income families. Meanwhile, decay was spreading, with housing abandonment reaching an alarming rate and housing losses (from demolitions and abandonments) believed exceeding completions of new units. A large number of families on welfare were forced to live in decaying but exorbitantly priced "welfare hotels."

spokesmen for New York's landlords and tenants. Those who have cast a sober gaze on the issue have generally concluded that the city's rent control structure, while far from the colossal villain in the New York housing picture that the city's landlords would have the world believe, nevertheless has contained features resulting in harmful inequities for some landlords and, ultimately, for tenants and the city's housing scene as a whole.

A holdover from World War II, when rent control was born as one of the federal government's nationwide measures to stem the upward surge of prices, rent control was gradually phased out after the war in every state except New York. There, as the 1970's began, some 160 localities still had the controls, the state having preserved them on the ground that a housing emergency, defined as a vacancy rate of less than 5 per cent, continued to exist. In New York City, which since 1962 has been responsible for its own rent control system, the furor over controls has been one of the most tumultuous political issues in a city not lacking for clamorous confrontations.

The World War II control system still applies to some 1.3 million of New York City's 2.1 million rental apartments, rigidly governing the rent that can be charged in the covered apartments (most of the city's privately built units constructed before 1947) and the circumstances under which tenants can be evicted from them. Until revised by the city in 1970, the rent control regulations provided that landlords of affected apartments could not increase rents beyond the prescribed maximum except in specific circumstances: when a new tenant moved into an apartment, in which case the landlord could raise the maximum rent 15 per cent provided that at least two years had passed since a 15 per cent lease increase had last been collected on the apartment; when a tenant in occupancy voluntarily agreed to a new two-year lease at an increase of up to 15 per cent (which was not often); when the landlord made major capital improvements on the property; when he increased services and facilities with the consent of the tenant; and when he showed that the existing rents in a building did not enable him to earn a "fair return" on his investment, defined as 6 per cent annually of his property's assessed valuation or purchase price (depending on circumstances) with an allowance of 2 per cent of the value of his building for depreciation.

The result of these regulations by the late 1960's was an irrational and often inequitable patchwork of rents in controlled apartments that, over all, was as unfair to numerous tenants as to many landlords. This was a view held not only by those implacably opposed to the entire concept of peacetime rent control but also by many who vigorously supported the basic idea of controls as necessary in a city starved for vacant housing that low- and middle-income families could afford.

Among the most important weaknesses of the regulations prevailing until 1970 was the provision for increases to assure landlords a "fair return." Aside from the administrative complexities involved in seeking increases under this provision—and for the nonprofessional who owned one or two small buildings, the effort could be discouraging or might entail a sizable expense for accountants—the exclusion of mortgage interest as an operating expense in determining whether an owner was earning his 6 per cent a year proved at times unrealistic. This was especially so as mortgage interest rates soared in the 1960's. With the interest having to be paid, in effect, out of a landlord's return, an owner of a building with large maintenance and operating expenses (themselves on a constant upward spiral in one of the nation's most inflationary regions) might find himself operating in or near the red even after being granted the so-called "six-and-two hardship increase" under the fair-return provision. Owners squeezed this way frequently cut back on maintenance and repairs to provide themselves with what they considered a fair return *in fact,* and the seeds of deterioration were thus planted.

Over all, the rent control laws on the books until 1970 resulted in a pattern of rents that in no way reflected housing quality or tenants' incomes. It was not unusual in New York in the 1960's to find financially comfortable residents of solid, well-maintained buildings in desirable middle-class areas paying $75 to $100 a month for spacious four- or five-room apartments while money-pinched families in decaying buildings in some of the city's worst slums were paying twice as much for squalid or smaller apartments. The reason was built into the too-rigid control structure: The tenants with the housing bargains had lived in their apartments for two decades or more, which meant no 15 per cent "vacancy increases" in all that time. Those in the costlier slums were living where there had been frequent turnover and thus numerous 15 per cent vacancy increases. Even within a single building one could often find sharp disparities: an apartment with little or no turnover since World War II renting for as little as half the amount of an apartment, of the same size and amenities, which had had several changes in tenancy and thus several 15 per cent vacancy increases over the two decades.

Undoubtedly, more than a few landlords recognized the blessings of frequent turnover and to encourage it, while incidentally cutting costs, provided a low level of maintenance and services in their buildings. In this regard, the rent control structure certainly provided what an economist would call "disincentives" to high-quality maintenance. Granted, the control law also had provisions designed to combat landlords' neglect—rents could be reduced where maintenance and services deteriorated—but, like the housing maintenance code in New York and every other city generally, these provisions were invoked far less consistently than the provisions for 15 per cent vacancy increases.

None of this is to exaggerate the impact of the rent control structure on housing deterioration in New York City. Despite the ritualistic cacophony of landlords to the contrary, the determinants of how well or badly any building is maintained are far more complex than any one factor such as rent control. As clearly indicated by now, they embody an often subtle interplay of economic, social, and psychological forces that owners act on and react to, forces that include basic motivation in ownership (long-term investment accompanied by diligent care as opposed to short-term speculative holding accompanied by minimal or indifferent care); the influence of federal income tax depreciation and local property tax assessment provisions; the influx of black and Spanish-speaking families into neighborhoods and the fear and uncertainty this induces in landlords and mortgage-lending institutions; and the wear and tear inflicted on a building by its tenants. Buildings had decayed in New York long before rent control, and solid neighborhoods have conspicuously turned to slums in cities where there is no rent control.

At the same time, the rigidities of the rent control structure still must be counted as one more element contributing to the decline of some portions of New York City's housing stock in the 1950's and 1960's. Following a series of studies reporting this, the administration of Mayor John Lindsay initiated an overhaul of rent control in 1970 with the aim of removing the inequitable and harmful features.

The revisions—denounced with equal vigor by landlords ("worse than before" and "institutionalizing further what should be abolished") and most tenants ("too much" and "rewarding bad landlords arbitrarily")—provided for interim rent increases in apartments where there had been low turnover, and then, in 1972, computer-calculated new maximum rents for every rent-controlled apartment in the city. The new maximums were to be based on landlords' expenses and their right to an annual return of 8.5 per cent of the valuation of their property, and were to be readjusted periodically. Rents below the newly calculated maximums were to be brought up to them in stages (although rents already above them were not to be lowered to them) and the old system of 15 per cent vacancy increases was done away with.

Just how well-conceived this revised rent control structure was —in reality rather than rhetoric—was, of course, still to be seen in 1971. Whether it would be seen was another question. At the behest of Republican Governor Nelson Rockefeller, and to the delight of the real estate industry, the New York State Legislature in 1971 enacted a measure mandating the removal from rent control of all controlled apartments voluntarily vacated by the tenants then in residence. The measure, which also prohibited the city from making rent controls any more stringent than they already were at that point, set off yet another furor.*

* Similarly remaining to be seen was the state's effect on still another rent-limiting measure in New York City, the Rent Stabilization Act of 1969. Affecting some 375,000 privately owned apartments not under the standard World War II rent controls—most apartments under rent stabilization were built after 1947—the stabilization measure was locally enacted after a controversy over steep rent rises in the city's noncontrolled apartments. It provided for ceilings on rent increases when expired leases were to be renewed and when new tenants took over vacant apartments. More flexible than the standard rent control system, it is administered in cooperation with the real estate industry. However, the industry agreed to participate only because it feared an even stronger measure otherwise, and it welcomed state action to phase out stabilization along with rent control.

While attempting to deal with some of the weaknesses of its rent control system, New York City's government has not taken action, at this writing, to modify what some housing analysts as well as builders consider another municipal act seriously injurious to housing: the city's zoning law.

Enacted in 1960 as a modern and enlightened measure to improve the quality of life in New York, the zoning ordinance provides for much less density and more open space than under the previous code. This has meant larger plots of land are needed to build a given number of apartments; in some cases only half the number of units possible under the old law can be constructed on a given area under the new code. Thus, among other things, the new law has entailed significantly higher land costs, increasing still further the already high cost of producing housing in New York. Whatever blessings the new zoning law might have afforded in open space and light, it has to be considered an additional factor against the construction of decent housing at decent rents, and in this respect it is still one more example of a big city government's helping to worsen its own housing problems.

The long catalog of circumstances that have rendered the governments of the nation's large cities unable to deal with the shelter needs of their constituents might give the impression that all big city governments have diligently sought to meet housing needs only to be thwarted at every turn by externally shaped or internally created handicaps. The impression would be false. Administrations in power in different cities across the country, or in a given city at different times, have shown widely varying degrees of concern over the state of housing in their jurisdictions and have given housing needs widely varying places on the scale of municipal priorities.

Nor is the catalog of municipal weaknesses meant to imply that big city governments have contributed nothing to the effort to overcome the housing woes of urban America. Spokesmen for the cities can point to a number of programs across the country in which municipal administrations have fostered the construction or rehabilitation of housing for those lacking a decent place to live. In fact, the federally aided public housing that has been built in the nation's large cities, however inadequate in quantity and quality, itself has resulted in large part from local government initiative and subsidy. This is because the federal acts shaping the public housing program call for local determination as to whether a city will participate and require local contributions (since 1949, in the form of property tax exemptions for the public housing and acceptance in lieu of taxes of 10 per cent of a project's rents.)

But the point is that, whatever priorities big city governments have given housing over the years and whatever efforts they may have made toward meeting housing needs, the basic fact remains that such governments have been rendered unable to make a perceptible dent in the housing problems of their constituents because of powerful forces beyond their control and equally powerful circumstances entirely of their own making.

The Suburban Noose

While the cities have choked on their housing problems, the suburbs surrounding them have provided an additional squeeze for good measure. Overwhelmingly white and far more robust than the cities financially, the nation's suburbs are determined to remain so, and their determination raises one of the most explosive barriers to meeting the nation's housing needs.

To retain perspective, it must again be pointed out that the suburbs are not without their own problems of decrepit housing and poverty. According to one estimate, some 5.7 million suburbanites, nearly 9 per cent of the suburban population, were poor by federal standards in the 1960's.* "The suburban slum-ghetto," Herman Miller, chief of the Census Bureau's population division, said in 1969, "is becoming a visible, although unmeasured, phenomenon in many large metropolitan areas, particularly those around older cities." In the two suburban counties of Nassau and Suffolk, east of New York City on Long Island, more than 100,000 persons were living in substandard housing in the late 1960's, according to a survey by a bicounty planning agency.

* In 1966, a nonfarm family of four was poor by federal standards if its annual income was less than $3,335.

Over all, however, America's suburbs are far better off than its cities. At the time the central cities were being ripped by racial explosions in the middle and late 1960's, they contained an estimated 30 per cent of the nation's population and 31 per cent of its poor; the suburbs, by contrast, contained about 35 per cent of the population (having pulled ahead of the cities during the 1960's) but only 20 per cent of the poor. Racially, the cities and suburbs have grown apart: While nonwhites were forming some 23 per cent of the total central-city population in the tumultuous late 1960's, they made up only about 5 per cent of the total suburban population.

Moreover, in the suburbs as in the cities, the poor and ill-housed are usually concentrated in older areas that have more in common, economically and socially, with the troubled big cities than with the newer, more affluent communities that give suburban America its sun-bathed, tree-lined, split-level stereotype. It is generally the more prosperous suburbia, not the older or "inner" suburbs, that contains the large amounts of land whose unavailability for low- and moderate-income housing is a major obstacle to the provision of decent shelter for millions of central-city slum dwellers. And it is in this suburbia where, for social, psychological, and economic reasons, the poor, the black, the Mexican-American and the Puerto Rican is usually as welcome as crabgrass.

The elements underlying the opposition to these groups, and to the housing that would attract them, are present in varying combinations in different towns and villages. Often the less acceptable of them, in terms of democratic rhetoric, are left unvoiced in public while opposition is proclaimed on grounds not in crude conflict with the ideals that supposedly underlie national life but all too often are the lie of national life.

The most pervasive and powerful of the elements rarely acknowledged in public—at hearings of the local zoning board or in the letters-to-the-editor columns of suburban newspapers—are, of course, racial hostilities and fears. Around backyard barbecue grills or in work-bound car pools, it quickly becomes apparent that, for numerous white suburbanites, the urge to keep blacks out arises from sheer distrust or dislike of all Negroes. For others, it stems not so much from hostility or distrust as from the fear that admission of blacks to a community will bring with it the same social tensions and discords besetting the cities, which many whites thought they were getting away from by moving to the suburbs. (Where hostility and distrust end and fear begins is often about as fathomable to a psychiatrist as property tax depreciation formulas are to a two-year-old.)

Sometimes the opposition to lower-income housing is founded on more a class than a racial prejudice. In some cases such prejudice is simple snobbery, the feeling that one has not "made it" unless he lives in a town devoid of lower-income families and less-than-$50,000 homes. In others, it is the conviction that housing for low-income or moderate-income families, especially rental housing, will attract families with little or no sense of responsibility for keeping their homes and the local public facilities in good repair, and that this will cause the general quality of life in the community to deteriorate.

This was the fear expressed in one suburban situation where there was no difficulty determining that the opposition was based entirely on class rather than race. The opposition—to a proposal that would have extended homeownership opportunities to low-income blacks—came from better-off blacks who already were homeowners. The situation (to be kept in mind by crusaders for social justice who sometimes forget that whites have no monopoly on deeply rooted prejudices) occurred in 1970 in North Hempstead, a suburb of New York City on Long Island. Black homeowners there bitterly contested a plan by the town's housing authority to erect in their community the first of a group of prefabricated $25,000 ranch homes into which selected public housing tenants, to be chosen on the basis of their potential for economic improvement, would initially move as renters. As the economic circumstances of these families improved, they would make higher monthly payments and eventually take title to their houses as mortgage holders. Faced with the angry opposition of the black homeowners, the town's officials killed the plan.

One of the blacks who had fought the proposal, a man with a painting of Martin Luther King, Jr., hanging in his $14,000 home, explained his stand by saying: "People who rent houses don't keep them up. Maybe what I am saying would be contrary to what Dr. King would say, but this is my opinion."

Still another sentiment working against the construction of low-cost housing in the suburbs is the feeling that suburbia should remain a semipastoral haven from the proximity-induced tensions of city life. Often this concept is interpreted not only to leave little or no room for multifamily construction but also to preclude fuller utilization of suburban land for single-family homes. And many times it is also accompanied by the notion that high residential densities invariably lead to slums ("congested instant slums," as one suburbanite referred to such densities).

While there is much to be said for the psychological benefits of distance between dwellings—though this is often a matter of personal temperament; many a city dweller does not feel at his best *unless* he is tripping over his neighbors at every turn—the equation of high densities with future slums has about as solid a foundation as a split-level suburban sanctum built without pilings on a bog. That high-density development by itself is not synonymous with "congested instant slums" is clear to any stroller along New York's Park Avenue between 59th and 96th Streets, where low density is hardly the term to describe the canyon-wall of tall apartment buildings standing shoulder to shoulder on each side of this famous millionaires' row. That plenty of distance often has little relationship to healthful housing is equally apparent to any visitor to the shacks of Appalachia or the hovels of a score of Indian reservations.

In any case, the arguments these examples are addressed to are a red herring. Fuller utilization of suburban land for housing need not entail city-type densities or anything approaching them, and most critics of the present patterns of suburban land utilization are not urging such densities. Rather, they contend that with careful and intelligent planning (garden-apartment clusters surrounded by large open space, for example) the healthful features of suburban tracts—their elbow room, grass and trees, and cleaner air—can be enjoyed by many who are now shut away from them, bottled up amid the simmering deterioration of the central cities.

Finally—but emphatically not least in importance—there are

significant economic factors motivating the opposition to lower-income housing in the suburbs. Their significance is understandable even to many critics of suburban exclusion of lower-income housing, because they stem from the same fiscal pressures beyond local control that afflict the central cities, namely, the pressures flowing from reliance on local property taxes for the major part of locally raised revenue.

Just as big city governments have been concerned with making urban renewal projects pay off in the biggest possible boost to the local property tax base, so the governments of suburban jurisdictions are concerned with developing their land to strengthen the local tax base, and the fiscal situation generally, to the fullest extent. Hence the opposition to housing for low- and moderate-income families. This housing not only fails to enlarge the property tax base as much as housing for well-off families or commercial and industrial development, but also leads to sizable additions in public expenditures, because it frequently brings into a community families with more children and a greater need for social services than does housing for the upper middle class or the rich. Greater numbers of children require more schools—outlays for education already form the largest portion of local budgets in most suburban communities—and this, added to the other municipal services often needed by lower-income families, prompts many suburbanites to object that housing for such families does "not pay its way." The fear that their own property taxes would have to be raised to make up the difference between the tax intake added by such housing and the new expenditures required for its residents gives suburbanites one more reason for opposing lower-income housing in their communities.

The sentiment resulting from all these reasons is fully and faithfully reflected by suburban local government, which brandishes its legal armor to stave off the unwanted housing. The most effective shield in this endeavor has been the local zoning law.

To critics of the suburban exclusion of lower-income housing, use of the zoning powers for this purpose represents a perversion of essentially desirable laws intended to safeguard the over-all public welfare and interest, as well as private property values, by providing a rational and orderly framework for development. As it has evolved over the past half-century, these critics say, the zoning power has become the deadliest weapon in the hands of those who are helping to shape an America that is guided more by their prejudice and fear than by the welfare and interests of all Americans. Suburbanites who defend their zoning practices maintain that they are perfectly in keeping with a major purpose of zoning: to prevent land uses incompatible with the "character and quality of life" in a community.

Actually, this division of opinion should not be surprising. From its start, the movement for public zoning powers, which grew steadily in strength in the late nineteenth and the early twentieth century, was based in two major camps: planners, motivated primarily by a vision of an environmentally healthier and more rational way of building communities than through the unguided functioning of the private real estate market; and property owners, whose main concern was to prevent changes in their areas that could conceivably lessen the value of their own holdings or enterprises. The different emphasis of each group helps explain the clashing views in the 1970's.

This clash really comes down to the different concepts of "community" behind the contending views. Those who oppose the use of zoning as a tool to exclude sizable segments of the population from sizable areas of the country extend the concept of "community" to the entire nation. The zoning function, they say, should be exercised within a framework of fostering the healthy development of the over-all national community without hindrance by parochial boundaries. Defenders of exclusionary suburban zoning practices have a less inclusive view of "community," which usually stops at the town line.

The above observation, when I made it in the presence of one suburbanite, drew this heated response: "It shows ignorance of some of the real strengths of American society—home rule, pluralism, heterogeneity, the blacks and whites and reds and yellows instead of a dull homogenized gray!"

The contention that racial and ethnic differences, traditions, and enclaves have enriched the nation and should have every opportunity to continue doing so is not, however, disputed. Nor is it disputed that a local voice in determining public policy is an important part of the democratic ideal. The point is that an even more important part of the democratic ideal is *freedom to choose* to be part of the black or white, the red or yellow, or the dull gray. Wherever public policy abridges this freedom for large segments of the population, "heterogeneity" and "home rule" are simply euphemisms for apartheid, star-spangled-banner style.

As the zoning power has developed over the past half-century, it has become such an abridgement. During the 1920's, the authority to zone was delegated by the states—in which it resided as a function of the "police power" to legislate for the public health and welfare—to localities of every size. By 1930, by which time every state had passed enabling legislation to permit all or some of their localities to enact laws governing uses and densities on the land in their jurisdictions, more than a thousand local zoning ordinances were in effect. In subsequent decades the number increased tenfold. Of the nearly 10,000 local zoning laws as the 1960's ended, slightly more than half were in the nation's metropolitan areas, with the vast majority in localities of less than 50,000 population.

In the Philadelphia region, about 200 of the 238 cities, townships, and boroughs have zoning ordinances. In Cook County, Illinois, more than 100 out of about 130 small cities, towns, and other jurisdictions surrounding Chicago exercise zoning power, as do some 100 suburban localities in the San Francisco metropolitan area and more than 500 jurisdictions in the New York metropolitan area.

As a result, whatever the over-all housing needs of a metropolitan area—and the regional view of housing requirements is held by most experts to be the only possible view if the housing problems of urban America are to be overcome—any efforts to meet them are subject to a multitude of vetoes that, taken together, form a wall around the ill-housed and the minorities in the old deteriorating central cities.

The zoning laws achieve their effect through several exclusionary approaches. One common provision limits most of a locality's residentially zoned land to single-family homes, thus excluding even small garden-apartment clusters. Fairly typically, less than 1 per cent of the residentially zoned undeveloped land in the suburbs of New York City was zoned for multifamily housing in the 1960's, according to the Regional Plan Association. Although multifamily construction has undeniably increased in the suburbs in recent years, the increase is minuscule if measured against the land that would exist for such construction if not for prohibitions against multifamily housing. Moreover, suburban land has generally been made available for apartments, when at all, in a way that discourages low-cost development. As the National Commission on Urban Problems explains it:

> In many suburban jurisdictions zoning for multifamily housing occurs only through a piecemeal rezoning process. There is at any one time little undeveloped land available for multifamily construction. The price of land zoned for such purposes is thus inflated because of the uncertainty about the total amount of land that may become available.

Accompanying the widespread exclusion of multifamily housing is the equally extensive requirement that single-family homes be built on large lots. A fairly typical example is the Cleveland area In Cuyahoga County, which includes Ohio's biggest city, two-thirds of the undeveloped land mapped out for single-family residential construction in the late 1960's was zoned for minimum lots of more than a half-acre. In adjacent Geauga County, 85 per cent of the residentially zoned land had to be developed with single-family homes on lots of an acre or more.

Still other exclusionary zoning practices take the form of minimum-floor-area requirements so high as to preclude low-cost construction, and prohibitions against mobile homes, a form of housing that has been increasingly advocated in recent years as a possible source of the low- and moderate-income units required to meet the nation's needs. (More about them later.)

The impact of these restrictions on the housing production process is severe. Large-lot requirements and the widespread exclusion of multifamily development drives up the cost of whatever housing is constructed in the suburbs—in the one case by preventing economies associated with multifamily construction, in the other by requiring greater expense for the installation of such facilities as sidewalks and water and sewer lines, all of which must stretch farther where single-family lot sizes are larger. Beyond this, large-lot requirements and multifamily exclusion, by restricting the supply of sites available for housing in a given metropolitan area, contribute to inflated costs of residential land all over the area, including the central city.

Finally, according to some researchers, suburban exclusion of low- and moderate-income housing pushes the number of sites down below what is required if all the new housing needed by many metropolitan areas and their central cities is to be built. These researchers point out that the supply of available land in many cities is so limited that even landfill projects and "air rights" construction (building over facilities such as schools and railroad yards) will not increase the number of potential housing sites enough. In the words of the President's Committee on Urban Housing, "regardless of the extent to which the nation chooses to tear down the central cities and rebuild them, a large share of the new housing, including subsidized housing, developed in the coming decade will have to be located outside of central cities."

The exclusion of low- and moderate-income housing from so much of suburbia affects more than just the housing supply. It separates unskilled and semiskilled jobs from the areas where blue-collar workers live, especially black workers. Along with the migration of middle-class whites, the 1950's and 1960's saw a sizable migration of industry and commerce from central-city to suburban locations. Between 1954 and 1965, according to the U.S. Department of Labor, more than half the industrial and commercial facilities built in the nation's metropolitan areas were built in the suburban rings. Four-fifths of the new jobs gained in the nation's large metropolitan areas during the 1950's and 1960's were gained in the suburbs, according to Paul Davidoff and Neil Gold, city planners who have served as consultants for, among other groups, the President's Committee on Urban Housing.

Whatever the extent of this trend, there is no question that the suburbs have been far more willing to accept industrial and commercial enterprises, especially when educational and other local government expenses have risen sharply and necessitated a wider tax base, than to accept the people who work in those enterprises. Hence the growing trend in "reverse commuting," especially by blacks, Puerto Ricans, and Mexican-Americans, who head from city homes to suburban plants in the morning and back in the evening, crossing paths with suburbanites negotiating the more traditional commuter route.

One of the most conspicuous reverse-commuter flows is found today in the Detroit area. Suburban-ring cities like Warren and Dearborn have automobile factories that employ thousands of blacks as well as white workers. But only the whites go home in the same cities; virtually no blacks live in them, and when the work shifts are over, the blacks stream back to Detroit. In varying degrees, but increasingly as more industries head for the suburbs unaccompanied by housing for the unskilled and semiskilled labor supply, the reverse-commuter phenomenon can be seen in almost every major metropolitan area.

The need for distant commuting presents a sizable difficulty for city-dwelling blue-collar people. Commuter rail and bus fares, usually far higher than city transit fares, take a heavy bite out of working-class paychecks. And because public transit frequently is spotty in automobile-oriented suburbia, commuting is time-consuming as well as expensive for any reverse commuter who is too poor to own his own automobile or unable to join a car pool, and whose factory is not within walking distance of a commuter railroad or bus station. These difficulties must certainly be considered factors in the high rate of unemployment among big-city blacks.

In an effort to remedy this handicap and other negative effects of suburban exclusion of lower-income and minority families, the National Association for the Advancement of Colored People announced in 1969 a major program of litigation against bias-based suburban zoning. The National Committee Against Discrimination in Housing, another prominent civil rights organization, also announced as the 1960's ended that it was embarking on a nationwide program of court action aimed at wiping out segregation through local land-use controls. "Until local governments have been deprived of the power to exclude subsidized housing and to manipulate zoning and other controls to screen out families on the basis of income and, implicitly, of race, there can be no effective progress in halting the trend toward predominantly black cities surrounded by almost entirely white suburbs—the geographic manifestation of 'two nations, one black and one white, separate and unequal,' " the committee declared, citing the conclusion of the National Advisory Commission on Civil Disorders in 1968 that American society was splitting into two nations.

To many urban affairs analysts, such litigation is unquestionably as important to the achievement of equal opportunity in housing as action to strengthen and implement the array of traditional open-housing measures enacted in the late 1950's and the 1960's. These measures—totalling in 1970 some 370 open-housing laws on the local level—are designed to deal with only one aspect of exclusionary housing practices: discrimination in the sale and rental of existing housing. They have no bearing on the equally consequential discrimination that so often hinders the construction of desperately needed new housing.*

But urban affairs experts, aware of the entire range of motivations for suburban exclusion of the poor and minorities, justly point out that court action toward ending such exclusion, while necessary and desirable, is not sufficient by itself. If suburban communities are to be compelled to admit lower-cost housing, hence new population requiring sizable increases in public services, then there must be new arrangements to help these communities finance the increases. Either federal grants will have to be provided to help offset the cost of the additional services or the system by which the suburbs raise their revenue must be sharply altered. Otherwise, many communities will be unable to afford the increased outlays for services, given the often limited tax bases represented by the property within their own jurisdictions.

One suggestion for fiscal change has been to expand the property-taxing jurisdiction in the suburbs beyond a single town or

* The traditional open-housing laws have had little impact on the discrimination they are supposed to deal with in the existing-housing market. Lukewarm or ineffective enforcement, vague definitions of illegal discrimination, and long and discouraging procedures for invoking these laws are widespread. At the same time though, the mere existence of open-housing measures has to be considered a sign of progress, and they provide a legal framework within which to press for equality of opportunity in housing. (The first local open-housing law covering the private market—and the first such law on any level of American government—was adopted by New York City on December 31, 1957.)

village (countywide, in some cases), as is already done to some degree in the form of school districts. This would mean a sharing of property tax revenues by a number of communities for many functions, including social welfare, police, fire, and recreational services and facilities. In this way communities with a tax base that might collapse under an influx of lower-income families would be fiscally buoyed by neighboring communities with a more solid base or with less of an influx. However, it goes without saying that such a widening of taxing jurisdiction would require acceptance in the suburbs and in state legislatures (where the necessary legislation would have to be enacted) of a definition of "community" that extends well beyond town boundaries, and such acceptance shows no evidence of mushrooming in the early 1970's.

In any case, the joining of the battle by prominent civil rights groups promises to make suburban exclusion of lower-income housing an issue as massive and bitter in the America of the 1970's as the struggle over school segregation was in the 1950's and 1960's. "This commission has had it up to here with communities that have to be dragged kicking and screaming to the Constitution," the Reverend Theodore Hesburgh, chairman of the United States Civil Rights Commission, declared with frustration in the summer of 1970. But "dragged kicking and screaming" is precisely how a great number of suburban communities will have to be brought to the point where they no longer exclude the less affluent and the black and Spanish-speaking minorities.

The Nixon Administration, it was clear at the time Father Hesburgh was expressing his frustration, was not to be counted on to do any of the dragging. If the Administration had any policy on opening up the suburbs to all Americans, it could be characterized only as aggressive nonaction. At first this was evident whenever George Romney addressed himself to the issue, as when he rushed to Warren, Michigan, in July, 1970, to try to stem the anger that had erupted in the suburbs of Detroit over reports that the Administration was considering some action in the area. As noted, Romney told the officials of the worried suburban communities that he was seeking not "forced integration," but only "affirmative action" toward desegregation as the price of a community's receiving federal urban renewal money. Exactly what did he mean?

According to one observer at the Warren session, "When Warren's mayor, Ted Bates, asked the secretary if any acceptance of affirmative action programs would be tested by looking for an increase in black residents, Mr. Romney did not answer directly but said the program would depend only on 'good faith' of the suburbanites."

For those who justifiably wanted fuller explanation of the Nixon Administration's policy on this major issue of American life, there was Romney's statement several weeks later to a Senate committee:

> The federal government should not, in my view, require a community to accept a housing development which does not conform to code or zoning requirements imposed for the benefit of the community as a whole and which are uniformly enforced. But neither should a community be permitted to exclude an otherwise conforming development just because of its eligibility for federal assistance.

Lest the slow of mind still be uncertain (most exclusionary suburban zoning requirements are "imposed for the benefit of the community as a whole," at least as far as the imposers are concerned, and often are "uniformly enforced"), Romney referred the senators to legislation that the Nixon Administration had quietly and unsuccessfully proposed to Congress three months earlier. It would have forbidden local government to use its zoning, planning, or building code powers to prevent, in areas in the path of development, the "reasonable provision . . . of low- and moderate-income housing eligible for federal assistance in a manner inconsistent with any state or local comprehensive or master plans for such areas," and it would have forbidden discrimination against low- and moderate-income housing "on the basis of its eligibility for federal assistance." To enforce the legislation, the United States Attorney General or any citizen eligible to benefit under a federal housing program would have been permitted to bring court action.

The proposal never made it out of a housing subcommittee in the House of Representatives, where the subcommittee's majority apparently considered the bill too un-American or too politically explosive or both. For Romney's part, the proposed legislation embodied a wise middle course of action in dealing with the extremely sensitive issue (as did the Department of Housing and Urban Development's policy, stated by Romney, of giving priority in awarding its limited housing and community development funds to localities that made an attempt to offer housing opportunities to poor minorities). To those affected or deeply troubled by suburban exclusion of lower-income housing, the bill, even if successful, would have meant little or nothing.

First, the requirement that an exclusion of a reasonable amount of federally aided low- and moderate-income housing, to be actionable, be "inconsistent with any state or local comprehensive or master plans" was seen as a watering-down of the attack, as few state or local governments had comprehensive or master plans calling for the racial, ethnic, and economic integration of the suburbs. Romney had an answer to that point: To qualify for various types of highly desired aid from the Department of Housing and Urban Development, state and local governments had to have master plans designed to promote "open communities" in ways acceptable to his department. However, because the criterion for open-community plans acceptable to Romney's department, as Romney told the mayor of Warren, would ultimately be the "good faith" of the communities adopting them, their value was open to question.

Second, the proposed legislation, like any civil rights legislation providing for remedies through court action, embodied an approach rife with the prospect of tortuous delays that would make it years at best before the legislation would have a meaningful impact, assuming actions under it were diligently pressed. And this was an assumption few critics were willing to accept, given the fact that the actions would depend to a great extent on a Justice Department headed by Attorney General John Mitchell.

Critics of the legislation said that, if the Nixon Administration were really serious about pressing the fight to open up suburban America to those now excluded, it would withhold federal aid—for such facilities important to the suburbs as schools, highways, hospitals and sewer systems—from suburban communities following exclusionary housing policies. Such a course was already sanctioned by civil rights legislation, specifically Title VI of the Civil

Rights Act of 1964, many legal experts held. And a study group on urban renewal that President Nixon had himself appointed recommended in 1970 that federal aid "of all sorts" be withheld to "break the suburban barrier around the central cities."

But George Romney in the same year consistently expressed the view that the federal government did not have the authority to withdraw such aid on a large scale and that, in any case, attempts to do so would arouse so much bitter opposition that the entire effort in behalf of open communities would be doomed.

That such opposition could be any more bitter than it already was in 1970 was doubtful, as Romney himself should have been aware after his visit to Warren. But the heart of the matter, of course, lay beyond anything that George Romney said—or could say, given the essential impossibility of his position. He was part of an Administration in which his appreciation of the damage inflicted by suburban exclusionary practices on American society, however troubled and sincere, had only the most marginal influence.

"In Washington," one journalistic observer of the Nixon Administration's day-to-day operations wrote at the time, "one gets the impression that Mr. Romney and his department are operating outside the main currents of the administration." The main currents, of course, had been influenced not by Romney, whose impact at the White House was generally agreed to be minimal at best, but by the real policy-shapers in the executive branch under Nixon: Attorney General Mitchell, chief domestic affairs adviser John Ehrlichman, and other White House "insiders," whose conclusions about the direction America had to take to make it a better place were far different from the conclusions George Romney had derived from statistics on the economic and racial polarization between the nation's central cities and its suburbs.

And it was the Mitchell-Ehrlichman conclusions that prevailed at the top. When President Nixon finally spoke to the nation on the issue, after having remained publicly silent about it for the first half of his administration, he declared in late 1970: "I can assure that it is not the policy of this government to use the power of the federal government or federal funds . . . in ways not required by the law for forced integration of the suburbs. I believe that forced integration of the suburbs is not in the national interest."

Asked later to explain his distinction between "forced integration" and the enforcement of the federal open housing law, which he promised to pursue, Nixon said:

> In the one case, the laws on the books deal, as they properly should, with human rights, the rights of an individual to buy . . . or rent a house or an apartment and not be barred because of his racial, religious or other background. In the other case, what we are talking about is economic considerations having to do primarily with the zoning. . . . It seems to me there is a clear distinction. The law does not require, and if it does not require in my opinion [it] does not allow, the federal government to use its monetary and . . . coercive power for the purpose of changing the economic pattern of a neighborhood. I think what the law does require is that there be open neighborhoods. The law does not require that the federal government step in and provide in a neighborhood the type of housing that an individual could afford to move into.

To civil rights leaders, this was a dubious if not disingenuous dichotomy. The "economic pattern of a neighborhood"—and of many a whole suburban city—is often what it is *precisely because* of racial discrimination, which frequently is the major underlying reason for the exclusion of the low-income and moderate-income housing that would change the economic pattern. The open housing law may not mandate that the federal government "step in and provide in a neighborhood the type of housing that an individual could afford to move into," but it does mandate that Washington take action when local public policies based on racial discrimination prevent federally aided housing from being built.

What's more, there will never be a significant degree of open housing in the United States until there is more lower-income housing in more communities. As the American Jewish Committee noted even before Nixon applied his sophistry to the subject, "more and more fair housing organizations . . . as they look for neighborhoods in which to integrate minority families, find a total shortage in low-cost housing units which makes any large-scale integration impossible."

But the realities of exclusionary suburban policies were not penetrating the walls of the White House in the early 1970's. In that august structure, another reality was considered far more important. That was that the Nixon Administration's constituency included the very people determined to continue these exclusionary policies, not the people whom the excluders considered too poor, too black, or too troublesome to qualify for a place in the suburban sun.

3. Washington and the Crisis—I

THE "MAGNA CARTA"

On August 1, 1968, on the sun-bathed plaza in front of the curving facade of the new Department of Housing and Urban Development building in southwest Washington, President Lyndon B. Johnson ceremoniously signed into law the Housing and Urban Development Act of 1968. To the dignitaries behind him and the lunchtime crowd of government workers jostling with television cameramen before him, the President proclaimed the act "the most far-sighted, most comprehensive, most massive housing program in all of American history." With a Texas-sized oratorical flourish to match the pomp of the occasion, he further declared that it "can be the Magna Carta to liberate our cities."

It was a proud moment for the Johnson Administration's Great Society—in fact, on a subsequent occasion the President would state that he considered the housing act of 1968 one of the ten most important pieces of legislation in the nation's history. It was a gratifying moment too for the many diverse elements of American society that had worked together to fashion what they described as a "landmark" or "breakthrough" measure. The act established a goal of 26 million units of new and rehabilitated housing to be created in America during the subsequent ten years, including 6 million government-subsidized dwellings designed specifically to meet the needs of the nation's ill-housed and "house-poor" families, and authorized a wide array of old and new programs to achieve this goal.

The programs embodied various approaches and embraced the views of many segments of American society that had often clashed on the issue of housing. There were provisions for vastly expanding the production of government-owned low-rent housing, which for years had been urged in some quarters as the only effective method of providing decent housing for those who could not afford it on their own; but there were also provisions for greatly increasing the role of private enterprise in meeting the needs of badly housed Americans, much to the gratification of the homebuilding industry. There were programs for reconstructing the decayed sections of America's existing cities, a task whose urgency few residents of these sections would dispute; but also provisions for facilitating the development of entirely new cities, which some experts have held out as the only real long-range solution to the nation's problems of housing blight and population growth. Greater participation in housing efforts by non-professionals through nonprofit and community groups was to be encouraged, but there was also machinery for enlisting the most accomplished professionals in the all-important task of advancing the country's housing technology.

In short, there was an array of programs and provisions to warm the hearts of those deeply concerned Americans who, from an assortment of social and economic perspectives, were united in feeling that it was time for the world's richest society to set about the task of providing decent shelter for the millions of its people who most emphatically lacked it. If there was dissatisfaction among proponents of the act, it was only because its goals understated the nation's true need, for reasons to be discussed in Chapter 7.

Little more than a half year later, even these relatively limited goals were being laid to rest in some quarters. Readers of the financial section of the Sunday *New York Times* on March 16,

1969, found the following banner headline over the views of several housing economists discussing the '68 act: "Housing Program, Still in Infancy, Already a Prospective Failure."

For those only vaguely familiar with the history of the federal government's housing activities, such a headline, coming little more than half a year after the highly publicized passage of the "landmark" act, no doubt was bewildering, to say the least. But those more experienced in the ways of federal housing policies over the previous three decades were hardly surprised. The history of federal effort in behalf of the nation's ill-housed families has been a history of rhetorically impressive promises followed by singularly unimpressive performances, of intricate programs long on solemnly avowed goals but short on the first thing needed to achieve them—*money*. In fact, the familiar handwriting was on the wall for the 1968 act even before the end of the congressional session in which it was adopted. The same session that authorized the programs making the act a landmark shortly afterward failed to appropriate anywhere near the funds needed for the programs to function at the authorized level.

This latest default by the federal government on its already overmortgaged credibility in housing was greeted by most experienced observers with a mixture of disappointment and resignation. Typical was the comment of James W. Gaynor, then Commissioner of Housing and Community Renewal in New York State, who told a meeting of local urban renewal officials:

> We are dismayed that in spite of the largess the Housing and Urban Development Act of 1968 apparently affords in new and expanded housing and community development programs, the actual appropriations by the Congress will do little to make these gains a reality. The pattern, unfortunately, has become a consistent one in the past several housing and urban development acts and is greatly to be deplored. A great deal of the credibility gap in urban affairs can be attributed to this tease-then-take-away procedure by the federal government.

No doubt Gaynor had in mind the most blatant previous "tease-then-take-away" saga in the history of federal housing legislation, the Housing Act of 1949. Similarly cited as a legislative landmark, this enactment, which proclaimed the goal of "a decent home and a suitable living environment for every American family," authorized the construction of 135,000 units of low-rent public housing a year for six years, or a total of 810,000 units by 1955. This total had not been reached in the *twenty years* after the 1949 act.

But if the "tease-then-take-away" routine—or the fact of Washington life that it is one thing for the national government to authorize a program and another for it to spend the money to see it through—has resulted in the most faltering steps toward providing for America's wretchedly housed, it has nevertheless created the illusion of a full-fledged federal assault on the problem. In Washington as the 1970's began there were some four dozen houseing programs with a maze of rules, regulations, and fine-print procedures. Anyone who saw such a stupifying bureaucratic array would have good reason to wonder how on earth a society could have a housing crisis with such a plenitude of official schemes to combat it. But just as all the architects' blueprints in the world can do little to keep a human being warm in the winter or dry in a rainstorm, so all the elaborately drawn and impressively titled schemes from the best brains of the housing bureaucracy mean little without the cash to back them up. And, in the words of the President's Committee on Urban Housing, a conspicuous fact of American life has been the "woefully inadequate scale of all government housing subsidy programs."

Just how inadequate becomes dismayingly clear when one realizes that, in more than thirty years, the federal government's grab-bag of housing subsidy programs has produced, at this writing, a grand total of approximately 1.5 million* housing units for the nation's poor and moderate-income families—or one-seventh of the "rock-bottom" need of 11 million units that the National

* A million and a half is the total number of new and rehabilitated units that have been completed (and existing units that have been leased and acquired without rehabilitation) as of July 31, 1970, under the low- and moderate-income programs of the U.S. Department of Housing and Urban Development and the Farmers Home Administration of the Department of Agriculture. Federal officials, however, argue that a full and fair picture of federal housing achievements would have to include units under construction as well. Though nobody lives in a housing "start," units under construction would raise three decades of federal housing "achievements" from 1.5 million units to about 1.75 million (again, as of July 31, 1970).

Commission on Urban Problems has found to exist among these groups. Moreover, as the National Commission has found, through 1968, the year of its report, "government action through urban renewal, highway programs, demolitions on public housing sites, code enforcement, and other programs *has destroyed more housing for the poor than government at all levels has built for them.*"

This kind of performance in the face of privation has led almost all observers of federal housing efforts, from the most knowledgeable to the most unsophisticated, into frustration and cynicism. Edward Logue, the urban redevelopment specialist whose work in New Haven, Boston, and New York State (as head of the state's controversial Urban Development Corporation) has brought him national attention, commented tartly in late 1968:

> What we have in our national government is like Macy's and Gimbel's. We have a new gimmick every year. But in the last ten years [during which there had been a proliferation of new housing and redevelopment programs out of Washington] we have successfully avoided facing up to that nice, simple problem of cash.

A woman resident of a New York City slum reacted in a similar vein that year during a community meeting. A city official was presenting an intricate explanation of how the federal government's newly developed "model cities" program had been designed to do for her neighborhood what a series of previous government upgrading efforts had failed miserably to do. "First you tried to urban renew us; then you tried to wage a war on poverty for us; now you say you want to put model cities on us," the woman said as her neighbors urged her on with shouts of "Amen!" and "Tell it like it is!"

"Now, I don't know anything but cookin', but I do know you can't bake, broil, and fry a fish at the same time," she told the red-faced official.

An officer of the National Association of Nonprofit Housing Organizations pinpointed another frustration arising from federal programs. "The newcomers to the low-income housing program—nonprofit sponsors and corporations—have been going through some difficult learning processes. They have had to become expert in a very short time in the intricacies of the several financing formulas under which they can operate: Sections 221 (d) (3), 235, 236, 202, 221 (h), Ginny Mae take-out, Fanny Mae back-up . . . it goes on," he complained, referring to the legislative section numbers and housing-agency acronyms and jargon that are as much a part of the housing bureaucrat's language as the most common nouns and verbs in Webster's.*

A typical conversation I had with one federal housing spokesman over a policy dispute between federal and local housing officials exemplifies the language barrier. Explaining Washington's position in the matter, the spokesman leaned forward earnestly in his chair and admonished: "You just can't make flip judgments in something like this. You first have to ask yourself—how will over-all goals be affected if, as a general rule, supplements plus 23's are allowed to total more than a fifth of a 236 or a d-3?" (Translation: . . . if, as a general rule, tenants receiving federal rent supplements, plus tenants in apartments leased by local public housing authorities under Section 23 of the public housing laws, are allowed to total more than 20 per cent of the tenants in a building constructed under Section 236 or 221 (d) (3) of the National Housing Act, which provide subsidies for the private development of housing for low- and moderate-income families.)

Whether expressed in bureaucratic jargon or in plain English, the federal government's efforts to meet the nation's critical housing needs—and to live up to its own commitments in this area—add up to the two words used by the Kaiser committee: "woefully inadequate." Moreover, besides being too little over the years, the efforts have been shamefully late in coming, particularly when compared with efforts that the governments of other developed countries have made to provide decent housing.

In 1931, a scholar of the American housing scene, Edith Elmer Wood, wrote:

> European countries have developed three major forms of housing activity which are all but unknown in the United States: (1) Slum

* "Ginny Mae," or GNMA, is the Government National Mortgage Association; "Fanny Mae," or FNMA, is the Federal National Mortgage Association. Their mission is, generally, to help keep the mortgage supply healthy, Ginny Mae in relation to subsidized housing, Fanny Mae in relation to nonsubsidized housing.

> clearance . . . carried out by public authorities as a health measure, nearly always involving considerable expense to the taxpayers; (2) housing loans at low interest rates, tending to be that of government bonds . . . (3) housing by public authorities, usually municipal, for those not otherwise provided for.

Noting that publicly aided housing had made significant strides in England even before World War I, and that between 1920 and 1930 more than 1 million additional government-aided units had been built in that country and in Scotland and Wales under various subsidy programs carried on while both Labor and Conservative governments were in power, she concluded that, in housing, the United States Government was a half-century behind the British.

A similar contrast was made with Germany, which between 1919 and 1928 created housing for more than 1.1 million families under a government loan program and a program of direct municipal construction, both of which had been developed before World War I. Between 1915 and 1930, the Netherlands "rehoused one-fifth of her population with public assistance," Mrs. Wood noted, and "nearly all other European countries have developed some form of housing loan at low interest rate and some form of municipal housing or a slightly disguised substitute for it."

But in the United States, where widespread housing squalor had been a blot on the landscape since the nation's earliest days, the federal government—as in so many other spheres involving the welfare of its citizens—had remained devoted to the notion, long discredited by reality, that sanctified private enterprise, unassisted by public efforts, could provide for the shelter needs of the citizenry. Except for a report on big city slums called for by Congress in 1892; the production of about 30,000 housing units—about half built as dormitories and all later sold—for civilian workers near major shipyards and munitions plants during World War I; and the development of a set of model building and zoning codes, the federal government had played no role in American society's efforts to house its population, even though one-third was still estimated to be living in housing that (in Mrs. Wood's words) was "definitely subnormal by any decent standard."

In fact, government effort on any level involving housing was largely confined to the restrictive aspect, in the form of state and local minimum-standard housing and building codes that had begun with New York's Tenement House Act of 1867. While these codes provided protection (if sometimes only on paper) against the worst manifestations of unsafe and unsanitary housing in the limited number of jurisdictions where they existed, they represented, as most European governments had already decided, only half the effort needed to assure decent housing. The other and equally important half was assuring a steady flow of new housing, and here America's governmental apparatus was woefully retarded compared with the rest of the developed world. For example, the pioneering New York State Limited Dividend Housing Companies Law of 1926 provided land-acquisition aid and property tax abatement to private groups undertaking construction of moderate-cost housing. Governor Alfred E. Smith and other proponents of public action in housing had urged far greater innovations. More than a dozen years before, the Massachusetts Homestead Commission had summed up the obvious when it had concluded that "in no country has private enterprise been equal to the task of properly housing the inhabitants." But the majority of New York legislators refused to go any farther than the 1926 act, which some of them already considered blatant Bolshevism.

The Works of the FHA

With the Great Depression, the role of government in housing, as in so many other basic spheres of American life, underwent a fundamental change—in theory if not always in practice.

The first federal responses to the housing side of the Depression crisis—construction of new housing plunged by the mid-1930's to one-tenth of the pre-Depression level of 900,000 units a year—were designed, in both the Hoover and the Roosevelt administrations, largely to bolster the existing home-financing system. In 1932, after a White House Conference on Home Building and Home Ownership that President Herbert Hoover had called the previous year, a system of regional Federal Home Loan Banks was created to advance home-financing capital to savings and loan institutions. Following this, the first year of the Roosevelt Administration saw the establishment of the Home Owners Loan Corporation, which was authorized to provide financial aid to families facing foreclosure. Between 1933 and 1936 alone, the corporation made available more than $3 billion to more than 1 million households.

Another early New Deal measure, creation of the Federal Deposit Insurance Corporation to insure bank deposits, also had an important influence in aiding the mortgage system. By reassuring depositors that they could put their money into banks without fear of losing it, the FDIC helped contribute to a stable supply of home-financing funds.

The New Deal "pump-priming" effort was combined with the effort to provide housing for the poor under a program in which the Public Works Administration built federal low-rent housing. Between 1934 and 1937, about fifty projects containing about 22,000 units were undertaken.

But these and other efforts, though they met the immediate needs of numerous families on the brink of losing their homes and brought basic stability to a shattered housing industry, were only first aid in an economic emergency ward. Far greater innovation was needed for long-term health, as was acknowledged by the Roosevelt Administration with the creation in 1934 of the Federal Housing Administration and its system of mortgage insurance—an innovation in American life that was to have a profound sociological influence far beyond the stimulation of renewed home construction in the economically bleak 1930's.

Under the FHA mortgage insurance program, a lending institution was guaranteed, in effect, that the mortgage loan it made for the purchase, construction, or repair of a home would be repaid even if the borrower defaulted. By providing this guarantee, the FHA removed much of the risk of making such loans and encouraged financial institutions and other lenders to make them on terms far more favorable to the homeowner than previously.

Before the FHA program, mortgage loans usually covered only one-half to two-thirds of the purchase price of a home, so that down payments of one-third to one-half were commonly required. Families unable to make such down payments had to take out second and sometimes even third mortgages, at additional high interest rates and other costs, to cover as much as possible of the part of the price not covered by the first mortgage. Interest rates on the first mortgage were also high. Repayment terms were short, frequently less than ten years, at the end of which a large lump sum covering the principal had to be paid, as the regular payments made during the term of the mortgage usually covered only the interest.

But with FHA guaranteeing repayment in case of default, lenders were willing to offer more favorable terms: higher loan-to-purchase-price ratios, resulting in smaller down payments and the avoidance of second and third mortgages; longer repayment terms; and gradual amortization of principal instead of the severe—and sometimes financially lethal—end-term "balloon payment." The costs of administering the FHA program, including outlays from defaults, were to be defrayed by a system of mortgage premiums (averaging .5 per cent of the unpaid balance of the principal) charged to the borrowers. At the start of the program the FHA was permitted to insure up to 80 per cent of the value of a home, enabling down payments of only 20 per cent, and to insure mortgages carrying terms as long as twenty years. Over the years the regulations were liberalized so that by the late 1960's the FHA was insuring the entire first $15,000 of value plus 80 to 90 per cent of the balance on mortgages bearing terms of up to thirty-five years.

Besides providing mortgage insurance for one- to four-family homes (under Section 203 of the National Housing Act, for those who want to sound authoritative at cocktail parties), the FHA has also provided mortgage insurance for apartment house projects under a variety of other sections. The Section 207 program, for example, has enabled private builders to obtain mortgage insurance covering up to 90 per cent of the appraised value of projects worth up to $20 million. Several of the federal subsidy programs for low- and moderate-income families developed in the 1960's (to be discussed in detail later) were placed under the jurisdiction of the FHA because of the tie-in of these programs with the mortgage insurance system. And in 1969 the FHA insurance system was extended to cover mobile homes, an aspect of the American housing scene whose already rapid growth in the 1960's was expected to be significantly accelerated by extension of the FHA umbrella to it.

What all this has added up to is financial fuel for an impressive output of housing over the past three and a half decades. Since 1935, more than 7 million homes and apartments, or approximately one-fifth of all privately financed nonfarm units built in the United States, have been constructed with FHA-insured mortgages. FHA officials and their supporters proudly point out that most of this housing has gone to young middle-class families that would not have been able to afford their own homes without the favorable financing terms induced by the agency's insurance program. They also note that, by mandating construction standards for the housing whose mortgages it has insured, the agency has brought an important degree of consumer protection to the housing field. And FHA insurance has also been granted to cover about 30 million loans for home improvements, many of which might not have been possible without the insurance.

None of this is disputed. But when one steps beyond the surface indicators of accomplishment, he finds himself in a field of controversy swept by a bitter crossfire of charges and countercharges. By far the great majority of FHA-insured homes have been built in the suburbs. FHA insurance was an important contributor to the rapid development of suburbia after World War II, and it is in this regard that the agency has had a sociological influence far beyond what its New Deal originators could have envisioned. Critics have berated the agency for the contrast between its extensive aid to new suburban areas and their middle-class residents and its meager aid to the old central cities, with their poor and near-poor.

Some critics of the FHA go so far as to heap on it most of the blame for the plight of America's cities today. For example, Martin F. Nolan, a Washington political commentator, in discussing the monumental tasks confronting the U.S. Department of Housing and Urban Development (of which the FHA has been a part since 1965), declared in *The Reporter* magazine in 1967:

> The Federal Housing Administration has, since 1935, issued more than $84-billion in mortgage insurance, creating suburbia and help-

ing to entice middle-income families from central cities without due compensation to the cities. This prejudice against cities and in favor of suburbs is the most grievous federal sin for which HUD must atone.

FHA supporters respond that the agency was not created especially to help the poor, that the purpose in establishing it was to revive homebuilding and stimulate homeownership, and that the FHA has been used as a scapegoat for the failures of those government agencies that have specifically been charged with meeting the housing needs of the poor. They point out—without exaggeration—that the agency has had to keep in mind the influential conservative congressmen who have ridden steady herd on it to assure that it does not take "excessive risks" and that its policies are "economically sound." The agency's defenders conclude that if anyone in Washington is to blame for a suburban bias in federal housing policies over the years, it is the national government in general, not the FHA in particular.

Whatever the merits of these arguments—and there is truth on both sides—the fact remains, as the National Commission on Urban Problems concluded, that "until recently, FHA benefits have been confined almost exclusively to the middle class, and primarily only to the middle section of the middle class." The Douglas commission went on:

> The poor and those on the fringes of poverty have been almost completely excluded. These and the lower middle class, together constituting the 40 per cent of the population whose housing needs are greatest, received only 11 per cent of FHA mortgages. . . . The experience of members of the commission and others convinced us that up until the summer of 1967, FHA almost never insured mortgages on homes in slum districts, and did so very seldom in the "gray areas" which surrounded them. Even middle-class residential districts in the central cities were suspect, since there was always the prospect that they, too, might turn as Negroes and poor whites continued to pour into the cities, and as middle and upper-middle-income whites continued to move out.

It should be pointed out that much of this was inevitable, considering the FHA's personnel over the years. Primarily recruited during the Depression from among "middle-class real estate men," the agency's original functionaries often "operated with the conventional racial prejudice characteristic" of this group, according to the Douglas commission. In fact, the commission added, "until 1948, when restrictive covenants or written agreements not to sell to Negroes were declared unconstitutional by the Supreme Court, FHA actually encouraged its borrowers to give such guarantees and was a powerful enforcer of the covenants."

In the middle 1960's, under a national leadership with a vigorously different attitude about FHA's mission, and against a background of the violent urban outbreaks that were to be a hallmark of the decade, new top-level instructions emerged from Washington. In 1965 Philip Brownstein, who had been appointed FHA commissioner by President John F. Kennedy in 1963 and who served through the Johnson years, urged his regional directors to "be alert to situations [in older areas] in which values can be stabilized and property upgraded by an infusion of capital." In 1967 he declared to his subordinates that the "FHA will not designate entire communities or areas as ineligible for participation in its mortgage insurance operations."

Meanwhile, liberal elements in Congress, unwilling to leave it to the FHA to clean its own house, took successful action themselves. In 1966, Section 203 of the National Housing Act was amended to permit the Secretary of Housing and Urban Development to waive the section's "economic soundness" requirement, provided that a property being considered for mortgage insurance was otherwise acceptable. According to the President's Committee on Urban Housing, this amendment resulted in a "dramatic" change in FHA activities. "At the time of the passage of the 1966 amendment," the Kaiser committee reported, "FHA loans in slum neighborhoods averaged less than 150 per week. By mid-1968, FHA averaged more than 2,000 such high-risk commitments per week." In the Housing and Urban Development Act of 1968, the FHA was further provided with a new "special risk insurance fund" and authorized to issue insurance to low- and moderate-income families whose irregular incomes or credit histories prevented them from meeting normal FHA credit standards and to insure mortgages in "older, declining" urban areas.

Just how faithfully these congressional intentions will be implemented over a long term remains, of course, to be seen. With a Republican Administration in power whose basic outlook on racial strife and urban difficulties appears to be more in keeping with the "traditionalists" still entrenched in many FHA regional and local offices than with the FHA national leadership that characterized the previous Democratic administrations, the outlook for continued liberalization within the agency seemed, in the early 1970's, uncertain at best.

When the Public Is the Poor

If the FHA's mortgage insurance system was the foundation laid by the New Deal for bettering the housing of middle-income America, then the Roosevelt Administration's counterpart for low-income Americans—in aspiration if not in subsequent achievement—was the system of public housing authorities created in the Housing Act of 1937. By that year, proponents of a strong federal role in housing realized that the three-year-old Public Works Administration program of direct federal construction of low-rent projects needed large-scale expansion and reform if meaningful results were to be achieved. To make possible such results, and, it was hoped, to meet some of the vigorous objections to the PWA program of direct federal construction, the United States Housing Authority was created as the cornerstone of a system in which federal and local governments would work together to meet the housing needs of low-income Americans.

Basically, the federal public housing program created under the act provides for local communities, through their own special housing authorities, voluntarily to develop, own, and manage low-rent housing. The federal government provides major subsidies to cover the costs of development and construction (originally through the U.S. Housing Authority, later through the Public Housing Administration, and today through the Department of Housing and Urban Development). The local governments provide additional subsidies in the form of property tax exemptions. The aim of these subsidies, as the 1937 act states, is to reduce rents sufficiently to make housing available to "families who are in the lowest income groups and who cannot afford to pay enough to cause private enterprise in their locality or metropolitan area to build an adequate supply of decent, safe, and sanitary dwellings for their use."

The act, late as it was, compared with what other countries had undertaken, was undisputably a landmark in the history of American social legislation. But that the program established under it has fallen far short of meeting the need for which it was designed—in terms both of total production over the years and of a financial structure that, until very recently, worked to exclude many families most desperately in need of decent housing—is also indisputable.

According to the Department of Housing and Urban Development, as of the summer of 1970 some 870,000 units of federally aided public housing were "in management" in every part of the country and in such possessions as Puerto Rico and the Virgin Islands. The total production figure rises to more than 970,000 if, as federal housing officials prefer, projects under construction are counted along with those in occupancy. In both cases the total figure includes units built directly by the local authorities, as provided for in the original 1937 act, and those leased or purchased by the authorities under more recent modification of the act. ("Public housing," to be absolutely clear at this point, refers specifically to the housing built or acquired under the 1937 act and its amendments or under its few counterparts on the state and local levels. The term is not used by housing professionals, though it often is by laymen, to denote all government-assisted housing. Housing built under programs involving government financial aid to private builders or nonprofit developers is referred to by the pros as "publicly assisted" housing.)

Taking into account units in the planning pipeline as well as those completed or under construction, approximately 3,000 localities in all fifty states and the several territories—roughly 15 per cent of all potentially eligible localities—had chosen to participate in the federal public housing program by the late 1960's. To urban dwellers who have become accustomed to thinking of public housing as a big city phenomenon, it will be something of a surprise to learn that approximately a quarter of the public housing units planned, under construction, or completed by 1970 are in localities of less than 25,000 population, and 17 per cent are in places of less than 10,000 population. Of course, the public housing programs in the smaller cities and towns are minuscule by big city standards. A recent study of 2,156 local housing authorities showed that 656 of them had fewer than fifty apartments each in their jurisdictions, while 431 others had between fifty and a hundred apartments. Only 296 of the authorities surveyed administered more than 500 apartments.

All the cities of more than 250,000 are involved in the program, though to widely varying degrees. New York City, with about 70,000 apartments under management in the federal program (in addition to 80,000 that the local housing authority has completed under similar state and city programs) is first in the nation. Chicago, with less than half of New York's population, has about half (38,000) the number of federally subsidized public housing units. Philadelphia has a quarter of New York's population and over a quarter (20,000) the number of its federally aided units. Houston, whose current population of 1.25 million is one-third the population of Chicago, has only one-thirteenth (2,900) the number of units Chicago has. Atlanta, on the other hand, with less than half the population of Houston, has about four times as many units.

As for cities that experienced the most violent ghetto outbursts of the 1960's, Newark, whatever the other faults of some of its municipal administrations, comes off rather favorably in public housing production. In the first thirty years of the federal program, the deeply troubled New Jersey city completed nearly 11,000 units for a total 1970 population of about 400,000. Los Angeles, with seven times; Detroit, with four times; and Washington, with twice the population, each completed fewer units during those three decades.

All told, as the 1970's began, about 3 million Americans, roughly 1.5 per cent of the total population, were living in housing built under the Federal low-rent program. From the previous discussion, it goes without saying that this figure is shamefully small in relation to the nation's housing needs. The inadequacy of the figure is further emphasized by the number of families seeking to enter public housing. The Department of Housing and Urban Development reported that, in the thirtieth year of the federal program, a total of 193,072 families were on the public housing waiting lists in the nation's fifty largest cities, while the number of vacant units in those cities totaled 6,864. True, not all families that put themselves on the waiting lists turn out to be eligible for public housing. But this must be balanced by the consideration that a sizable number of families whose financial eligibility and need are uncontested never apply simply because they are discouraged by the long waits in most places, or because they feel that past behavior by members of the family will prevent them from meeting screening standards that, contrary to popular middle-class notions, a large number of local authorities maintain.

To those who do place themselves on the waiting lists, there is little question that public housing, whatever its often-cited faults, is nevertheless superior to housing that these families, with their limited resources, might obtain on the private market. (The median public housing rent in 1970 was about $50 a month, including utilities.) But over all in the United States an appreciation of public housing is, to put it mildly, anything but overwhelming. Throughout its three decades, the program has been the target of bitter attacks and vehement and often highly emotional resistance. The deep-rooted opposition—based on a complex of social, economic, and philosophical elements—has been a major reason why public housing has fallen far short in relation to need, and in relation to the goals that Congress itself has set for the program in rhetorically expansive moments. At times in its history, the public housing program has ground to a virtual standstill.

Philosophically, the opposition has stemmed from the star-spangled belief, more prominent in the program's early days than in recent years, that it is alien and pernicious socialism for the government to be involved in producing housing for the citizenry. Like so many of the New Deal's innovations, the passage of the Housing Act of 1937, despite the hope that it would mollify critics of the PWA's program of direct federal construction, was greeted by tradition-bound Americans with outcries of indignation and denounced as one more example of the spiritual decadence into which the nation was being plunged. For many, this view no doubt arose from deeply felt ideology. With others, however, especially members of the homebuilding industry and allied businesses, it was not easy to tell where ideology left off and self-interest began.

Today the public-housing-is-un-American argument is encountered far less frequently as a growing number of generally conservative Americans, including many members of the homebuilding industry itself, have come to realize that, the resources of the poor being what they are in relation to the high costs of building and maintaining sound housing, profit-motivated private enterprise cannot by itself provide for shelter needs at the lower end of the economic scale. Debates over the principle of public housing now generally center on whether construction by public authorities is as efficient as governmental subsidy methods involving participation by the private sector. These disputes, though sometimes degenerating into clichés about the "innate superiority" of "inventive private enterprise" over "lethargic government bureaucracy," nevertheless are a long and wholesome way from the scare shouts of impending Communism.

But if the ideological opposition to public housing has abated in recent years, the opposition grounded on sociological factors has sharply increased. More and more, public housing has become bound up with the racial hostilities, fears, and tensions ripping away at American life. To try to understand the limited achievements of the program without recognizing this relationship is like trying to appraise a new house built in the middle of a garbage dump without taking into account the dump.

In its early days, public housing was rarely thought of as "black housing," originating as it did during a Great Depression in which so many of the poor were working-class white families victimized by a collapsed economy. During the 1940's, only about one-third of the country's public housing apartments were occupied by black families. But by the early 1970's the situation had sharply changed. Today the proportion of black families is more than half with perhaps 10 per cent more of public housing families (speaking now only of the continental United States and not Puerto Rico) estimated in 1970 to be Puerto Rican or Mexican-American

In short, at least 60 per cent of the families residing in public housing now are from the poorer elements of America's black and Spanish-speaking minorities, and in many cities the ratio is far higher than the national average.

To realize the significance of this, one need only attend a gathering of residents in a middle-class white neighborhood—within the cities as well as out in the suburbs, in the North as well as the South—for which a public housing development has been proposed. (Again, however, as the North Hempstead, Long Island, episode in the previous chapter made clear, some of the most vigorous objections to public housing have come from middle-class *black* homeowners living in neighborhoods where developments have been proposed. The bias against public housing is not only racial or ethnic in character but of a class nature as well.)

Still more criticism of public housing has come in recent years from the poor themselves and from many advocates of increased governmental activity in housing. Here the criticism is directed not so much at the principle of the public housing program as at its practice over the years. For example, the critics note, too little public housing has been built in most places for an especially house-poor segment of the population: *large* low-income families. This has resulted from a combination of federal financial pressures and local attitudes. The financial pressures have been in the form of limitations frequently imposed by Washington on the amount of money local authorities have been permitted to spend on the construction of a single housing unit, which have tended to restrict the number of units with three, four, and five bedrooms. Many local housing authority officials have felt that large families tend to be troublesome and that their numbers should be limited to insure the tranquility and good repair of a project. This combination of reasons helps to explain why roughly one-half the public housing units started during some years of the 1960's were for the elderly.

Similarly criticized by many who favor the principle of public housing is the depressingly sterile, stigmatizingly institutional form that far too much public housing has taken, which has made many public housing occupants as sensitive to the word "projects" as they are to a racial epithet. Although not all public housing developments are the "high-rise chicken coops" many of the critics refer to—in smaller cities one commonly finds garden-type structures, and even Chicago has built some public housing in the form of single-family homes—the fact remains that, far too frequently, monotonously massive construction has been undertaken whose architectural bleakness and jarring disproportion to the surroundings are anything but uplifting.

Undoubtedly such construction has often been the result of an unforgivable insensitivity on the part of many public housing officials to the relationship between design and psychological well-being. But the blame cannot be placed entirely on "unimaginative bureaucrats." The truth is that American society at large, because of its generally grudging attitude about the kind of housing that should be built for the poor, and because of the widespread concern that this housing not be built near the middle-American hearth, is largely responsible for the deplorable nature of so much public housing. Confronted by the pervasive notion, in and out of Congress, that government-built housing should contain nothing but the most essential physical facilities; generally forced, because of opposition to public housing in middle-class and suburban areas, to build in a restricted number of neighborhoods; and having always to work with a fraction of the funds they desperately need, even enlightened local housing authorities often have had little choice but to build big and with Spartan austerity if they were to build any meaningful amount of housing at all.

Over and over again I have spoken with middle-class people, many of them well-educated, who have condemned the "high-rise monstrosities" and "big brick barracks" in which "nobody should be forced to live," but who, just as vehemently, have opposed proposals for public housing in their own areas, no matter how small or imaginatively designed the proposed developments were. One usually perceptive magazine writer explained to me why he endorsed the view of a politician opposed to erecting public housing in middle-class areas: "Putting low-income people in middle-class neighborhoods only creates further tension and a heightened sense of envy among the low-income people," the writer said. "Also, what is gained by putting these people in high-rise slums?" he added in virtually the same breath. It never occurred to him that there might be a connection between the "high-rise slums" he deplored and a social philosophy that severely limited the amount of land where low-rent housing could be built so that high-rise concentrations were often unavoidable if a meaningful number of apartments were to be built in his housing-starved city.

In the same vein, those opposed to the entire notion of public housing delight in pointing to its most spectacular failure, the Pruitt-Igoe project in St. Louis, as if all their arguments are justified by the tragic history of that ill-fated development. Pruitt-Igoe, a complex of forty-three eleven-story buildings, was built in the mid-1950's at a cost of $36 million. By 1970, with most of the construction debt still remaining to be paid, twenty-six of the buildings were vacant and being boarded up, and it was not clear how long the other seventeen would continue to be occupied. The massive, 57-acre complex was succumbing to vandalism, crime, and deterioration. Life there had been so miserable and unsafe that, despite a severe shortage of low-income housing in St. Louis, many poor families shunned Pruitt-Igoe, preferring to live in squalid tenements at higher rents. At one point in the late 1960's, when the over-all vacancy rate in federally subsidized public housing across the country was 2.2 per cent, the vacancy rate in St. Louis' public housing was 13 per cent, largely because of Pruitt-Igoe.

Although foes of public housing will not see it this way, the tragedy of Pruitt-Igoe resulted as much from the opposition to public housing as from any defects in the program itself. While there is no question that administration of the project left much to be desired and that its design was in some respects abominable, the major reason for the development's severe difficulties was that it concentrated too many starkly poor, unstable, and problem-ridden families in one place, without providing an adequate level of the social services which were indispensable if these families were to overcome their problems. Most of the tenants were women and children on welfare—in a state where welfare payments ($124 a month in 1969 for a mother with three children) are among the nation's lowest—and narcotic and behavior problems were widespread.

The very need to concentrate these families in one place without sufficient social services, and to make that place a massive and psychologically cold assemblage of masonry and glass in a sea of existing slums, was the result ultimately of the widespread opposition to public housing that hems it into existing ghettos and prevents adequate amounts from being spent on it and on the needs of disturbed families in it. Ironically, or perhaps inevitably, the same people whose feelings are responsible for such constriction and for the inadequacy of funds are the quickest to brand public housing a "failure."

Obviously, prevailing attitudes will have to change sharply before widespread improvements can come about in the design and atmosphere of public housing. However, in an effort to force some improvements, Congress provided, in the Housing and Urban Development Act of 1968, that high-rise developments could no longer be approved by the federal government for families with children unless it was shown that there was no practical alternative to such construction.

The 1968 act, and also the Housing Acts of 1969 and 1970, contained additional provisions designed not only to improve the public housing program but also to rescue it from the very serious difficulties besetting it in recent years. The acute effect inflation was having on the program was among the most severe problems. Before the Housing Act of 1969, public housing, by statute, could not be built at a cost greater than $2,400 per room generally or $3,150 per room in high-cost areas like New York City. (The construction cost ceilings were higher for accommodations designed for the elderly.) In addition to the legislative ceilings per room, the Department of Housing and Urban Development, as noted, often placed administrative limits on construction costs per apartment. Both sets of ceilings were so unrealistic in the face of the sharply rising land and construction costs of the 1960's that, in high-cost areas, construction starts in public housing dwindled drastically as the 1970's approached. The New York City Housing Authority reported in December, 1969, that, despite a sharp nationwide increase in public housing starts that year, no new construction under the program had begun in that city since the previous July. As a result, the authority reported, slum neighborhoods in the city were scarred with brick-littered lots cleared of decayed tenements but equally barren of construction activity.

Responding to the situation, the Senate took the initiative in 1969 to raise the per room construction cost maximums, and the next year Congress eliminated the statutory dollar ceilings altogether and accepted a Nixon Administration recommendation for a flexible ceiling formula based on the costs of prototype construction in a given area. These reforms followed another welcome step, the provision in the 1968 act making available financing for the construction or acquisition of more than 300,000 public housing units during the three-year period ending June 30, 1971. This production target was part of the goal of well over a million public housing units to be started through 1978, with the latter figure itself part of the over-all goal of 6 million public and publicly assisted units envisioned under the 1968 act by 1978.

Whether the congressional actions will actually result in such a ten-year output of public housing remains highly uncertain, despite a good start in 1969 and 1970. During the 1969 calendar year, for example, the Department of Housing and Urban Development reported 82,000 public housing starts. This figure comprised 36,000 new units undertaken through the conventional approach of construction by local authorities; 30,000 new units begun under a recent innovation permitting local authorities to purchase projects built for them by private developers (the so-called "turnkey" procedure, designed to reduce the often criticized time span involved in conventional public housing construction); 6,000 new units begun under provisions allowing the local authorities to lease units built by private developers; and the start of rehabilitation work on nearly 10,000 existing units that the authorities had contracted to lease from private owners.

But these figures, as welcome as they are in contrast to public housing production in previous years, cannot obscure the big question marks on which the prospects for meeting the over-all ten-year goal hang. One of the biggest involves the availability of relatively inexpensive sites, and here the outlook is none too bright for many housing authorities.

For one thing, there remains the opposition to public housing that forces its construction closer to the center of cities where, as the National Commission on Urban Problems notes, land costs are high. For another, some housing officials fear that successful attempts to make sites available in more areas could actually contribute to a reduction of public housing starts. This argument was advanced after a federal district court in 1969 ordered the Chicago Housing Authority to build three-quarters of its future housing outside the city's black ghettos. Judge Richard Austin found the authority to have practiced racial discrimination in its site-selection and tenant-assignment policies, and he directed it to undertake 75 per cent of its future housing in census tracts having less than 30 per cent nonwhite population.

The decision was hailed by civil rights and open housing advocates, who have brought additional suits in the hope of obtaining similar rulings elsewhere, and by housing officials who believe that, in the long run, the public housing program cannot survive on a meaningful scale unless much new land is opened to it. On the other hand, a number of housing officials expressed concern that resistance to public housing in middle-class and white areas would continue to be intense—if in fact it did not become even more so as attempts were made to conform to court directives such as the Chicago one—and that many local governments, finding themselves under such directives, would simply take the course of least political resistance and seek to build nothing beyond the small proportion permitted them in largely nonwhite areas.

Similarly contributing to the uncertainty over the latest public housing goals is the precarious financial condition of a number of local housing authorities. In June, 1969, George Romney reported that fifteen of the country's larger authorities were "on the verge of bankruptcy" and that perhaps 200 more would fall into financial difficulty if prevailing patterns continued. Though officials of some of the fifteen cited by the Cabinet official indicated that his warning of imminent bankruptcy was exaggerated, officials of the others said that there was no exaggerating their financial plight. Actually, a study by the Department of Housing and Urban Development found that in 1968 forty-three of the nation's eighty-two largest authorities (those with 1,250 or more units in management) had financial problems of varying magnitude, compared with only twenty authorities in 1965. Of the forty-three, twenty-four had run deficit operations in the 1967 fiscal year. These had included the Washington, D.C., authority, whose routine expenses had been 106 per cent of its income and whose reserve fund had been completely used up, and the St. Louis authority, whose routine expenses had been 103 per cent of its income and whose reserves had been three-quarters used up.

Such financial predicaments stemmed from the fact that the traditional financing structure of the federal public housing program had grown outmoded in the face of the economic realities of post–World War II America. Under the traditional structure, federal subsidies paid the costs of developing and building public housing (through annual contributions to retire the bonds that financed these activities). Maintenance and operating costs, however, were not covered by the federal subsidies but had to be financed largely out of rental income. In many localities, housing maintenance was one of the most inflationary elements of the 1950's and 1960's, its costs far outpacing the ability of low-income families to pay commensurate rent increases. In Detroit, for example, public housing maintenance and operating expenses rose 106 per cent between 1952 and 1969, while the income of public housing tenants rose by an average of 9 per cent. In New York City, routine maintenance and operating expenses in federally aided public housing rose 125 per cent between 1952 and 1967; the income of tenants in this housing rose an average of 65 per cent during the fifteen years.

Grimly viewing such realities, Albert Walsh, then head of the New York Housing Authority, warned a seminar of the National Association of Housing and Redevelopment Officials in 1968:

> Public housing is not heading for a fiscal crisis: it is already in a fiscal crisis. . . . Public housing dwelling units will soon be priced out of the low-income market and a social crisis of major proportions will develop as low-income tenants face the difficult choice of paying a catastrophic proportion of their income for rent—or returning to the slums.

Actually, there was a third alternative open to public housing occupants, as the beleaguered St. Louis Housing Authority found to its dismay when it attempted to increase rents to avoid bankruptcy. This was the alternative of a rent-strike protest, a course that the St. Louis tenants took with devastating effect for nine months in 1969 in response to the rent-rise move by their authority.

Many would argue that Walsh's warning that public housing was being priced out of the low-income market was already too late. Although the median annual income of public housing families was less than $3,000 in the late 1960's, indicating that the program was certainly benefiting many extremely poor families, housing experts noted that many other abjectly poor families had been necessarily excluded from the program, especially in areas where operating costs required relatively high rent schedules. To quote the Douglas commission:

> Operating costs come in some cities to as much as $65 or $70 a month for a three-bedroom apartment. This in itself would require a yearly payment of from $780 to $840. Allowing 25 per cent of the family's income for rent, this would require a yearly income of from $3,100 to $3,400. This would exclude all the abjectly poor and a large proportion of the poor.

The traditional financing system also had unwelcome repercussions aside from the exclusion of many families most desperately needing decent housing. With funds for maintenance and operations shrinking sharply over the years in relation to need, a good number of housing authorities had to cut back on repairs and upgrading efforts, sometimes to the point where a spiral of deterioration set in. They also had to reduce many of the social and protective services that are often so vital in public housing.

In 1968 and 1969, Congress finally took major steps—or so it seemed—to remedy these problems. The 1968 Housing Act provided for an additional subsidy to local authorities of ten dollars a month for large families and families of unusually low income. The act also authorized special federal funds for social-service programs such as counseling on household management and on educational and job opportunities. However, to the distress of local housing authority officials, the $15 million authorized for the tenant services program in the 1969 fiscal year was never actually appropriated by Congress, and the $30 million authorized for the program in the 1970 fiscal year was never even requested by the Nixon Administration.

Similar disappointment followed passage of a 1969 provision sponsored by Senator Edward Brooke of Massachusetts that sought to make the fundamental change needed in the public housing subsidy structure. It authorized an additional $75 million a year from Washington to help financially beset local authorities meet the maintenance and operating costs that could not be met from rental income and to supplement rents so that no family in federally aided public housing would have to pay more than 25 per cent of its income. However, in March 1970, the Nixon Administration requested Congress to appropriate only $20 million of the authorized $75 million, leading local public housing officials to complain bitterly that financially plagued authorities could not possibly be helped to the extent desperately needed, and prompting the head of one major city's authority to denounce the Nixon Administration's action as a "grotesque subversion of the plain and manifest intent of Congress."

In fact, of course, the activities of the Nixon Administration will perhaps be the major determinant of whether the public housing program achieves the goals set for it under the 1968 Housing Act. Many public housing advocates cannot forget the fate of the goals set in the 1949 housing legislation: instead of 810,000 units begun by 1955, as called for in the 1949 measure, barely one-quarter that number were started between 1950 and 1955. The 810,000 figure, as already noted, had not even been reached twenty years later.

Something for the Soldiers

Like the Great Depression, whose legacies in federal shelter legislation were public housing and the FHA mortgage insurance program, World War II also prodded Washington to recognize its obligations in housing. As part of the GI Bill of Rights to make up for the sacrifice of wartime service and to help returning servicemen readjust to civilian life, the Veterans Administration's mortgage guarantee program was established in 1944. It was later made available to men who served full time in the armed forces at any time after the outbreak of the Korean War.

Under a "GI home loan," the government guarantees a private mortgage lender against any loss up to 60 per cent of the amount of a loan extended to an eligible veteran, subject to a fixed maximum. Until 1968, when it became $12,500, the maximum guarantee on a single home mortgage was $7,500. Because veterans who bought houses in the late 1940's and early 1950's rarely paid more than $12,000, and because few lenders in those resurgent post-war days were worried about losing more than 40 per cent of the value of a home loan in that price range, many were willing to provide VA-backed mortgages to cover the entire cost of a house, thus requiring no down payment.

Like the FHA mortgage insurance system, the VA guarantee program made possible home ownership for many young and middle-class families that otherwise would not have been considered acceptable mortgage risks. By the start of the 1970's, about 7 million GI home loans had been made, roughly three million for the purchase of new homes and the rest for the purchase of existing houses. The VA program has had more of an impact on the lower middle class than has the FHA program, according to figures cited by the National Commission on Urban Problems. For example, 29 per cent of the VA-guaranteed mortgages issued in 1966 were taken out by families whose annual incomes were between $4,800 and $6,000. By contrast, perhaps 10 per cent of FHA-insured mortgages extended to home purchasers in 1965 went to families in this income range.

Over all, the Douglas commission concluded, "by virtually eliminating down payments, the VA apparently reached further down the income scale than did FHA." On the other hand, the commission noted, as with the FHA program, the poor have been "largely left out" of the VA program. Only 1.6 per cent of the VA-guaranteed mortgages taken out in 1966 went to families earning $3,600 or less, a scant improvement over the comparable figure cited for the FHA program.

4. Washington and the Crisis—II

Renewal for Whom?

Although neither Depression nor world war was besetting the nation at the time, 1949 was the next big year in the evolution of federal housing programs. The housing law of that year was spurred by Washington's belated recognition of a calamity of another sort: the rapidly spreading blight chewing away at America's cities. Urban decay had intensified during a decade and a half of Depression and world conflict in which economic deprivation followed by the needs of a war-oriented society had severely restricted maintenance and upgrading. Slums had gone from bad to worse and marginal housing had become slum housing. Cities already burdened with large concentrations of the poor were beginning to feel the growing migration of those cast up from the countryside by advances in agricultural technology. Middle-class white city dwellers were starting their own flow to the suburbs, while the cities' poor, and especially their black poor, having no such alternative, found themselves mired in steadily spreading squalor. It was to reverse this decay, and to help realize "as soon as feasible the goal of a decent home and a suitable living environment for every American family," that the Housing Act of 1949 was passed.

In addition to the ill-fated public housing commitment already noted and to various modifications of the 1937 act designed to strengthen the public housing program, the 1949 legislation brought into being another federal program that was to have a controversial impact on housing in America. This was "urban renewal"—a term that, two decades later, was being spat bitterly from the mouths of slum dwellers as often as it was rolling pridefully from the tongues of mayors and chamber of commerce officials. The hostile reaction to urban renewal among the poor, and especially the minority poor, was understandable. While more than 400,000 houses and apartments occupied mostly by low- and moderate-income families were wiped out by urban renewal during the program's first eighteen years, housing for only *one-tenth* the number of such families was built on urban renewal sites. "Urban renewal is Negro removal," a familiar charge among poor blacks and their supporters, was far more than the exaggeration of a few malcontents that proponents of the program often declared it to be.

Urban renewal, of course, has been responsible for important achievements in the battle to preserve the health of America's cities. Under the renewal program—in which local governments buy and clear land and resell it cheaply to developers, with federal and local government sharing the loss, or "writedown"—blight and deterioration have been dramatically reversed in hundreds of cities across the country. From Scollay Square in Boston to Bunker Hill in Los Angeles, the decay of residential slums and the moldering drabness of obsolete commercial clusters have given way to the gleam of mid-twentieth-century office towers and shopping plazas, to modern apartment buildings and garden-type developments, and to public complexes such as the Lincoln Center for the Performing Arts in New York City and the civic center in St. Paul, Minnesota. Large downtown stretches of Baltimore and Philadelphia have been virtually reborn, as have extensive districts of Chicago's South Side. Urban renewal efforts have also revived areas of many smaller cities. Of the 1,947 urban renewal projects undertaken or in planning by 1968, more than one-third, 664, were in cities and towns of less than 25,000 population; 130 were in places of less than 5,000 population.

Thanks to urban renewal, land whose value had been declining has risen sharply, providing cities with badly needed revenue through increased property taxes. Business enterprises, encouraged by the rejuvenation stimulated by government-induced redevelopment, have often been attracted to cities with urban renewal projects while other businesses have expanded in them, providing increased jobs. The new housing on urban renewal sites has kept in the city many upper-middle-class families that might otherwise have joined the suburban migration and made even worse the growing separation of the comfortable and the deprived, the white and the black, into burgeoning suburbs and beleaguered central cities.

All of these trends, proponents of urban renewal argue, ultimately benefit the poor and ill-housed as well as the upper middle class and the business and financial entrepreneurs for whom urban renewal has meant vast and highly profitable new investment opportunities. Without a healthy tax base, these proponents point out, local government cannot finance the social service and low-rent housing programs so vital to the welfare of the poor, and without a thriving commercial life a city cannot provide the job opportunities which so often hold the key to the economic and social betterment of the poor.

All this, of course, is indisputable—in theory. But the *theory* of what urban renewal will do for a city's poor and ill-housed and the *reality* of what it most often has done are a world apart—a fact that Washington finally tried to deal with meaningfully in the Housing and Urban Development Act of 1968, nineteen years after the federal urban renewal program began.

Before 1968, a total of 404,000 housing units had been demolished in renewal areas. The vast majority of them had been occupied by poor and lower-middle-class families, frequently black or Spanish-speaking. By contrast, the number of new units completed for low- and moderate-income families in urban renewal areas through the middle of 1967 totaled 41,580, one-tenth the number demolished, and two-fifths the total number of new houses and apartments completed on renewal tracts. Moreover, as the Douglas commission noted in presenting these figures, "most of the 'low- and moderate-income' housing construction . . . is actually designed for those in the upper ranges of the moderate-income category"; only 10,760 units of this construction had been in the form of low-income public housing. Ultimately, according to plans as of 1967, a total of 74,000 units of low- and moderate-income housing were to be built in the same urban renewal areas (compared with 122,000 units for higher-income groups). But ultimately, also, according to the plans as of 1967, a total of 760,000 units would have been demolished in these urban renewal areas—again a ten-to-one ratio of housing demolished to new housing for the poor and those slightly better off.

However, simply citing these statistics is unfair and misleading, urban renewal officials have often told me. They argue that families displaced by renewal projects, even if not provided with new housing on the renewal sites themselves, have nevertheless benefited from the program in that the vast majority have been relocated from substandard or deteriorating accommodations to "decent, safe, and sanitary" ones as called for by federal law.

At best, this assessment is highly debatable, and it has been vehemently debated. The families that were relocated into low-income public housing no doubt did make a change for the better in most cases. But even though low-income families displaced by urban renewal have been among those having first priority for public housing, most households uprooted by renewal projects over the years have not moved into public housing. Many preferred not to, and others could not qualify because their incomes, though not high enough to afford sound housing without great sacrifice, were still above public housing maximums. But, for the most part, there simply has never been enough public housing available in most cities to absorb a significant portion of families dislocated by urban renewal. Public housing and urban renewal undertakings have not generally proceeded with any degree of coordination, and most public housing has not become available at the time households uprooted by urban renewal have needed it. Even if, by some miracle, such synchronization had been achieved, the amount of public housing built in many cities still would have been insufficient as a relocation resource. In ten of the nation's fifteen largest cities, the number of housing units demolished to make way for urban renewal projects between 1949 and 1967 exceeded the number of public housing units built during those years. In the fifty-one largest cities, units demolished on urban renewal sites totaled 222,832, while public housing units built in those cities totaled 207,272.

For the families relocated in the private housing market, urban renewal has brought changes in housing quality that, taking into account relocation over the years and throughout the country, can only be described as mixed at best—despite the consistent view of renewal officials that the changes have largely been for the better. In 1964, William L. Slayton, then federal urban renewal commissioner, told a Senate subcommittee on housing that according to reports from cities across the country, 80 per cent of the families dislocated by urban renewal had "gone into decent, safe housing." Only about 7 per cent, he said, had had to move into substandard housing, while the rest had left the city or "disappeared" without leaving forwarding addresses. By contrast, a 1963 study of forty-one cities by Harry Reynolds, Jr., Professor of Public Administration and Political Science at the University of Southern California, had found that 60 per cent of the families relocated from urban renewal sites were still living in deteriorated conditions.

Such wide variations between official sources and independent research, still a prominent element of the urban renewal controversy, can be attributed in part to the different places and periods covered by the various reports, as well as to divergent views of what constitutes "decent, safe, and sanitary" housing, certainly not surprising in a society where such a definition is anything but developed. Some official reports consider relocation housing acceptable if it passes muster according to the Census Bureau definitions of housing quality, whose gross inadequacies will be discussed in Chapter 7. A study that the bureau made for the old Federal Housing and Home Finance Agency showed that, in a sampling of 2,300 families uprooted by urban renewal in 1964, 94 per cent were relocated into "standard housing." Given what we will see are the census criteria, one can safely assume that a sizable portion of this "standard housing" was hardly a significant improvement over the quarters left behind.

But the differences between official and critical evaluations go much deeper than differences of definition. Chester Hartman, a sociologist who has closely followed developments in urban renewal relocation, put his finger on this aspect when he wrote in *The Journal of the American Institute of Planners:* "As long as relocation remains a secondary interest in the renewal process and the primary impetus for renewal is to replace low-income housing with 'higher' uses, there will be strong pressures to use compromised standards and to understate any adverse impact of the relocation process on displaced families." Inasmuch as the primary impetus for most urban renewal over the years *has* been the replacement of low-income housing with "higher" uses, few who are familiar with the inherent bureaucratic need for self-approbation will dispute this.

In any case, as I learned when I encountered the results of practice rather than promise, for too many families uprooted by urban renewal, especially before improvements in relocation policies and procedures began to be felt in the mid-1960's, the renewal program has meant little more than a forced and sometimes traumatic move from one decrepit apartment in a decayed area to an apartment possibly a shade or two better—and most likely more expensive—in an area offering little perceptible improvement over the one left to the bulldozers.

Over all, the National Commission on Urban Problems concluded, urban renewal relocation made welcome gains during the 1960's but still had a long way to go. "In basic legal authorization, rules, and organization, and almost surely in results, relocation has been improving, particularly in the past few years," the commission stated, noting also that the urban renewal program "has not been as indifferent as the highway program, which in the past has demolished several hundred thousand homes without showing until recent years the least tangible interest in what happened to the occupants." But the Douglas commission also observed that

> it seems hard to escape the conclusion that the primary purpose of [urban renewal] relocation practice, if not of announced policy, has changed but little. In the earlier stages of renewal it might be summarized: get the site occupants out of the way of project construction with as little delay and outright hardship as possible. More recently a clause might be added to the preceding sentence: 'and with as much improvement in their housing as market conditions

allow and with some respect for their dignity as human beings.' . . . But is [this] good enough? . . . Why should anyone—legislators, administrators, or concerned members of the public—be reasonably satisfied when surveys show that the housing of those displaced improved a little on most counts and was not much worse on a few others?

By the mid-1960's, resentment bred by the traditional approach of urban renewal toward the poor and ill-housed began to have its effect in Washington. In 1965 Congress stipulated that residential renewal had to afford "a substantial number" of housing units for low- and moderate-income families and had to "result in marked progress in serving the poor and disadvantaged people living in slum and blighted areas." Two years later the Department of Housing and Urban Development stated that future urban renewal proposals should include housing primarily for the poor and those economically just above them. The Housing and Urban Development Act of 1968 was finally specific, providing that, in the future, a majority of housing units created in renewal areas would have to be for low- and moderate-income households, with at least 20 per cent for low-income families unless that amount of low-income housing was found not to be needed in a community.

In the last months of the 1960's the results of these changes were being seen. During the three fiscal years ending June 30, 1969, the number of new low- and moderate-income units begun on renewal sites nearly equaled the number of such units begun in the entire sixteen years of the renewal program before that.

Other indications that urban renewal might at long last become responsive to those most in need of improved housing include the procedures which some cities have adopted to alleviate the hardships of families affected by renewal. In some cases these procedures have been directly forced by the growing political militancy of slum dwellers, a trend of the 1960's that also has had a significant affect on housing. Such was the case in Philadelphia, where residents of the Washington Square West area waged a battle that ended with a city council resolution calling for at least 400 units of low- and moderate-rent housing to be built in their area before any renewal displacement of residents could take place. Also typical of the "staging" of renewal activities to minimize disruption of site occupants were the plans announced for the West Center City urban renewal project in Wilmington, Delaware, in 1969. In contrast to that city's previous urban renewal undertakings, in which massive relocation and clearance had preceded reconstruction, the West Center City plans required none of the 8,000 renewal area residents to leave the neighborhood. Instead, new housing in the area was to be made available as occupants of housing to be torn down had to move.

The Housing and Urban Development Act of 1968 included modifications of the urban renewal program designed to foster precisely this kind of departure from the traditional urban renewal approach. Under the so-called neighborhood development program in the act, cities could begin building facilities in an urban renewal area even before detailed planning for the long-term development of the area was completed, a change from requirements of the past. Besides giving cities more flexibility in handling problems of displacement and relocation as they arose, the neighborhood development program, by telescoping the planning and execution phases of urban renewal, was designed to speed up the often agonizing length of time it had taken to carry out urban renewal projects. Large projects had commonly taken ten to fifteen years, some even longer, and this added greatly to both financial cost and human hardship.

Unfortunately, the number of cities permitted to adopt the neighborhood development program approach was limited by the Nixon Administration. Of more than 300 cities applying for the program, only 80 would be permitted to participate, the Department of Housing and Urban Development announced in 1969. Administration officials said the limitation was necessary because Congress had not provided sufficient urban renewal funds to permit accelerated activities on a wider basis. It was also clear, though, that expenditures under the program would run counter to President Nixon's goal of limiting government spending to reduce inflation—a stand that, by early 1970, had forced severe cutbacks in urban renewal plans over all in cities throughout the country. Though Congress had authorized $2.3 billion for urban renewal, the Nixon budget for fiscal 1971 called for only $1 billion (the President subsequently vetoed an appropriation providing $1.35 billion), indicating, among other things, that the increases in low- and moderate-income housing mandated in renewal areas by the 1968 Housing Act would be even slower in materializing than many experts had expected.

Thus, in the early 1970's, the urban renewal program still appeared to be a long way from making amends for the over-all indifference it had previously demonstrated to the plight of Americans most severely in need of the "decent home and suitable living environment" promised by the 1949 act that had created urban renewal.*

Another Fine Theory

The 1950's saw, besides the abandonment of the first big public housing commitment and the diversion of urban renewal from the problems of the ill-housed, a dearth of innovation in federal housing policy. The most significant housing act of the Eisenhower years, passed in 1954, added various conservation and rehabilitation provisions to urban renewal and, perhaps most consequential, established the requirement that before a locality could qualify for federal aid for renewal and public housing, it had to fashion a "workable program" for dealing with the problems of slums and community development confronting it. To be federally approved, a workable program had to include such elements as housing and building codes, long-range plans for orderly growth, arrangements for relocating renewal-displaced families and businesses, and procedures for citizen involvement in renewal planning. Subsequently, the workable program requirement was extended to some of the housing subsidy programs for low- and moderate-income families developed in the 1960's.

Behind the workable program mandate was a solid aim: to get the cities and towns of America to contribute their own efforts toward meeting their problems of slums and growth, and to dis-

* If President Nixon had his way, urban renewal would end as a federal program altogether. As part of the so-called revenue-sharing system he has advocated, urban renewal would be among the programs turned over to the cities and states to continue, alter, or terminate. More on revenue sharing in Chapter 8.

courage the localities from "letting things slide" in the hope that this approach would hasten the coming of federally aided renewal. Albert Cole, administrator of the old Federal Housing and Home Finance Agency, explained to a congressional committee in 1954:

> This workable program requirement does not mean that a community must first exhaust all its efforts and resources in meeting these problems before it finally comes to the federal government to be rescued. Nor does it mean that a community must undertake a protracted period of detailed and clairvoyant planning and forecasting of the city's future for the next several generations before it can make an appropriate case for federal assistance. It does mean that a community must find out where it really stands and where it intends to go, and determine what present resources it can mobilize to get started in the right direction.

One of the clearly beneficial effects the workable program requirement has had on housing is in having spurred the development of badly needed local housing codes. In the mid-1950's fewer than 100 local governments had such codes; by the late 1960's, the number had risen to at least 4,900. But just as clearly, the workable program stipulation has also served to thwart the construction of housing under some of the federal subsidy programs to which it was attached in the 1960's. These programs, providing financial assistance to private developers of housing for low- and moderate-income families, did not in themselves require the consent of local governments for projects to be built under them. But these governments had, in effect, the power of approval in that they were able to refuse to adopt a workable program where they did not want housing constructed under these programs. It was partly in recognition of this reality that Congress, in 1969, eliminated the workable program requirement from some of the housing subsidy programs to which it had earlier been attached, and did not tie it at all to the major new subsidy programs established in the 1968 Housing Act.

New Directions, New Disappointments

As previously indicated, the 1968 act was the culmination of a decade of innovation in federal housing legislation. To some housing experts, the proliferation of new programs during the Kennedy and Johnson administrations of the 1960's was a welcome sign that the national government was willing to experiment and to seek the kind of broad-based approach to federal housing efforts that some analysts felt was badly needed. To others, like Edward Logue, the variety of new programs added up primarily to "gimmicks" designed to compensate for the one indispensable element that Washington was consistently short on in its housing endeavors: money.

The first of the major new tacks, in 1961, was designed to encourage a large-scale effort by private developers to build and rehabilitate apartments for low- and moderate-income families (though, in practice, the program quickly became one for the moderate-income sector and even for families with somewhat higher income).* The program—known to housing professionals as 221 (d) (3) BMIR, a mouthful standing for the section of the National Housing Act that established it and for the below-market interest rates that were its subsidy method—was intended to cut construction and development costs sizably by reducing mortgage interest.

Under the program, private developers were provided with FHA-insured mortgages at interest rates substantially below the prevailing rates for such mortgages—since 1965, a maximum of 3 per cent under the program. Financing costs were further reduced because the normal FHA insurance premium, .5 per cent, was waived. In return, the developer was required to limit rents or, in the case of a cooperative project, carrying charges.

The result was rents and carrying charges about 25 per cent below what they would have been had the housing been built with mortgage loans at the unsubsidized, market interest rates. In general, BMIR apartments have rented for between $22 and $30 a month per room, depending on the varying construction costs in different areas. This compares with monthly rents of $12 to $20 a room in most public housing.

* While the definition varies with family size and local cost of living levels, moderate-income households are often thought of as being in the $4,500 to $8,000 a year income range.

Income eligibility requirements for admission to BMIR housing have varied from city to city. The minimums have usually begun where public housing maximums have ended. The BMIR maximums have been based on local median income for families of various sizes, or on the rent necessary to support developmental and operational costs of an apartment. In Birmingham, Alabama, as an example, the maximum income permitted a family of three or four seeking entry into BMIR housing in 1968 was $6,200 a year. It was $8,000 in Gary, Indiana, and $10,250 in Honolulu, the highest in the country. First preference for BMIR housing has gone to families displaced by urban renewal or other governmental programs. BMIR developers, in accordance with the 1961 law, have included nonprofit sponsors such as philanthropic or community groups as well as profit-motivated organizations whose annual return has been limited to 6 per cent of equity.

All together, as of the summer of 1970, 175,000 BMIR apartments had been started in projects across the country and 140,000 of these had been completed. Considering that the original goal of the program had been to produce at least 40,000 apartments a year, which would have meant more than 350,000 starts through mid-1970, the actual output is anything but impressive—especially when one considers that it took *five* years for the number of total starts under the program to exceed the first year's goal.

There are several reasons why the BMIR program lagged. Profit-motivated developers were not overwhelmed by the opportunity to earn 6 per cent when far more attractive investments appeared elsewhere—though, it should be pointed out, the actual "yield" under the program, as opposed to the cash return, could be much higher for certain developers. (As the President's Committee on Urban Housing explained it, because of the tax savings on over-all income that can result when a builder takes advantage of depreciation deductions available on newly constructed housing, some investors in BMIR developments could obtain "an over-all yield, including tax savings to those in the 50 per cent tax bracket, approximating that required by many industrial corporations—better than 15 per cent per year.") But most builders preferred the still higher yields that resulted when tax savings were combined with cash returns greater than those permitted under the program.

In the case of the nonprofit sponsors, the numbers participating often were kept down by a lack of expertise in housing matters, for which no amount of community spirit and enthusiasm could substitute, and by the absence of funds, or "seed money," to obtain the professional guidance needed to plan a housing development. In addition, for several years the application procedure itself was a formidable hurdle, even to the most experienced builders. "Complexities and bottlenecks in processing applications by FHA often frustrated the program," the National Commission on Urban Problems reported. "The manual of successive steps which must be taken under 221 (d) (3) comes, with the illustrative forms, to 283 pages. This discouraged all but the most persistent sponsors."

Finally, though certainly not least in importance, BMIR was one of the programs hindered by the workable program requirement, which remained tied to it until 1969. No matter how interested a residential construction company or community group might have been in building under BMIR, its hands were tied if the local government had no workable program and refused to adopt one, as was the case in more than a few suburban areas that did not want BMIR housing.

As the 1960's ended, removal of the workable program requirement, the speeding up of FHA processing procedures, and a sharp and welcome increase in production under BMIR would normally have been grounds for rejoicing about the future of the program. But in fact the program had no future; it was being phased out in the early 1970's in favor of still another, supposedly superior, mortgage-subsidy scheme that had been created in the 1968 Housing Act.

Another Recipe: Rent Supplements

A second legislative concoction of the 1960's in which production crawled far behind promise was the highly controversial "rent supplement" program enacted in 1965.

Narrowly passed by a sharply divided Congress, rent supplements provided an additional means of producing federally aided low-rent housing.* In contrast to the traditional method of producing federally subsidized housing for the poor, involving development by public authorities, the rent supplement program called for development by the same private sponsors permitted to participate in the moderate-rent BMIR program: profit-motivated organizations willing to accept a limited return, nonprofit groups, and cooperatives. Under the rent supplement setup, these developers were to finance their construction or rehabilitation with FHA-insured mortgages at market interest rates (unlike the below-market rates of the BMIR program). The subsidy under rent supplements was to be in the form of federal payments to the developer amounting to the difference between 25 per cent of an eligible tenant's income and the "market rent" of his apartment as computed in accordance with the law.

As the program was enacted, tenants were eligible for rent supplement apartments if they met the admission standards for public housing in their localities. However, the developer of a rent supplement project did not have to rent only to families eligible for the supplements; he could rent also to any other tenants willing and able to pay the market rent, which was usually in the middle-income range. In fact, the Johnson Administration, in proposing the rent supplement program, had envisioned that it *would* become a vehicle for mixed tenancies, facilitating racial and economic integration in housing. Finally, many proponents of the program were hoping it would serve as a method of building federally aided low-income housing in middle-class and suburban areas, where, it was hoped, the mixed tenancies envisioned under rent supplements would be more welcome than orthodox public housing with its low-income-only occupancy.

It was these hopes, in part, that led to the vigorous opposition to the rent supplement proposal in Congress that nearly killed it and that drastically hampered production under it subsequently. Between enactment in 1965 and the middle of 1970, only 55,000 apartments had been started in rent supplement projects, with only 33,000 of these completed. Considering the scope of achievement that had been hoped for under the program, such a produc-

* In proposing the program, the Johnson Administration had wanted it used largely for moderate-income families.

tion figure must be considered no less disappointing than production under almost every other federal subsidy program aimed at meeting the housing needs of the poor.

The reasons for the rent supplement showing offer a vivid case study in how a grandly conceived program can be choked by short purse strings and long red tape. Congress authorized $150 million for the program through 1968; it actually appropriated $42 million for the period, including nothing at all in 1967. The original statute creating the supplement program did not require local government approval or the existence of a workable program for a supplement project to be undertaken; a rider attached to the 1966 appropriations bill for the program required that at least one of these conditions be present, all but wiping out prospects that the program would serve as a means of entry for poor and minority-group families in middle-class and suburban areas.

Additionally, "to mollify congressional pressures," according to the President's Committee on Urban Housing, the Federal Housing Administration (which has administered the supplement program) "has been forced to impose regulations on the program which have made it increasingly unworkable." Among these was the ruling that a supplement to a family could not exceed 70 per cent of the market rent of an apartment, a requirement that made the program inapplicable to many low-income families in areas of high construction costs. Limits imposed on the construction costs themselves and on amenities permitted in rent supplement projects made it increasingly difficult to design developments that would appeal to the unsubsidized middle-income families that, it had been hoped, would form part of the tenancy and would make such developments attractive to builders hesitant to invest in projects housing low-income families only.

And, of course, there were the FHA tendencies which hardly needed congressional prompting. As the National Commission on Urban Problems tells it, potential rent supplement sponsors, especially nonprofit groups, "were repelled by what they regarded as cold, bureaucratic, and at times actually hostile treatment at the -nands of FHA." Despite the apparently sympathetic attitude of top FHA officials, the Douglas panel stated in its 1968 report,

> testimony before our commission revealed [that] the rank and file officials in district and local offices were, in many cases, highly unsympathetic. They were accustomed to dealing with the conservative real estate and financial community. They did not feel at home in having business dealings with churches and philanthropists whom they tended to regard as soft and impractical. Nor did they welcome having the poor as their constituents.

And so it went, a catalog of obstacles as depressing as it was prolific.

A Model Idea

Hardly had rent supplements entered the housing bureaucrat's bulging vocabulary than, one year later, another grand design was packaged in Washington as a major departure from old-line federal policies affecting housing. This was the "model cities" program of 1966, designed to demonstrate how poverty and blight in America's cities, including substandard housing, could be overcome if the programs required for the task were concentrated and coordinated in a way never previously attempted.

Traditionally, government efforts to better the lot of deprived Americans had involved a number of undertakings in a piecemeal approach. Programs involving housing, education, jobs, health, recreational facilities, police protection, and municipal and social services had usually functioned with little relation to one another, so that a slum neighborhood's gains in one area of need would frequently be offset, or mean little over all, because of continued shortcomings in the other areas. (Although urban renewal did offer a comprehensive approach, it either ignored many of the worst slums or, as discussed previously, rebuilt them largely for other than their original inhabitants, who were simply shifted elsewhere.)

It is not surprising that the construction of public housing in a slum that otherwise remained unchanged, while providing decent dwellings for some fortunate families that previously lacked them, by itself usually contributed little to the over-all physical and social needs of the neighborhood. Even for the occupants of the public housing, such construction, at best, often was only a first and incomplete step in creating a "suitable living environment." Garbage-littered streets prowled by muggers and narcotics addicts, inferior schools, overcrowded and poorly equipped hospitals, the lack of vocational training opportunities, poor transportation facilities—all added up to an environment in which the new housing was often swallowed up in a sea of continuing physical and social depression. Yet instead of recognizing that *much more* than just building new housing was needed to wipe out the ills of slum life, opponents of public housing often branded this housing a failure because it, by itself, had not somehow magically alleviated all the ills.

In the same vein, even the most diligently maintained old building in a slum has often stood little chance of remaining a decent and safe place to live if the efforts to maintain it have not been accompanied by attempts to upgrade the entire area socially and economically as well as physically. It is a cliché among many middle-income and well-to-do Americans that the nation's slum problems would all but end if, as one suburban matron put it, slum dwellers "cleaned up their living—like stopped sending their garbage air mail out the window." One need not subscribe to this simplistic view of the slum environment to recognize that this environment nevertheless is synonymous with some harsh social realities that make it an uphill battle for even the best-intentioned landlord seeking to preserve his building as an island of cleanliness and good repair.

The Citizens' Housing and Planning Council of New York knows this well. A civic group devoted to improving the quality of life in the nation's largest city, the council, in 1962 and 1963, bought and rehabilitated a decrepit tenement in Manhattan's Lower East Side slum. With $115,000 of donated money, it installed new kitchens and bathrooms, replaced the old plumbing and wiring, replastered and repainted, and made various other improvements to convert a crumbling relic of the 1880's into decent and comfortable accommodations for the 1960's. The council had been motivated in its undertaking partly by the desire to gain firsthand knowledge of matters that, like so many similar groups, it had long theorized and philosophized about.

By 1967, a visit to the building showed garbage a foot deep

in the air shafts, broken windows, defaced hallways, and mailboxes vandalized by drug addicts—conditions that recurred almost as rapidly as they were remedied. Like the unimproved structures all around, the council's modernized building had an annual tenancy turnover rate of 80 per cent. It was a discouraging outcome for the civic group and its well-wishers, but at the same time it once more emphatically illustrated the multifaceted nature of the slum problem, and the need for a multifaceted and comprehensive approach in dealing with this problem.

It was to provide the first steps toward establishing such an approach nationwide that the Johnson Administration presented to Congress what developed into the Demonstration Cities and Metropolitan Development Act of 1966, the first half of which quickly became known by the catchy appellation "model cities." To demonstrate what could be accomplished when order and orchestration rather than confusion and contradiction prevailed in government programs involving the urban slum, the model cities program provided financial inducements for cities to concentrate—in some of their worst neighborhoods and under comprehensive plans for upgrading these neighborhoods—the various programs involving housing, education, social services, and other areas of need.

Specifically, the act authorized the federal government, in addition to contributing its normal share in financing such federally aided programs, to contribute up to 80 per cent of the share usually contributed to these programs by the cities themselves—a *supplemental grant,* in the bureaucratic tongue, a *bonus* in layman's language, a *bribe* in the view of critics who contend that no other word describes what is needed to induce many cities to make a sustained effort on behalf of their most deprived inhabitants. The act also provided for Washington to finance up to 80 per cent of the cost of developing and administering the kind of comprehensive programs envisioned under model cities, tasks that were to be carried out with "widespread citizen participation."

One can hardly fault the theory behind the coordinated concentration of public services envisioned under model cities. And because of the scope of the program, and the magnitude of the task for which it was designed, it will be many years before a fair judgment can be rendered on the merits of the approach in practice. However, a view of the first years of the program, and of the Nixon Administration's handling of it, leave one justifiably skeptical that model cities will achieve much that the nation's ill-housed can be thankful for.

For one thing, Congress has been true to form in appropriating funds for the program. For fiscal 1969 it slashed nearly 40 per cent from the Johnson Administration's request of $1 billion. The requested amount, according to most urban affairs experts, was the minimum required if model cities was to have any meaningful impact. For the 1970 fiscal year, the Nixon Administration did not even call for the full $1 billion that the 1968 Housing Act had projected for model cities for that fiscal year; instead, the Administration requested only $675 million, and even this was cut by Congress to $575 million. President Nixon's budget request for fiscal 1971 was at the level of the previous year's appropriation, indicating a continuation of model cities funding at about half the level earlier envisioned. Considering that model cities money was potentially to be distributed among the 150 cities that had qualified for planning grants by 1969, proponents of the program despaired of its future, convinced that continued appropriations at such levels would make the program precisely what one critic had already branded it: "just another poor man's pork barrel—empty."

But if well-wishers of the program were discouraged by portents of its financial future when model cities was limited to 150 localities, they became even more discouraged when the Nixon Administration began restructuring the program. As conceived in the Johnson Administration, model cities was to be limited to a given number of neighborhoods until results were shown in these places. As progress in the first model neighborhoods was demonstrated—and with sufficient additional funds—the program could be extended until it became the *modus operandi* in all areas of urban poverty and blight. The Nixon Administration, however, undertook to extend the model cities concept at once, *without* a corresponding increase in federal financing. Instead, Administration officials indicated that private enterprise would be relied on to join in and provide funds on a large scale.

The desire for rapidly extending the model cities approach was not limited to the new Administration. A number of mayors and congressmen, feeling pressure from slum dwellers outside the model neighborhoods who demanded "equal treatment" for their own areas, also advocated immediate extension of the program, as did those urban affairs experts who felt that the coordinated concentration of model cities, being the only realistic approach in the battle to reverse urban depression, should prevail everywhere.

But the fact remained that a "stretch-out" of model cities without a commensurate increase in federal appropriations (few believed that investment by private enterprise would be sufficient to make up the deficit) would simply mean that a low level of funding would have even less of an impact when spread thin over a broader area. While one could agree in principle that the comprehensive approach of model cities should prevail everywhere, the reality of available funds dictated that a premature step in this direction would virtually wipe out the original hopes of accomplishment under the program. In the words of one economist, "The model cities program will never have a chance to meet [its] challenges if each municipality must make its meager federal allocation serve for a whole urban revival."

At the same time, it must be pointed out that low-level funding, though boding ill for the future of the program, was not the primary reason why model cities lagged behind expectations in its first few years (to the point where ground-breaking for the first new housing development under the program did not take place until the summer of 1969, nearly three years after the program's enactment). A major reason why even the limited funds appropriated in the early years were not put to work as quickly as hoped was the delay-causing disputes arising in many cities from the provision calling for "widespread citizen participation." This provision had been put into the model cities act largely as a response to the growing demand of slum dwellers in the 1960's for a voice in shaping the decisions affecting their lives and neighborhoods.

Much has been written about the myths and realities of "citizen participation," and its effects on the housing production process will be seen in a later chapter. In the case of model cities, implementation of "widespread citizen participation" often led to acrimonious disputes on several levels: between City Hall and the community representatives of model cities neighborhoods for control of model cities programs; among various groups of the poor themselves over which needy areas should be included in the model cities program; and, within model cities areas, among groups competing to shape and administer the local effort. In New York City's South Bronx slum one August night in 1969, a 26-year-old employee of a community organization was pushed in front of a car and killed during a dispute with members of a rival community group competing for model cities funds.

The Johnson Administration sought to develop arrangements for the residents of model cities areas to share control, through their representatives, with city officials. But the Nixon Administration decided, as George Romney told an appreciative audience of the United States Conference of Mayors, that "the ultimate responsibility at the local level will have to be that of the mayor and local officials." This decision aroused bitterness and charges of betrayal among many community control partisans, and court suits were launched by residents of model cities areas in an attempt to reverse Nixon Administration actions.

However, the still uneasy relations between traditional decision-makers and community representatives did not appear, in the early 1970's, to pose the greatest long-run threat to the model cities program, nor did the squabbles among the community groups themselves. In fact, many urban analysts viewed these conflicts as inevitable in the formative stages of a program like model cities, just as competition among business enterprises for dominance in a newly developed commercial market is unsurprising. As decision-making and administrative relationships solidified and as lines of authority became stabilized, many reasoned, the initial contests for control were likely to wane and attention would turn to the problems for whose solution model cities had been conceived. At this point there would still be the possibility that a sufficiently funded model cities program would produce less in the way of decent housing and other improvements than in the way of a new class of neighborhood bureaucrats. On the other hand, there was the *guarantee* that, if insufficiently funded, model cities would produce one more unfulfilled blueprint on the pile of paper promises that litter the history of Washington's housing policies.

The Latest Promises

As if uncertainty over model cities, rent supplements, public housing, and urban renewal were not enough to keep analysts of the American housing scene busy in the 1970's, the Housing and Urban Development Act of 1968 swamped them with another dizzying array of legislative and bureaucratic creations. If one man's far-sighted innovation is another man's elaborate gimmick, then the 1968 act represented either a bold and multidirectional onslaught against one of America's most pressing domestic problems or a vast and meaningless bureaucratic mishmash.

In addition to the already mentioned provisions relating to public housing, urban renewal, and other existing programs, the omnibus 1968 act brought into being several new programs and "instruments" that were trumpeted as additional routes toward the act's ten-year goal of 6 million homes for the nation's ill-housed families. These programs and plans incorporated the suggestions of numerous government officials, of business and labor organizations, and of such groups as the National Association of Housing and Redevelopment Officials, the United States Conference of Mayors, the President's Committee on Urban Housing, and the National Commission on Urban Problems.

One of the most important new programs was a scheme designed to bring home ownership within the reach of more than 1 million lower-income families by 1978. Known as the "Section 235 program," it sharply reduced home-financing costs for eligible families—largely in the $4,000–$8,000 a year income bracket—by slashing their mortgage interest payments to as little as 1 per cent. An eligible family* would pay 20 per cent of its income

* Eligibility for the program was limited to families whose incomes at the time of their home purchases generally were not above 135 per cent of the maximum incomes they could have and still be eligible for admission to public housing in their localities. A smaller number of families, however, were permitted to have somewhat higher incomes: up to 90 per cent of the maximum that would be permitted them for entry into 221 (d) (3) BMIR housing in their areas.

toward the cost of financing its home purchase, and the federal government would make up whatever was needed to complete payments on the mortgage, an FHA-insured loan provided by a private lending institution at the full market interest rate (more than 8 per cent in 1970). The maximum federal payment would be the amount needed to reduce the family's own contribution to the equivalent of paying off the mortgage at a 1 per cent interest rate.

As the program was enacted, mortgages were to cover the entire purchase price, generally were to be for a maximum of $15,000 (they could go up to $20,000 for large families in high-cost areas), and could be repaid in as much as forty years. To assure that the program served mainly to stimulate the production of new housing rather than merely enabling eligible families to compete with better-off families for existing housing, Congress provided that only a minority of the Section 235 commitments could involve existing homes.

Developers of housing under the program were not limited to a statutory cash return, nor were they hindered by the workable program requirement, which was not attached to Section 235. Both these factors, besides the traditional appeal that the idea of homeownership has had to the spirit of Middle America, help to explain why the real estate industry, which vigorously promoted the 235 concept, responded enthusiastically in working under it. By August 1, 1970, exactly two years after the program was enacted, nearly 110,000 houses had been put into construction or were already being occupied under Section 235.

Over all, the program appeared more likely to approach its 1978 goal of some 1.3 million starts (the goal the Nixon Administration was projecting for it in 1970) than other federal housing subsidy programs to approach their goals. Despite an inadequate initial appropriation, influential segments of Congress were expected to be friendly to a program backed by the real estate industry and designed to spur such apple-pie American features as homeownership and free-enterprise ingenuity—the latter because, without a statutory limit on a developer's return, the more economically he could produce an FHA-acceptable house within the program's mortgage ceilings, the more of a profit he could earn.

On the other hand, there were large uncertainties about any program depending for its financing on the vicissitudes of the private mortgage market (where, as the 1970's began, prevailing interest rates were at some of their highest levels in the nation's history). It was also feared that inflationary rises in land and construction costs could make the program virtually inapplicable in many high-cost cities, given the ceilings placed on its mortgages. (This danger was clearly indicated in a regional breakdown of the 20,266 homes that, on May 31, 1969, had received final or preliminary FHA commitments for Section 235 subsidies. Only 621 of the houses, by far the smallest number, were in the high-cost Northeast, while nearly 5,500, the largest number, were in the low-cost Southeast.)

Equally important, not all members of Congress were satisfied with the program. In 1971, the House Banking and Currency Committee announced that its investigators had found widespread and fraudulent abuses on the part of real estate speculators participating in 235 and blatant negligence—at the least—by the FHA in permitting the abuses. "In the area of new 235 construction, FHA has appraised houses for figures that are inflated by several thousands of dollars above the true value of the home," the committee said, adding that "the construction of these homes is of the cheapest type of building materials, and, instead of buying a home, people purchasing these houses are buying a disaster." The committee found that some existing housing approved for purchase under the program was "of such poor quality that there is little or no possibility they can survive the life of the mortgage." Rundown housing, it said, had been cheaply bought by speculators, given a superficial "paste-up or cosmetic" rehabilitation, and resold under 235 at a handsome profit.

Although the committee emphasized that there were Section 235 houses "in excellent shape and fairly priced," and although FHA officials announced tighter inspection and certification standards to combat the abuses, some congressmen remained basically dissatisfied with the program, adding to the uncertainty over it.

Finally, it was unclear how moves to consolidate and simplify federal housing programs generally, under way in 1971, might affect production—and goals—under the subsidized interest approach. There was some feeling that these moves would amount to yet another major overhaul of the federal housing effort.

A second innovation of the 1968 Housing Act was the rental- and cooperative-apartment counterpart of the Section 235 homeownership program. Under the "Section *236* program," multifamily housing could be put up by the same private developers eligible to work under 221 (d) (3) BMIR: profit-making organizations accepting a limited return, nonprofit groups, and cooperatives. But instead of financing with a mortgage at 3 per cent interest, as under the BMIR program, the developer under 236 would obtain an FHA-insured mortgage at the full market interest rate. The families in 236 apartments—income eligibility requirements were made the same as under the 235 homeownership program—would pay 25 per cent of their income for rent (carrying charges in the case of a cooperative) and the federal government would pay the amount needed to make up the difference between each family's contribution and the "fair market rental" of its apartment. In similarity to the 235 ownership program, the maximum subsidy to a family under 236 was to be the amount needed to reduce its rent to the level that would prevail if the building had been financed with a mortgage bearing 1 per cent interest.

The Section 236 approach was designed to supplant the 1961 BMIR program. With maximum subsidies that provided rents at the equivalent of 1 per cent mortgage financing, the newer program was presented as achieving lower rentals than BMIR with its 3 per cent financing. The difference in rents that can result from a two-point difference in mortgage interest means that a one-bedroom apartment costing $139 a month under BMIR can cost $123 a month with a maximum subsidy under Section 236.

Such calculations will be the bureaucrat's doodling, however, unless production under the later approach is meaningful. And in its first two years the 236 program was off to a disappointing start. Whereas the Johnson Administration had envisioned the start of construction or major rehabilitation on some 90,000 apartments by the summer of 1970, actual production totaled two-thirds of that target. The main reasons for the poor beginning were a mortgage market in which home-financing funds were unavailable, except at very high interest rates, and initial congressional funding for the program at a level far below what Congress itself had authorized.

These same elements, congressional appropriations and the mortgage market, will be major determinants of whether the subsidized-interest apartment program comes anywhere near achieving its over-all goal (as of 1970) of 1.3 million units by 1978. Still other determinants will be the willingness of Congress to keep construction cost limits abreast of actual rises in such costs, continuance of the program's exemption from the workable program requirement or any other form of local government veto, and—as with the homeownership program—the nature of any consolidation or overhaul of federal housing programs generally.

The 1968 legislation also brought into being several other highly touted creations, among them a system of "national housing partnerships" to stimulate private corporations and nonprofit groups to become involved in production of low- and moderate-income housing; a program of financial assistance to spur the construction of new cities across the country; and provisions for greatly increasing governmental research to foster improved and less costly methods of housing construction.

Under the housing partnerships provision, formation of a government-sponsored private corporation was authorized that would seek local partners—both profit-motivated companies and nonprofit groups—with which to enter into residential development ventures under the various federal subsidy programs. By 1971, such a national corporation had been initiated, had raised more than $40-million in capital through the sale of stock, and had entered into equity partnerships with local investors in housing ventures across the country, putting up a share of the funds often required as developers' equity under the programs.

In addition to offering local partners a share of cash return from investment in housing construction under these programs, the partnership arrangement was designed to pass along to the local partners the tax advantages generally available to owners of residential property, including "book losses" possible as a result of the sizable accelerated-depreciation deductions permitted on new housing—"losses" that could be used to reduce over-all income for tax purposes. Such an incentive, it was hoped, would prove attractive to companies that might not otherwise be interested in subsidized housing construction as an investment.

The provision to encourage the development of new cities authorized the federal government to guarantee bonds and other obligations issued by developers of such ventures and to provide them with additional assistance designed to avoid some of the financial pitfalls often encountered in undertakings on so massive a scale. In return, the developers were required to adhere to various guidelines, including provision of an acceptable amount of housing for low- and moderate-income families. One urban affairs official high in the Johnson Administration indicated the administration's hope for the so-called "new towns provision" of the 1968 act when he predicted that the measure might ultimately prove as significant as the nineteenth-century Homestead Act, which helped spur the settlement of the West after the Civil War.

The prediction quickly proved outsized. By late 1970, commitments to guarantee loans had been made for only five new cities, to range in population from 50,000 to 110,000 upon completion over the next two decades.* Considering that the National Committee on Urban Growth had just suggested the creation over the next 30 years of 100 new communities of at least 100,000 population each, plus ten new cities of at least a million population each, this showing was a good deal less than had been hoped for. The housing act passed in 1970 contained provisions for greatly strengthening the new communities program, and it was hoped that the changes would make possible the kind of development that had not emerged under the original legislation.

In contrast to the new towns program, the program for greatly expanded federal efforts to stimulate housing research got off to an encouraging start. The research provision of the 1968 act had been designed partly to overcome the past deficiency of federal housing research, which had been carried out over the years on a scale that could only be considered pathetic when compared with federal research expenditures in other areas. In the 1966

* Jonathan, Minnesota; St. Charles Communities, Maryland; Park Forest South, Illinois; Flower Mound, Texas; and Maumelle, Arkansas.

fiscal year, for example, the Department of Housing and Urban Development spent $1.4 million on research and development activities (and not all of this involved housing, inasmuch as HUD was also concerned with such matters as community development and public facilities). This kind of expenditure—by a department dealing with one of the basic needs of every single American—contrasted with research and development expenditures that year of $8.3 million by the Department of Labor; $50 million by the Office of Economic Opportunity; $160 million by the Department of Transportation; $230 million by the Department of Agriculture; $830 million by the Department of Health, Education, and Welfare; and $6.7 billion by the Defense Department.

It is true that federal departments other than Housing and Urban Development have also carried out programs involving housing research and development down through the years—among them Defense (as part of its attempts to cut the cost of providing military family housing); Health, Education, and Welfare (especially on the relationship of health to housing conditions); Agriculture (in its rural housing programs); and Commerce (through its Census Bureau and other units involved in the collection of data on the housing industry). But, as the President's Committee on Urban Housing reported in 1968, "Despite this lengthy list of federal agencies which have played a part in housing R and D in the past, the sum of their efforts has been insignificant in comparison to the needs."

To help reverse the past insufficiency, the 1968 act provided for a new Assistant Secretary of Housing and Urban Development who would be in charge of research and technology, and it directed the department to undertake a program of experimental housing production to determine the extent to which housing costs might be cut through mass production techniques. Despite an initial congressional appropriation of about half the $20 million the Johnson Administration had requested for HUD research and development for 1969, the department moved quickly to implement the legislative mandate. Harold Finger, a highly regarded veteran executive of the National Aeronautics and Space Administration, was named by President Nixon to the new assistant secretary post, and a program was undertaken to construct some 2,000 prototype units of housing involving nearly two dozen privately developed building systems that, it was felt, offered the best possibilities for adoption on a mass production basis.

The prototype program formed the strongest element in the Nixon Administration's much-ballyhooed "Operation Breakthrough," an otherwise weak-kneed design for kicking over the economic, social, and technological barriers that have hindered the development of a mass production approach to housing in the United States—barriers that, in addition to rising costs of land, labor, materials, and often financing, have included restrictive local zoning and building codes and restrictive labor practices and industry traditions. (More on Breakthrough later.) Construction of the prototypes began in 1970 on the first of nine sites across the country. "Completed prototype components, units, and systems will be tested in accord with recommended standards to assure their safety and durability," George Romney announced, promising a sustained federal effort to foster the advancement of housing technology.

Just how sustained this effort would be and, assuming it did not lag, what it would eventually mean to those in need of decent housing—and to the way Americans were sheltered in general—was anybody's guess in the early 1970's.

Beyond Legislation

So much for the staggering array of legislation through which the federal government has specifically sought to stimulate the housing production process. However, as I soon learned while viewing the complex of forces that bear on housing, to look simply at the national government's many housing programs still leaves one with only a partial picture of Washington's impact on the state of American housing. Just as consequential have been the federal government's policies and actions in areas that, to the layman, seem only distantly related to the process that puts walls around him and a roof over his head.

This has certainly been the case regarding the government's efforts to control inflation. By now it is certainly clear that inflation itself potentially poses one of the major obstacles to the nation's realization of its proclaimed housing goals—the general one of a decent home and a suitable living environment for every American family, and the more specific goals in the 1968 Housing Act.

As the cost of land, labor, building materials, and mortgage financing (in the form of high interest rates) sharply rise, the number of families at the lower end of the economic scale that can afford decent housing on their own diminishes, inasmuch as the incomes of such families usually rise far slower than prices in an inflationary economy. At the same time, the government programs designed to provide decent housing for lower-income families themselves become less effective. This is so because, as the cost of subsidizing each housing unit increases, as it must when the cost of producing or maintaining the unit increases, the funds appropriated for these programs subsidize fewer total units. Where construction costs have risen so high as to exceed the statutory construction cost limits that have been part of the various programs, housing production under these programs has faltered and even come to a halt—the case, as we have seen, with public housing in New York City in 1969. The housing prospects of many middle-income families, too, suffer from the inimical consequences of inflation.

Other effects of inflation on housing are equally serious. Savings deposits, for example, often decline in periods of rapid inflation, because people invest their money where they can get a higher return as a hedge against inflation. This reduces the savings institutions' funds for making mortgage loans, hindering still further the process of building housing.

For these and other reasons, there is no question that efforts to stem inflation are as vital to the fulfillment of the nation's housing needs as they are to economic and social well-being over all. Yet *how* inflation is fought by Washington is also important to the housing-production process, for some federal efforts to harness inflation can hurt residential construction as severely as inflation itself can.

This has been proved true on the several occasions since World War II when Washington has sought to fight inflation with a so-called tight money policy, which means encouraging a rise in interest rates and a reduction in the lendable assets of banks. The hope behind a tight money policy is that it will slow economic activity, and thus the rise in prices, by making the borrowing that finances a good deal of business activity more expensive and difficult. Yet whenever it has been invoked, the industry that has been "cooled down" far more than any other has been homebuilding.

There are several reasons why residential construction is more sensitive to a tightening of the credit supply than most other business sectors. First, of course, borrowed money plays a much more dominant role in construction than in most other industries. Second, in residential construction, the party that bears the cost of an interest rate rise is the party that is usually least able to afford it—the individual family using the housing. In the case of the homeowner, the burden is directly felt: He pays the interest to the bank that provides his mortgage. In the case of the apartment renter, it is indirectly but similarly felt: The builder's interest costs will be figured into the rent.

When all this comes on top of the extremely high portion of the consumer dollar that housing eats up to begin with, it is not surprising that a rise in mortgage interest can put new or improved housing beyond the reach of many families.* Residential builders, appreciating the effect of increased interest on marketability, reduce their activity when interest rates rise, compounding whatever slowdown may result in tight money times from a decline in funds available for mortgages.

It was with these economic realities in mind that Eugene Gulledge, then president of the National Association of Home Builders (and subsequently a top assistant to George Romney), took critical note in 1969 of the "very uneven impacts" of a federal tight money policy. "The 1967 report of the President's Council of Economic Advisers," he said, "observes that in the 1966 credit crunch, *home building bore almost 90% of the total cut-back in the entire economy. Home building is only 3.5% of all economic activity.* The inequity of this is so clear as to beggar comment." (Emphasis Mr. Gulledge's.)

* As an illustration of what rising interest rates mean in housing, monthly payments on, say, a $10,000 mortgage being paid off over twenty-five years are 15 per cent higher when the home buyer is paying 7.25 per cent interest than when he is paying 5.75 per cent.

The National Commission on Urban Problems similarly observed of the 1966 attempt to control inflation by federally stimulated interest-rate rises that

> the only segments of the economy that cooled off were housing and small businesses (both highly susceptible to changes in monetary policy). It became clear to most people that fiscal policy (including such factors as budget cuts and tax increases rather than mere increases in interest rates) would have to be used to cool off the economy, and that it was unfair to impose the full burden of control upon housing and small businesses.

The commission's 1968 report, however, was pessimistic about the prospects for a departure from the view of housing "as a contracyclical industry," a view that it found still widely held in Washington. On the other hand, some observers were heartened by developments in 1969 and 1970 that indicated a possible change in this view. Early in 1970 President Nixon acknowledged that "housing and the industry which provides it are bearing a disproportionate burden of both current inflationary pressures and the anti-inflation measures instituted to restore price stability." He promised efforts to remedy the situation. His Administration did take steps to "cushion" the impact of the tight money policy then again prevailing. Typical was the authorization by the Federal Home Loan Bank Board for savings institutions to pay higher interest on certain deposits (in the hope that this would cut withdrawals and thus reduce the amount of savings lost to the supply of potential mortgage funds).

Such steps did keep the level of housing starts from dropping as sharply as it had during the previous credit squeeze in 1966. But people concerned with the nation's housing needs looked for far more fundamental actions to show them that the inimical effects of tight money on housing had an equal share of attention in Washington with the hoped-for positive effects on price stabilization.

The Tax Man Cometh

The federal government's policies in levying the income tax also have a sharp impact on housing. By its arrangement of deductions and reductions among the nation's taxpayers, Washington over the years has significantly influenced the activities that supply new housing and that affect the maintenance of a good deal of the existing housing stock. The extent of this influence has already been indicated in the previous discussions of various federal programs—236, BMIR, the national housing partnerships—all of which were conceived, in part, to use tax incentives to spur investment in housing production for low- and moderate-income families. The relationship between federal income tax policies and housing was further emphasized during debates over major tax reform legislation passed by Congress in 1969, when preserving the incentives involving housing became one of the controversial aspects of the intricate legislation.

The income tax regulations affect housing in several ways, and, over all, for bad as well as for good. As already noted, one of the most important relationships involves the depreciation deductions permitted real estate owners. These deductions allow a landlord of an income-producing building to reduce his income tax by claiming losses that theoretically measure the decline in the value of his building—a decline that, in fact, is frequently nonexistent or at most far less than the amount permissibly claimed for income tax purposes, especially in the case of a new building or a used but solid one.

So-called accelerated depreciation enables a landlord to show in the early years of ownership even greater paper losses than the "straight-line" depreciation method of equal annual installments over the life of the structure. Accelerated depreciation can be at a rate that permits more than 40 per cent of the cost of a new apartment building to be depreciated over the first quarter of its theoretical life span, and up to three-fourths of the cost to be depreciated over the first half of its estimated life.

In accountants' jargon, the accelerated formulas bear such dry names as the "200 per cent declining balance" and the "sum of the years digits," but in plain English they add up to two juicy words: *tax shelter.* Accelerated depreciation often enables a landlord, in his early years of ownership, to pay little or no income tax at all on his earnings from a building and, in many cases, to show a paper loss that can be used to reduce his total taxable income from all his income-producing endeavors.

During debates over the 1969 tax reform legislation, which had been introduced in Congress partly because of widespread public resentment against tax "loopholes" favoring the wealthy, the point, in effect, was made—and prevailed—that tax shelters appearing inequitable on the surface were justified if they fostered socially worthy endeavors such as producing decent housing for those lacking it. Accelerated depreciation was held to be a justifiable shelter because of its influence in attracting funds for housing investment. As the case for accelerated depreciation was stated by the National Association of Home Builders before a congressional committee during the 1969 debates:

> Compared to other available instruments, even under the most favorable circumstances, residential real estate is just not attractive to a builder or a real estate investor if the return is solely from the net rental proceeds of the property after payment of taxes, operating expenses, and mortgage interest and amortization. We say categorically that should accelerated depreciation for real estate be eliminated, the construction of income producing real estate—particularly multifamily housing—would drop to a fraction of its present level—to a negligible amount compared with the need for it during the next ten years.

Similar views, at least as they affected housing, were voiced also by a number of public officials whose position could not be easily dismissed as colored by the self-interest of an industry under fire. Jason Nathan, then serving as New York City's Housing and Development Administrator, was among those who warned that erasing the tax incentives for residential realty investment would pull the rug from under the 1968 housing legislation, the goals of which depended largely on programs involving substantial private investment in housing for lower-income families.

Swayed by such warnings, Congress passed a tax reform act that, while sharply reducing accelerated depreciation levels for new *nonresidential* construction, permitted continuation of the previous generous levels for new *residential* construction. As for depreciation deductions permitted new owners of existing buildings, the 1969 tax reforms abolished accelerated depreciation on nonresidential structures but continued such depreciation, though at a reduced level, on residential buildings with an estimated remaining life of at least twenty years.

While depreciation incentives are lauded for their favorable effect on housing, they are also cited as having in many cases a pernicious influence. Accelerated depreciation has been among the factors encouraging frequent turnover of property by real estate investors who, having taken advantage of the larger deductions flowing from the accelerated formulas in the early years of ownership, have had little interest in continuing ownership when the tax shelter has diminished, preferring to put their money into new holdings and restore to their tax returns the fatter depreciation allowances that have grown slender on their old portfolio. Experts note a "high correlation between frequent turnover and poor maintenance practices, especially for 'slum' housing," as the National Commission on Urban Problems summed up their findings.

One hopes that the 1969 tax reforms, by limiting accelerated depreciation to those existing apartment houses with a useful life of at least twenty years, and by lowering the rates permitted qualifying buildings, will lessen this negative influence.

Yet another aspect of the federal income tax with important ramifications for housing are provisions regarding upgrading expenses. Generally, outlays that a landlord makes for repairs and ordinary maintenance are tax-deductible as a current operating expense, while outlays made for improvements are treated as capital expenditures (nondeductible) that supposedly add to the value of the building. In theory this is a valid distinction; but applying this distinction to slum buildings in the same way as it is applied to solid middle-class or luxury apartment houses is unrealistic and inimical to the rehabilitation of deteriorated buildings. As explained by Professor Richard Slitor of the University of Massachusetts:

> In the case of slum properties, expenditures which constitute improvements in the eyes of the tax law represent in reality long overdue repairs accumulated over years of neglect and deterioration. They may be equivalent to a bunching of repairs which would have been deductible currently if made year by year. . . . The rehabilitation expenditures of the particular taxpayer often add little

> to the current earning power of the property and possibly little to its anticipated resale value. Yet, in addition to failing to qualify for a current income tax deduction, rehabilitation outlays may lengthen the estimated useful life of the property and thus reduce depreciation rates and increase exposure to federal income tax, [and may] result in a higher local assessment and thereby increase property tax costs.

The dampening effect of all this on upgrading the slums will also, it is hoped, be reduced by the 1969 tax reforms, which provided for a special five-year amortization deduction for the rehabilitation of low-rent housing.

Besides the income tax factors affecting *investment* in housing—and those we've just seen are not the only ones—other tax factors have helped influence decisions on the *consumption* end of housing. The person who owns his own home or a share in a cooperative apartment house is permitted deductions on his federal income tax for the property taxes paid to his local government and the interest on the mortgage. The person who rents his housing is not permitted such deductions, even though a portion of his rent pays for the landlord's property tax and mortgage-interest expenses.

The fairness of providing these hefty tax benefits to the homeowner and co-op dweller but not the renter have been debated over the years. Whatever one feels about the equities involved, there is no disputing that the income tax laws, by so encouraging homeownership, have helped to influence countless families over the years in their choice of buying rather than renting their housing. One estimate is that in the middle 1960's the "typical" homeowning taxpayer was realizing income tax savings from his ownership that offset about 12 per cent of his yearly housing costs.

Issues in Black and White

No view of Washington's influence on the American housing scene is complete without an understanding of federal activity—or the lack of it—in the area of civil rights in housing, or "open housing," as it is more commonly referred to.

In the early 1970's, the most significant actions on the federal level to foster open housing had only just been taken. It was thus hope generated by these actions, and not any meaningful results that had yet flowed from them, that prompted the view that they constitute a watershed in the history of American housing and civil rights. The two major developments, both coming in 1968, were passage of a civil rights act that prohibited racial, ethnic, and religious discrimination in the sale, rental, and financing of most of the nation's housing, and a United States Supreme Court decision that outlawed racial discrimination in the sale and rental of all housing.

The Civil Rights Act of 1968 was passed by Congress in April of that year, several days after the assassination of Martin Luther King, Jr. The murder of the civil rights leader appeared to have influenced the outcome of the bitterly contested legislation in the House of Representatives, although its advocates insisted that they had gained sufficient support there even before the assassination to assure passage of the bill, which the Senate had already passed before King's murder. Whatever the truth, the success of the open housing measure marked a sharp reversal in Congress, where, only two years before, open housing legislation had been talked to death in a Senate filibuster. In fact, the change was even more marked when one considers the widespread opposition that greeted an executive order by President John F. Kennedy in 1962 that prohibited discrimination solely in federally aided housing—housing built with *public* funds or assisted under the insurance programs of *public* agencies.

When Title VIII of the Civil Rights Act of 1968 went into full effect in 1970, its strictures against discrimination applied to all housing in the nation except most privately owned buildings containing two to four dwelling units, one of which was occupied by the landlord (the "Mrs. Murphy's boarding house" exemption), and most single-family homes sold or rented by the families owning them without the aid of real estate brokers and without advertising. It was estimated that the exemptions would total only 20 per cent of the nation's housing units.

To enforce its provisions, Title VIII authorized several courses of action against violators. The Department of Housing and Urban Development could receive complaints of discrimination and, where no local or state agencies existed to grant the complainants "substantially equivalent" opportunities for relief, the department could investigate immediately. If it found a complaint warranted, it could attempt to resolve the matter by conciliation and persuasion. The department could not, however, issue binding orders to force a halt to the discrimination. Where a local or state human rights agency existed under laws offering the complainant "substantially equivalent" rights and remedies, the department had to refer the complainant to this agency and could assume jurisdiction only if the local or state body did not act on the matter with "reasonable promptness," generally within thirty days.

If under the act a complainant chose to forgo administrative procedures, or if he received no satisfaction through them, he could bring a court suit—in federal court if no "substantially equivalent" judicial remedy was available to him under state or local law, in a state court if such a remedy was available. If the plaintiff won his case, he could obtain a court order requiring that he be rented or sold the housing at issue, provided it was still available, and he could be awarded actual damages and up to $1,000 in punitive damages. The law further permitted courts to award attorney's fees to a successful complainant too poor to afford them, and to make available free legal services and waive court costs where necessary to permit the filing of a suit.

Finally, Title VIII authorized the United States Attorney General to undertake federal court action against any group or individual he believed to be engaged in a "pattern" of discrimination in violation of the law, a provision that proponents of the 1968 legislation hoped would become an effective tool for assaulting discrimination by large developers and apartment management firms.

In the early 1970's, the provisions of Title VIII, much though they promise on paper, have had little practical meaning for the millions of Americans whose color or origins are an important reason why they cannot improve their housing. And it will be many years—at best—before these provisions do take on a practical significance. First, the time and will needed to pursue an action under the legislation—and sustained and widespread efforts will be required to overcome resistance to the rights granted by the 1968 act—are often beyond the capacity of the people most keenly affected by housing discrimination. Second, the groups that might encourage and assist the kind of protracted legal actions necessary, such as community legal aid and civil rights organizations, though more numerous than in the past, are still dwarfed by the magnitude of the task confronting open housing advocates. And finally, the act itself, by limiting the Department of Housing and Urban Development to conciliation attempts, with time-consuming court action still needed when the department's mediation efforts fail, adds further to the obstacles to swift implementation of the rights granted.

On the other hand, there is no question that simply by declaring discrimination in the sale and rental of 80 per cent of the nation's housing to be illegal, the open housing legislation of 1968 is of major symbolic significance in a country rent by racial strife. And while its effects will not be seen on a widespread scale for many years, if at all, the act does establish a badly needed legal foundation on which Americans determined to make a reality of open housing may mount their efforts.

The same evaluation can be made of the June 17, 1968, decision by the United States Supreme Court in the case of *Jones v. Mayer*. In a landmark seven-to-two ruling, the nation's highest court turned a forgotten civil rights statute of 1866 into a far-reaching affirmation of the right of black Americans to purchase and rent housing—no units excepted—as well as all other real and personal property, without prejudice because of their race.

The 1866 law had been enacted to enforce the Thirteenth Amendment, outlawing slavery and ratified in 1865. The law provided that citizens "of every race and color, without regard to any previous condition of slavery . . . shall have the same right, in every state and territory in the United States, to make and enforce contracts, to sue, be parties, and give evidence, to inherit, purchase, lease, sell, hold, and convey real and personal property . . . as is enjoyed by white citizens."

This was interpreted by the 1968 Supreme Court majority to forbid racial discrimination in housing when it was practiced by private citizens as well as governmental agencies. Because such discrimination was "a relic of slavery," the court held, Congress had been fully justified in legislating against it. Thus the court overruled lower federal courts that had found in *Jones v. Mayer* that neither the Constitution nor the 1866 law prohibited racial discrimination by private owners (in this instance the Alfred H. Mayer Company, which owned the suburban St. Louis subdivision from which Joseph Lee Jones, a black bail bondsman, and his white wife had been excluded).

Like the Supreme Court's landmark decision outlawing school segregation in 1954, *Jones v. Mayer* signaled the beginning, rather than the climax, of a long legal battle. Just as in the case of officially segregated schools, so with housing discrimination it was one thing for nine men in judicial robes to declare a long-standing and deeply-rooted feature of a sizable part of American life illegal, and quite another for that declaration to be translated into actuality. Moreover, the *Jones* ruling itself left unanswered a number of important questions that had to be resolved in further court cases before one could even begin estimating how much of an impact the decision might have in wiping out residential segregation.

Among these questions were whether a successful plaintiff under the 1866 law was entitled to monetary damages as well as injunctive relief, an entitlement that would put teeth into the Reconstruction-era law and that was provided in the 1968 open housing legislation; whether "class actions" would be permitted to enforce the 1866 law, as opposed to actions by—and the granting of judicial relief to—one plaintiff at a time; and whether *Jones v. Mayer* would be held enforceable in state courts.

In addition to the *Jones* ruling and the 1968 civil rights act, there were other recent developments on the federal level important to open housing proponents. Federal court decisions like the one ordering Chicago to build three-quarters of its future public housing in predominantly white areas were expected to multiply as an increasing number of suits were being brought in the federal courts to challenge state and local laws and practices which perpetuated racial and ethnic segregation and thwarted the production of lower-income housing. Among the most important of these practices and laws, of course, were the zoning activities of suburban governments discussed previously.

In one important case, in 1971, the open housing forces suffered a major defeat in the Supreme Court. In a five-to-three ruling, the high court upheald the constitutionality of referendum laws in several states that permit a majority of voters in a locality to veto a local-government proposal to build a public housing project. The court rejected a ruling by a lower federal court that had held such referendum provisions unconstitutional in a case involving the California one. The lower court had found that, by requiring a proposed public housing project for the poor to be passed on in a referendum, while permitting public agencies to build housing for college students, public employees, and other groups without the need for approval in a referendum, the California provision discriminated against the poor and thus violated the equal-protection clause of the Fourteenth Amendment.

The Supreme Court rejected this reasoning, stating that the thrust of the Fourteenth Amendment was to forbid public policy distinctions based on race, and that there was no evidence that the California provision was aimed at any racial minority. Rather, the court found, the statute was a "procedure for democratic decision-making" that gave the residents of a community a say in policies that would increase their taxes, weaken the tax base, and thus affect community development.

What this decision might mean for the open housing campaign over all was not immediately clear. The ruling appeared directly applicable only to public housing undertaken by public authorities. Whether it was also applicable to *publicly aided* housing—housing undertaken by private developers working under the various law- and moderate-income government subsidy programs—was doubted by some lawyers but thought to be a matter for future court determination by others. Similarly, some open housing lawyers remained confident that local-government actions would continue to be cverturned in the federal courts where racial discrimination was shown to be a factor, but other open housing advocates were worried that such discrimination might be successfully presented to the courts as economic considerations.

First Things Last

Beyond housing laws, and beyond all the monetary, fiscal, and civil rights activities discussed, the underlying determinant of the federal government's affect on the nation's housing situation is the importance that the policy-makers in Washington attach to America's housing needs relative to its other needs—or alleged needs. In short, to drag out an overworked but still most descriptive phrase, it is a matter of "national priorities." Despite the status of shelter as one of man's basic needs, and despite the abundance of rhetoric and the string of legislative enactments in the 1960's, the fact remains that housing continued in that decade to have a low priority in Washington, as attested by the evidence that counts most—the federal budget.

"From fiscal 1962 through 1967, $356.3 billion was spent for national defense, $33.2 billion for stabilizing farm prices and income, $24.2 billion for space exploration, and $22.2 billion for federal highway construction. In contrast, $8.1 billion was budgeted for *all* programs under housing and urban renewal, and only $1.25 billion for federal housing subsidies," the President's Committee on Urban Housing reported.

Despite the pride that the policy-makers of Lyndon Johnson's Great Society took in the fact that starts under federal low- and moderate-income housing programs rose sharply as a legacy of Johnson Administration policies, there was, in fact, only the barest reason for a sense of accomplishment. The $4.1 billion outlay under the budget heading "community development and housing" in fiscal 1968—by far the highest annual dollar outlay in this category in the 1960's—represented only 2.3 per cent of total budget outlays for that year. Granted that this was an improvement over fiscal 1960, for example, when policies of the Republican Eisenhower Administration had resulted in an outlay ($971 million) that had represented 1.1 per cent of the total budget.

But in the context of housing needs and of "national defense" outlays of $80 billion (about 45 per cent of the total budget) during fiscal 1968, the amount for housing and community development could hardly be said to represent a meaningful "reordering" of national priorities. Moreover, because of inflation, the *real* value of the budget increases for housing and related subjects was far less than the dollar figures imply.

The truth is, of course, that however strongly committed Lyndon Johnson might have been to meeting the nation's critical domestic needs, including housing, he was driven, and ultimately subverted, by the delusion that America could pursue a tragic and costly military adventure in Southeast Asia and still have the resources to overcome its deficiencies at home. But a national government that was spending more than $25 billion a year on a war—as much in a single month as its entire year's outlay for all housing and community development programs in 1969—was hardly in a position to provide the funds needed if the nation's shortcomings at home were to be dealt with to any effect. It was commonly observed by housing experts that the money the federal government was making available for housing for the entire country in the late 1960's could have been used by New York City alone. Further, as the major cause of the inflation which was dealing housing an especially severe blow, the war in Indochina was aggravating the housing situation over and above the diversion of vitally needed public funds that it entailed.

But, as already indicated, the war was not the only example of priorities gone askew in the 1960's. The Johnson Administration embarked on an expensive antiballistic missile system of dubious need that was expected to cost between $6 billion and $7 billion. Nonmilitary programs that by no stretch of the imagination could be considered of higher priority than eliminating wretched housing for millions of Americans—programs involving the development of a supersonic commercial airliner, continued extensive construction of superhighways, costly farm subsidies to many with already lucrative incomes—ate up additional billions of federal dollars, while housing, like programs to eliminate hunger, had to scramble for relative pittances.*

The Nixon Administration offered little prospect for improvement, despite President Nixon's declaration that his proposed budgets for 1971 and 1972 begin "the necessary process of reordering our national priorities." True, there was a much-vaunted trimming of defense expenditures proposed for 1971, amounting to $5.8 billion, so that these expenditures would total "only" $73.6 billion out of a total budget of nearly $201 billion. But the Nixon budgets' provisions for social programs such as housing and urban

* The supersonic transport madness was finally ended by Congress in 1971, after an expenditure of nearly $1 billion in public funds.

redevelopment could hardly be said to reflect the vast magnitude of unfulfilled tasks in these critical areas of American life. The President proposed $3.8 billion in these areas for 1971 and $4.5 billion for 1972, levels that, given inflation, represented insignificant gain over the previous few years and, given the nation's desperate needs, represented no gain at all. They still amounted to a pathetic 2 per cent of the budget.

Taking Stock

To sum up federal efforts to improve the housing of the American people over the years:

During nearly four decades, Washington has immeasurably aided the housing circumstances of middle-class America and the segments of the construction and financing businesses that cater to it. In the depths of the Depression, the million families saved from foreclosure by the Home Owners Loan Corporation were primarily middle-income families by the economic standards of those days, and the corporation was just as salutory to the lending institutions to which foreclosure would have given ownership of housing that, in the circumstances of the time, would have been difficult if not impossible to find new buyers for. Since the darkest days of the Depression, homes for some 7 million families, the vast majority of them middle-class, have been built under the FHA mortgage insurance program, which also has been an incalculable boon to the homebuilding and home-financing sectors.

In contrast to such benefits to middle-class America—and to many families today forming part of the Richard Nixon "silent majority," which resents the clamor of the poor and the wretchedly housed for government aid—three decades of federal activity in housing have produced pathetically little for the poor and nearly poor. As previously noted, all of Washington's housing subsidy programs for low- and moderate-income families had resulted, by mid-1970, in 1.5 million units, or one-seventh of the "rock-bottom" need found by the National Commission on Urban Problems as the 1960's ended. (See the table on page 131.)

To be sure, starts under these programs soared in the most recent years to the point where they totaled half a million units in the 1969 and 1970 fiscal years. But this was an impressive achievement only in relation to the past inadequacy of federal activity, not in relation to the nation's housing needs as the 1970's began. In fact, the half-million units represented a 30 per cent "shortfall" even in relation to the goals for these years originally set as part of the "production path" toward the 6 million units called for by the 1968 Housing Act—a shortfall that will have to be made up rapidly if the over-all ten-year goals of the act are to be realized.

Moreover, the federal government's future efforts in behalf of the ill-housed will continue to show the same severe imbalance against the rural areas as Washington has shown in the past. These areas contain at least half of the nation's substandard housing. Yet of the 1.5 million units produced under Washington's subsidy programs by mid-1970, only one-fifth resulted from the low- and moderate-income programs of the Farmers Home Administration of the Agriculture Department, which ministers to the housing needs of rural America, off as well as on the farm. Under the projections as of 1970, only a quarter of the hoped-for 6 million units authorized by the 1968 act were envisioned as resulting from Farmers Home Administration programs.

Of course, one will always find those who see the bright side of everything, and in relation to the national government's housing efforts, these people urge that the situation be looked at "positively" and "with historical perspective." It was barely four decades ago, they note, that Washington even acknowledged that it had a role to play in helping the American people fulfill the elementary human need for decent shelter, and although a million and a half subsidized units might not be all that the country can use, it certainly is a hell of a lot better than none at all. Moreover, the federal contribution is bound to increase, optimists say, as the momentum of Washington's programs increases, and it is just a matter of "being patient" and remembering that "institutions don't change overnight."

I have heard such views expressed numerous times by persons both inside and outside the national government. When it is a federal official holding forth, one cannot help but think of a fire chief who—his company having arrived late at the scene of a block-long conflagration and having then been hampered by insufficient equipment—takes comfort and even pride in the fact that his men saved a single-family house or two from burning down while a dozen large apartment buildings were destroyed.

PRODUCTION UNDER FEDERAL LOW- AND MODERATE-INCOME HOUSING PROGRAMS
(Through July 31, 1970)

Program[a]	Completions[b]	Starts[b]
Public housing[c]	867,000	973,000
Rent supplements	33,000	55,000
221(d)(3) BMIR	140,000	175,000
235 (home ownership)[d]	68,000	110,000
236 (rental and cooperative)	9,000	64,000
Other low- and moderate-income programs under Department of Housing and Urban Development[e]	56,000	67,000
Low- and moderate-income programs of Farmers Home Administration[f]	330,000	350,000
Totals	1,503,000	1,794,000

[a] Units built in urban renewal areas but receiving no subsidy under a low- or moderate-income program are not counted, even though such units are federally subsidized in that the land "write-down," which lowers the cost of developing the units, is largely financed by federal funds. However, units receiving only the write-down subsidy have not usually been in the range of low- or moderate-income families, as the discussion of urban renewal has made clear.

[b] Unit figures are rounded to nearest thousand and are for all fifty states and the territories (Puerto Rico, Virgin Islands, Guam).

[c] Includes conventionally built public housing, leased units, and units built under the "turnkey" procedure (purchased by the local housing authority upon completion by a private builder).

[d] Includes new and rehabilitated units and existing ones purchased without substantial rehabilitation.

[e] These programs have provided such aid as low-interest loans for rental housing for the elderly and handicapped (the Section 202 program), grants and loans for rehabilitating property in urban renewal and certain other areas (Sections 115 and 312), and low-interest loans for renovating housing for resale to low-income families (Section 221[h]).

[f] These loan programs aid construction and rehabilitation of single-family homes and of rental and farm-labor housing, and aid the purchase of existing housing.

Sources: Department of Housing and Urban Development and Department of Agriculture (Farmers Home Administration).

5. The States and the Crisis

States' Wrongs

If the sin of the federal government against housing has been to acknowledge its role grievously late and then consistently to deliver far less than it promised, the sin of the state governments is that, with few exceptions, they did not even *begin* to acknowledge more than an onlooker's role for themselves until three decades later, and over the years delivered *exactly* what they promised: almost nothing. "Beyond passing enabling legislation which allowed local authorities to act, or which delegated state police powers over zoning and building and housing codes to the cities, most states have played a minor and a passive role in housing the American people, including those with low incomes," the National Commission on Urban Problems stated in its 1968 report.

Actually, even this comment presents the states in a more favorable light than their performance over the years warrants. Rather than merely being passive and uninvolved, state governments by and large played a decisively negative role in housing as the decades passed in that their actions, or refusals to act, contributed significantly to intensifying the nation's shelter problems. The states' wholesale ceding to local government in the 1920's of their police powers involving zoning and building codes became in later years a source of many of America's housing woes. And the widespread refusal in state capitals to provide cities not only with adequate funds critically needed to help meet housing needs but even with enough local taxing authority to raise such funds has been a significant factor in housing decay and in the inadequate level of publicly aided construction.

There are two ways of viewing the states' poor showing. Apologists for the states have argued that without the kind of resources made available to the national government by the federal income tax, state governments, with far more restricted revenues, could not possibly have been expected to make the same contribution to meeting housing needs within their borders that the federal government has been able to make. There is certainly some truth in this. But there is even more truth in another explanation of the states' extensive remissness over the years: With malapportioned legislatures frequently dominated by rural conservatives and reactionaries—often in league with suburban delegations no less hostile to spending large sums on low-income housing and slum clearance—and with administrative bodies outmoded and inadequate to mid-twentieth century social and economic tasks, most states over the years had little inclination or ability to assault the problems of physical and social blight plaguing their cities (and, sometimes forgotten by those who chastise state legislatures for a "history of indifference to urban problems," plaguing their rural areas as well).

With these realities in mind, as well as with the memory of his own experiences and frustrations, former Mayor John Collins of Boston summed up a widely held view when he told the Urban Land Institute in the late 1960's: "The states, by and large, with a few exceptions, have displayed all the dynamism, all of the desire for innovation, of the dinosaur."

But even as the former Boston mayor was saying this, there were welcome if tentative indications that a significant number of states were beginning to wake up to the fact that they, too, had an important role to play in the effort to provide a decent home and suitable living environment for every American. During a decade of court decisions mandating fairer representation for urban areas in state legislatures, and with riots rocking black slums across the country and sending out shock waves perceptible even in the most anachronistic statehouses, state governments began adopting in the 1960's an assortment of measures in response to housing and related needs.

These measures varied widely in effect—from councils with no more than advisory powers to agencies empowered to provide mortgage money for the construction of low-income housing—and the all-important funding support given the new creations differed sharply from state to state. Nevertheless, the mere adoption of these measures indicated that, though only the barest beginning had been made, and though traditional state legislative behavior was a long way from dying, possibly significant change from the past was occurring in the predominant attitude of state government toward involvement in the battle to overcome America's housing deficits.

Exceptions to the Rule

The lean history of state involvement in housing began in 1856 in New York State, which, throughout the nation's history, has been the leading exception to the general pattern of state government behavior. At that time, the New York legislature appointed a five-member committee to investigate conditions in the crammed and squalid tenements that had sprung up in the then separate cities of New York and Brooklyn ("New York City" in those days having been the island borough of Manhattan).

Even this initial state move, however, was many years late in coming. As immigration into New York City and Brooklyn had increased after the War of 1812, the new arrivals had jammed into decaying houses, rickety shacks, and dingy multifamily "tenant houses" thrown up for renting at a quick and handsome profit. By the 1830's and 1840's, these constructions were being repeatedly cited by local health officials and groups devoted to bettering the lot of the poor as foul, festering breeding places for crime and cholera. But not until 1856, after a host of additional tenements had been added to the scene without any regulations governing minimum standards for ventilation, light, sanitary facilities, and density, did the state act—or at least simulate "action."

The committee of five legislators, guarded by a police detail and accompanied by health officials and members of the press, "penetrated to localities and witnessed scenes"—in the words of the lawmakers' 1857 report—"which in frightful novelty far exceeded the limit of their previously conceived ideas of human degradation and suffering." In vivid detail, the legislators described the often windowless holes rented for exorbitant profits in stench-laden, rodent-ridden buildings with rotting floors and walls; the backyard privies spilling their contents from overflowing vaults; the ubiquitous filth and unbelievable crowding. One 12-by-12-foot room, the legislators reported, was serving as home to five families comprising twenty men, women and children.

I did not cover the excursion, of course, but with only a bit of imagination I can readily picture the scene on this pioneering politicians' safari: The legislators and their entourage picking their way through the muck and garbage with a pack of ragged, jabbering children dogging their heels; older residents of the area staring with a mixture of curiosity and sullen, muttering resentment; the shock and indignation expressed by the official visitors at every turn, especially when a member of the press was close at hand to record the outraged observation.

Except for the absence of untethered goats and pigs, except for a decline in the slum-dwellers' curiosity and an increase in their scowls and resentment (a century later such treks to the slums had become as commonplace as the conditions they never remedied), and except for the television cameras, which had become far more important to the official visitors than the scribbling newspaper reporters, little had changed in the ritual of such political slumming a hundred years later.

Still another precedent was set by the first legislative exploration: Nothing at all came of it, aside from the committee's fifty-four-page report. Thus, by the Civil War things had changed in no way except for the worse in old New York—a fact volcanically brought home by four days of tumultuous and bloody rioting in July, 1863. Sparked by a conscription law that blatantly discriminated against the poor, thousands of Irish slum-dwellers rampaged through the city in a massive eruption of arson, pillaging, and murder that was as much an insurrection against their abysmal living conditions as against a draft law that enabled a man to buy his way out of military service by paying the government $300 or hiring a substitute. Hundreds died and countless more were injured in the New York Draft Riots, in which pitched battles were fought between the mobs and artillery-firing troops, and the outbreak did not end until thirteen Union Army regiments were rushed to the city from the battlefields of the Civil War. The riots dwarfed anything that America was to see in its black ghettos in the 1960's.

And still it was not until several more years after this brutal and costly expression of pent-up bitterness and frustration, after further reports and further anguished and angry appeals for action by civic groups and reformers, that the state finally passed the pioneering Tenement House Act of 1867.

This first exercise of the state police power in behalf of rottenly housed Americans, actual and potential, provided, among other things, that cellars could not be used for dwellings unless their ceilings were at least one foot above ground level, that a water-closet or privy had to be provided for every twenty inhabitants of a tenement, that city water had to be available in every tenement or its yard, and that various rudimentary steps had to be taken regarding sanitation and repair. A local board of health, which had been established only the year before, was to be the enforcing agency.

Landlords and tenement builders in New York City and Brooklyn, where the act applied, howled with dismay. Defenders of the sanctity of private contracts thundered with indignation, for in this land of individual initiative and free enterprise, were not the conditions of hearth and home a matter to be settled entirely between landlord and tenant, the latter as free as a soaring seagull to move if not satisfied?

In truth, the first of the tenement regulation acts, like housing codes ever since, wrought no drastic change for the worse in the fortunes of slumlords, nor any revolutionary improvement in the circumstances of their tenants. As would be the case for a century thereafter, it was one thing to mandate minimum housing standards on paper and quite another to enforce them so that requirements in legislation became realities in living conditions.

In 1879, a second tenement house act was passed by New York State, again applying only to the two largest cities, New York and Brooklyn. This act called for, among other things, at least 600 cubic feet of air space for each adult resident of a building, a janitor on the premises where there were more than eight families, and—what turned out to be more a curse than a blessing—a window that opened to the outer air in each room of all newly built housing.

The last requirement was widely met by building tenements containing air shafts, often barely two feet wide but up to sixty feet long, separating the interior of one building from that of the next—"fresh air" features that rapidly became foul, illness-breeding depositories for garbage. The sorry results of the 1879 tenement act are still to be seen in abundance in New York City slums today, especially on Manhattan's Lower East Side, where they serve as home for thousands of Puerto Rican families, part of the latest wave of immigrants in a neighborhood that has traditionally been a first settling place for new arrivals in America.

In 1901, still another major tenement house law was passed by New York State, this time applying to New York City (since 1898 comprising the five boroughs it does today) and Buffalo, which had succeeded the formerly independent Brooklyn as the state's other "city of the first class" in population. The result of the work of a tenement house commission that Governor Theodore Roosevelt had appointed in 1900 and of a wave of agitation for reform growing out of the writings of such chroniclers of late-nineteenth-century New York City slum life as Jacob Riis, the 1901 law mandated standards for construction and maintenance, as well as for ventilation, light, sanitation, and other conditions directly affecting health, that were a vast improvement over the provisions of the previous acts. Generally regarded as the nation's "first modern housing law," the 1901 act precluded further construction of the air-shaft type of tenements fostered by the 1879 measure (which after 1901 were referred to as "old law" tenements) and placed enforcement in New York City under a new tenement house department rather than under the board of health.

In the first years of the twentieth century, amid the heady spirit of Progressive-era reform, a minority of other states were also prodded to recognize the need for some kind of action to regulate basic housing conditions and mitigate the worst of the slum conditions that abounded in all of the nation's major and many of its lesser cities. But the process of recognition was agonizingly slow, and by the time of American entry into World War I, only eleven states had adopted minimum-standard housing acts of one sort or another, most of them patterned on the 1901 New York law. These states, besides New York, were Pennsylvania, New Jersey, Connecticut, Wisconsin, Indiana, California, Kentucky, Massachusetts, Michigan, and Minnesota.

In subsequent years, state enactments covering housing maintenance increased and became more diversified. Many states passed legislation authorizing all or some of their local governments to enact their own housing maintenance codes (though these states often prescribed, in the enabling legislation, how the local codes were to be enforced). Other states continued adoption of state housing maintenance regulations and applied them to various categories of cities. Some states with housing maintenance statutes also allowed cities to enact their own codes, so long as they were consistent with the states' standards. The result by the 1970's, from a national perspective, is a vast and varied body of state and local enactments that fill many pages in law books but, because of frequently inadequate enforcement by local government and an often insufficient range of sanctions permitted by the states, have done little to assure the minimum standards of health and safety they call for—as millions of slum-dwellers are keenly aware.

Just as New York had been the first state to seek to enforce minimum standards of decency in housing, so it was the first of the few—until quite recently—states to become active in the necessary second half of any governmental effort to assure decent dwellings: fostering the production of *new* low- and moderate-cost housing.

In 1920, Governor Alfred Smith, whose origins in New York City's Lower East Side slum had made "the housing problem" a more poignant reality for him than it could be for the most ardent middle-class-born foe of slums, called a special session of the legislature to demand a "permanent housing program" for the state—a program that would include steps to encourage private industry to put up housing the working class could afford. But the lawmakers' principal response to Smith's call for reduced housing costs was a measure permitting cities to abate real estate taxes on new residential construction for ten years. While this led to a massive building boom in new apartments, especially in New York City, the law contained no restriction on rents that the tax-relieved landlords could charge, hence its effect was hardly what Smith had had in mind.

Finally, in 1926, in response to the Democratic governor's continuing pressure, the Republican-dominated legislature did approve a program specifically aimed at encouraging the construction of moderate-cost housing: the so-called limited-dividend housing companies law. This pioneering measure lowered housing costs in three ways. First, by enabling the private organizations working under it to acquire land with the aid of public condemnation powers, it lowered the costs usually incurred when developers had to deal on their own with property-owners, many of whom held out for inflated prices. Second, it sizably reduced the sponsoring organization's operating costs by authorizing cities to exempt housing built under the law from local real estate taxes for up to fifty years, with the taxes to be paid on the sites amounting only to what had previously been paid on them. Finally, the sponsoring and owning groups were limited to paying their stockholders a maximum annual dividend of 6 per cent on their investments, and the organizations' financial affairs were subject to state supervision.

Admission to limited-dividend projects was restricted to families with incomes no larger than six or seven times the rent (carrying charge, in the case of cooperatives) to be paid for the apartments, the larger multiple applying to larger families. Monthly rents and carrying charges in the earliest limited-dividend housing averaged about $10 a room, within the means of the lower middle class of that day. In the late 1960's the averages in these early projects had generally risen to between $18 and $25 a room.

The limited-dividend program as enacted did much less to lower the cost of housing production than Governor Smith had wanted. He had proposed as well, for example, that low-interest mortgage loans be provided by public agencies to bring down the all-important cost of mortgage money. But, as noted in Chapter 3, it was as far as the Republican majority of legislators would go. By the 1950's, when it was phased out in favor of a program that did provide the kind of low-interest loans Smith had urged, the limited-dividend housing program had produced more than 11,000 apartments—all in New York City, because the state's other municipalities had been unwilling to grant the tax abatement central to the program.

The 1955 program that did provide the lower-than-market-interest mortgages Smith had sought was adopted with passage of the so-called Mitchell-Lama Law, named for the legislators who sponsored it, State Senator MacNeil Mitchell and Assemblyman Alfred Lama. This act made available low-cost financing with repayment terms of up to fifty years and permitted local property tax abatement for up to thirty years. As under the limited-dividend law, the return to developers and owners was restricted to 6 per cent of equity, which was raised to 7.5 per cent in 1970.

Mitchell-Lama mortgages could be provided by the state or by a city, with the interest rate based on the interest paid by the state or city in selling the bonds to raise the loan funds. In the 1950's, interest on Mitchell-Lama mortgages was 4 per cent at a time when the market rate was 6 per cent; in 1970, Mitchell-Lama interest was about 7 per cent while conventional mortgages in the state were, in effect, costing 9 and even 10 per cent. As with limited-dividend developments, admission generally was restricted to families whose incomes did not exceed six or seven times the rent or cooperative carrying charges.

The Mitchell-Lama program was intended for lower-middle and middle income families, with monthly rents and carrying charges generally in the range of $20 to $25 a room in the program's early years. But as construction costs rose sharply in New York during the 1960's, and as the interest that the state and New York City had to pay in selling bonds for the program also rose, even the lower-than-market-interest mortgages and generous tax abatement of the program could not keep the cost of producing housing at a level where rents or carrying charges could be within lower-middle-income means. In the late 1960's it was not unusual for rents or carrying charges in new Mitchell-Lama units to monthly average $50 or more a room, making it hardly the kind of housing for families in the $6,000–$9,000 a year income bracket. In 1971, some developments in the planning stage were expected to average more than $80 a room.*

Altogether, more than 60,000 units of Mitchell-Lama housing had been completed as of 1970, with the mortgages for about half having been provided by the state and for the other half by New York City. No other municipality had provided Mitchell-Lama mortgages, and the vast majority of the units financed with state mortgages had themselves been built in New York City.

Regarding low-income housing, New York State had taken important action in 1939, when it began its own public housing program to supplement the newborn federal efforts in this area. The state program, sanctioned by the voters in a referendum the previous year, provided low-rent units separate from those produced in the state under the federal program; in fact, mingling funds from the state and federal public housing programs in the same project was prohibited by the state.

Nearly 65,000 low-rent units were produced under the state program by the mid-1960's, when the people of New York State had a change of heart about the virtues of spending for public housing. In 1964 and 1965, and again in 1970, they decisively

* A family with two or three growing children of different sexes needs at least three bedrooms, or five rooms in all, counting the living room and kitchen. At $50 a room, this would entail rent of $250 a month, or $3,000 a year: half of an annual income of $6,000 and a third of annual income of $9,000. At $80 a room, the same family, even if it were able to squeeze into four rooms, would require about $15,000 a year in income, assuming that rent ($3,840 on an annual basis) is 25 per cent of income. Hopes were high in New York that there could be widespread grafting of the federal government's Section 236 program, with its subsidies reducing rents to as low as those permitted by 1 per cent mortgage financing, onto the Mitchell-Lama program, thus reversing the trend of steadily higher Mitchell-Lama costs. Actually Mitchell-Lama housing had already been subject to a good deal of "piggybacking" of subsidies, in that 20 to 30 per cent of the units in a number of Mitchell-Lama projects had been given over to low-income families under the federal government's public housing leasing program, and under a state rent-supplement program called "capital grants."

defeated in referenda proposals to make funds available for additional units, and thus the state program, so far as new construction was concerned, was inactive at this writing.

Two other states were also playing relatively vigorous roles before the 1960's in aiding the production of housing for families unable to afford the output of the unassisted private market. State programs in Massachusetts had produced a total of about 35,000 units for the low-income elderly and for veterans with low and moderate incomes by 1970. Connecticut programs had resulted in the construction of 17,000 units for low- and moderate-income residents of the state. Some historians of American housing also count Illinois among the states taking noteworthy action in the past: In the late 1940's it joined with Chicago in a program that resulted in nearly 1,000 subsidized units.

Aside from these efforts, however, and aside from some contributions to the federal urban renewal program that a small handful of states had made to supplement local contributions, state government had done virtually nothing until the 1960's to help bring into being decent new housing for their poor and working classes.

THE NEW LOOK

With the 1960's rumbling ominously on, and with the United States Supreme Court mandating a measure of justice in the geographical make-up of state legislatures, the first stirrings of widespread response to such needs as housing and the eradication of urban slums took place in the nation's statehouses. To some wishful proponents of a greater state role in the war against America's domestic ills, these stirrings were evidence that, as one spokesman for the states put it, "state government has moved into the mainstream of the urban crisis facing the nation." Others, however, more realistically preferred to wait before plunging in with such proclamations, holding that a splash along the shoreline, however welcome, could hardly be considered a dive into the mainstream.

Among the most significant of the splashes in the 1960's was establishment in thirteen states of agencies having the authority to issue tax-exempt bonds to finance such activities as providing mortgage loans for construction of low- and moderate-income housing and buying such mortgages from private lending institutions. States creating agencies of this kind by mid-1970 were New York, Massachusetts, Connecticut, Vermont, Delaware, Illinois, Maine, Michigan, Missouri, New Jersey, West Virginia, Maryland, and North Carolina. Legislation to create similar agencies was expected to pass within a year or two in several other states, though court challenges against already established agencies were also under way or planned in a few states.

A second welcome housing-related trend of the 1960's was the creation in many states of executive bodies to deal specifically with urban or community affairs. By the middle of 1970 such agencies existed in twenty-eight states—often, though, with little real power and just as little money. A survey reported by the National Governors' Conference indicated that in all the remaining states, specific agencies or officials had been assigned responsibility for community and urban affairs, including, in some cases, coordinating the programs of an assortment of agencies that had an impact on such affairs.

Still other states took beginning steps in the 1960's to help meet housing needs with a variety of additional approaches. Under a California measure adopted in 1968 to stimulate the flow of mortgage money where it was most needed, commercial lending institutions were permitted to deduct from their state corporate income taxes an amount equal to 1 per cent of loans made during a year to low- and moderate-income families for the purchase or improvement of privately owned homes.

Hawaii, Illinois, Michigan, and New York were among states authorizing rent-supplement assistance of one sort or another. In 1969 Rhode Island began a program of leased housing for low-income occupants under which private investors were to rehabilitate rundown dwellings and rent them to eligible families. Arkansas, Pennsylvania, New Jersey, and New York enacted their own "mini" model cities programs, designed to help localities participate in the federal model cities program and to coordinate various state programs in federal model cities areas. New Jersey, for one, allocated $1.28 million in state funds to nine cities to help them prepare applications and plans for the federal model cities program and to permit the start of local projects in housing and other areas of need while over-all model cities plans were developed.

Several states also took action in the 1960's to bring some order out of the chaos of the more than 8,000 local building codes and the nearly 10,000 local zoning ordinances. New Jersey, California, Indiana, North Carolina, Ohio, and Wisconsin adopted modern, mandatory statewide building codes for apartment construction. Several other states developed model building codes for local adoption. In 1969 most of the fifty states were represented at the first National Conference of States on Building Codes and Standards. Also that year, Massachusetts enacted a bitterly controversial law permitting the state, under specified conditions, to overrule local building and zoning laws to enable public housing agencies or limited-dividend and nonprofit private corporations to build low- and moderate-rent housing in suburban communities. A new California law exempted prefabricated housing from building codes and substituted a state code permitting the components for the housing to be checked at the factory by state inspectors; local inspections were to apply only to on-site hookups of such elements as power and water lines.

By the middle of 1970, twenty-seven states had passed open housing laws applying to the private housing market to one degree or another, beginning with Colorado in 1959. But, as with the local open housing laws, the over-all effect has been negligible, partly because of lukewarm or ineffective enforcement in a number of states, partly because of basic defects in the laws themselves, sometimes because of both.* But on the theory that a first step, however faint-hearted and faltering, is better than no movement at all, the states' open housing laws of the 1960's had to be

* Most enforcement agencies limit themselves largely to acting on specific individual complaints rather than undertaking widespread investigations to determine where patterns of discrimination exist and then initiating action to fight such discrimination. One exception, however, is the New Jersey Division on Civil Rights, which in 1970 required landlords of apartment houses with twenty-five or more units to file annual lists designating the race of their tenants and reports on apartment turnover and the race of applicants for vacancies. These were to be used to determine the existence of any systematic patterns of discrimination.

considered some sort of advance, offering at least the hope of more vigorous action in the future.

Still other indications of a possibly significant trend toward state action in housing came from political rhetoric that previously had ignored housing needs. For example, in 1968, for the first time in Illinois history, both major political parties included planks on housing in their state platforms. "This singular event," the National Association of Housing and Redevelopment Officials rejoiced, "reflected a growing recognition that state government could no longer leave the solution to housing and other urban problems solely in the hands of a distant federal bureaucracy or to financially and jurisdictionally weak municipalities."

LOGUE'S LEGIONNAIRES

All these developments, however, paled by comparison next to the boldest state move to assert a meaningful role in housing and related matters: creation in 1968 of the New York State Urban Development Corporation.

Proposed in February of that year by Governor Nelson Rockefeller and passed by an initially reluctant legislature after Martin Luther King's assassination in April—and after the shock of the assassination was reinforced by Rockefeller in a dazzling display of legislative arm-twisting—the Urban Development Corporation was endowed with an unprecedented array of powers with which "to help renew New York State's cities and towns and to plan and develop the orderly growth of urban areas." The UDC could undertake the development of residential, commercial, industrial, educational, and recreational facilities, as well as entire new towns, anywhere in the state, building the facilities directly or arranging for their construction by private developers and other public agencies. It could condemn land, sell revenue-raising bonds, and—perhaps most significantly of all—override local zoning and building codes and undertake renewal projects where they were opposed by local government.

To say that Rockefeller's UDC proposal was not kindly received by many mayors and spokesmen for local government is like saying that canaries in a cage are somewhat disturbed when a starving tomcat is tossed into their midst. Throughout the state, cries were heard that the proposed "superagency" flagrantly violated the concept of home rule and threatened to ride roughshod over local desires and a local voice in shaping the nature and quality of life in New York State's cities and towns. Vigorous opposition came not only from suburban communities that saw in the UDC a drastic threat to their determination to keep the poor and minorities a good train ride away, but also from Mayor John Lindsay of New York City, a leading proponent of massive governmental action to help provide decent housing for the nation's slum dwellers and certainly no sympathizer with suburban exclusion of the poor and the minorities.

Whatever the political and personal factors at work involving his relationship with Rockefeller, Lindsay commented that the powers proposed for the UDC presented the danger of a "distantly operated bulldozer" that would bash its way into communities with insensitivity to over-all local needs and no fear of obstruction. Lindsay insisted that the state agency, should it try, would find it "impossible to evaluate the impact of its projects on local transportation, education, environmental protection, and all the other facets of human life." For his part, Rockefeller maintained that the proposed "public benefit corporation" was one of the "extreme measures" that had to be taken in the battle against urban blight. (No doubt, being one of the most political of political animals, he also viewed it as one of the "extreme measures" needed at the time to build up his image as a daring and innovative problem-solver worthy of the 1968 Republican Presidential nomination.)

The certainty that the UDC would be steeped in controversy arose not only from its powers but also from Rockefeller's selection of the man to head it: Edward Logue. The most prominent of that new breed of professional city-rebuilders who have spread their works across the land—for good or bad, depending on one's perspective—Logue had earned a reputation through his efforts in Boston and New Haven as either a far-sighted man of action who forged ahead and got things done while lesser figures hemmed and hawed and tried to determine which way the political wind was blowing, or as a self-righteous bully who bulldozed his way across the townscape with as much regard for the people uprooted as for the bricks and mortar of the decaying buildings demolished.

Whatever the truth of his past propensities, Logue treaded relatively lightly during the first two years of the Urban Development Corporation's life. He made clear, for example, that despite its authority to do so, the UDC would not go into any cities where its urban renewal work was not wanted; enough municipalities had invited the corporation's aid to provide it with more than a sufficient number of tasks, he said. His restraint was not necessarily an indication that Logue had had a change of heart about the aggressiveness with which he felt a successful city-rebuilder must operate. It *was* an indication that he fully appreciated the political reality that what a legislature has given, a legislature can take away. "A lot of people would have us go ruthlessly ahead and then would sit by while the legislature repealed our power," the UDC chief said.

By late 1970 two dozen localities had signed agreements to work with Logue's corporation on more than fifty projects, which envisioned, among other things, the construction of a total of more than 40,000 housing units. One of the cities was New York, whose Mayor Lindsay invited the UDC to join in working in eight redevelopment areas—but on a restricted basis that allowed the city to retain the powers of local planning that Lindsay had been so adamant about in his original battle against the UDC.

All together, about 12,000 units of housing were scheduled to be built in the eight projects, 5,000 of them in the most ambitious of the undertakings: the transformation of Welfare Island, a two-mile-long sliver of unsightly, glaringly underdeveloped land in the East River off Manhattan's East Side "gold coast," into an economically and racially integrated "new town" of 20,000 people. As in UDC projects generally, one-fifth of the housing planned for the island was scheduled to be for low-income, nonelderly families and one-tenth for the low-income elderly. Nearly half the apartments were to be for moderate- and middle-income families and the remaining quarter—the only apartments not to be built under one or another public subsidy or assistance program—were to be in the luxury category.

This kind of housing mix indicates why the UDC, as potentially powerful as it is, will never be the master of its own fate, at least as far as at its housing goals are concerned. To subsidize all the low- and moderate-income apartments that the agency plans in its projects—a task far beyond the resources of the state—requires heavy reliance on federal housing programs. If programs such as public housing and federal mortgage interest subsidies remain generally underfunded in Washington, all the expertise in the world on the part of Logue and his staff in plowing through the labyrinthine federal housing bureaucracy will not take them far toward realization of the UDC's housing goals.

In this regard, the UDC offers at this writing an excellent test of the Nixon Administration's "new federalism," designed to give the states a greatly enlarged role in helping to meet the nation's domestic needs. The UDC is the strongest measure yet taken by any state to attack the problems of substandard housing and urban decline and certainly is evidence of the sort of willingness to act vigorously on the state level that the "new federalism" supposedly is all about. But the UDC's plans to help meet New York State's massive housing needs—a million new and rehabilitated units in the 1970's just to replace deteriorated and overcrowded dwellings, and a million more to keep up with the expected growth in population—depends, of necessity, on sizable federal assistance. Whether or not this assistance is forthcoming will determine whether Nixon's "new federalism" has the kind of dollar-and-sense meaning that builds desperately needed housing, or whether it is just the newest nondollar, nonsensical rhetoric out of Washington.

A number of states were closely following the fortunes of the New York UDC in 1970, and there was little doubt that the triumphs or trip-ups of Logue's legionnaires would have a strong bearing on whether similar agencies were created elsewhere. At the same time, it was clear that even a spectacularly successful New York UDC would not make similar creations the rule among the states in the foreseeable future. For the states' stirring in the 1960's toward helping housing in no way indicated that the predominant inaction and indifference of the past were disappearing.

Far more typical than the New York Urban Development Corporation, or than the assortment of other state creations and enactments of the 1960's designed to facilitate the production of low- and moderate-rent housing, was the behavior of the Missouri legislature at the height of the previously discussed public housing rent strike crisis that hit St. Louis in 1969. With the virtually bankrupt St. Louis housing authority desperate for income to meet its operating expenses, and with a large and determined portion of its tenancy refusing to pay the rent increases that the authority needed but that the recalcitrant tenants, many on welfare, claimed they could not afford, state assistance was sought as a possible way out of the ruinous impasse. It was noted that payments under Missouri welfare programs were so low (again, a mother with three children received $124 a month) that, by adjusting rents to income, the St. Louis authority, in effect, had subsidized the state's welfare system, which was certainly one reason for the authority's financial plight.

Although both housing and welfare officials urged that the state rectify the situation, and with the public housing picture in the state's largest city disintegrating, the pleas fell on deaf ears. The state legislature turned down a bill that would have given a monthly $20 grant to local public housing authorities for each of their families on welfare or other forms of fixed income.

It was one more clear illustration that, despite the welcome winds of change in the 1960's, pervasive pockets of stale, strongly clinging attitudes remained to be blown away before the great majority of states assumed a role on the American housing scene commensurate with the standing in the American power structure that proponents of states' rights so vocally fantasize for them.

6. Business and Labor and the Crisis

THE HOUSING NONINDUSTRY

The sector of the economy that provides the walls around the American people and the roofs over their heads is as far-flung and diverse as American society itself. The wealthy professional builder who alters a city's skyline with a forty-story luxury apartment tower or converts acres of suburban greensward into a new "bedroom community" for $50,000-a-year executives is in the same "industry" as the immigrant landlord of a four-family building, one of whose apartments he and his family occupy, in a drab working-class neighborhood. The president of a bank is as much a part of the housing business as the owner of a lumber mill; the wood products industry is the most important single supplier of materials for housing construction, but without the foundation of mortgage credit laid by the banks and other financial institutions there would be little need for the lumber, because nobody but the richest would be able to buy houses or build apartments. The plumbing subcontractor whose firm installs some of the vital amenities of modern residential construction is an integral part of the housing business, and so is the professional housing consultant whose firm sells its knowledge of the *bureaucratic* pipeline to developers wanting to build under federal housing subsidy programs but baffled by their intricacies.

In short, the "housing industry," as the above sampling of members indicates—and it is only a small sampling—is not one industry but a collection of many industries and professions, scattered widely through the American economy, as are the individuals who run these industries and services over the spectrum of social and political views.

Even if the definition of the housing industry is narrowed to those businesses closest to the center of the housing provision process—the real estate and construction industries—and excludes such vital but once-removed enterprises as materials manufacturing and legal services, the industry is still wide-ranging in its interests and views. For example, the Council of Housing Producers, made up of fourteen of the nation's largest homebuilding companies, has constantly voiced its opposition to local zoning and building laws that hinder the production of low-cost housing. By contrast, when the Nixon Administration made its unsuccessful proposal against the use of zoning and other local powers to prevent the "reasonable provision" of federally aided low- and moderate-income housing, the proposal, weak as it was, was denounced by the president of the National Association of Real Estate Boards. The system of local zoning powers is "an important measure for achieving local aspirations in environmental quality that our cities and towns must retain," he declared.

Similarly, one often finds a wide divergence of views (and a good deal of antagonism) between small-scale landlords—the dentist or grocer who owns a small apartment building or two as a long-term investment—and large-scale professional real estate investors and management specialists who own or operate scores of large apartment structures and often become involved in urban renewal projects as well.

To New York City's tenants, for example, there is little to choose between two arch-foes of rent control, Edward Sulzberger, president of the Metropolitan Fair Rent Committee and head of one of the city's largest real estate concerns, and Vito Battista, head of the "little man's" United Taxpayers party and a perennial gadfly in behalf of the small-scale property-owner. But as far as the flamboyant Battista is concerned, there is as much difference between him and Sulzberger, and between the people they represent, as there is between one of the giant new apartment towers that Sulzberger's company manages on urban renewal sites in Manhattan and a four-family building owned by an Italian immigrant on a tree-shaded street in the distant (from Manhattan) Bay Ridge section of Brooklyn.

As Battista once explained to me, "Sulzberger is interested in the large owners and they work against us. Whatever he says about rent control in public, the Sulzberger group is willing to accommodate itself on controls so they won't lose their urban renewal contracts or commercial advantages." Battista defined the latter as "the opportunities to buy out small landlords cheaply when they find themselves going under because of rent control."

Such suspicion of the "big boys," especially those involved in urban renewal, is not limited to New York. In cities across the country, the conviction is expressed time and again by "little landlords" that the "urban renewal profiteers" are working hand in glove with the government in a conspiracy to foster the deterioration of neighborhoods and ripen them for the bulldozings that will enrich the big-time professionals.

The Homebuilders

Such fragmentation in spirit and outlook reflects the general fragmentation that characterizes the housing business even when defined in its *narrowest* sense: the companies directly engaged in building housing.

According to the Department of Housing and Urban Development in 1970, there were about 50,000 homebuilding concerns in the country, and the average one produced about thirty housing units a year. "No single producer captures as much as 1 per cent of the conventional housing market," HUD reported. The President's Committee on Urban Housing found that the fifty largest producers of all types of housing turned out a total of less than 15 per cent of the country's annual housing output. Levitt & Sons, the largest builder of single-family homes in the United States, noted in 1969 that it was accounting for only 0.3 per cent of the nation's yearly production of new housing. In short, not only is there no "big three" or "big five" in the homebuilding business, but this sector of the American economy still has a long way to go before it even reaches a "big fifty" or a "big hundred."

This fragmentation reflects and reinforces the local character of the American housing market, which stems both from the necessities of the homebuilding process itself in the United States and from public policy in the form of local building and zoning ordinances.

The necessities are related to the sheer size and meteorological variations of the country. The same automobile can be purchased for use in Minnesota and Florida. The same house cannot, cutting down the market for the output of any housing production line. Automobiles can be shipped long distances; unless the entire nation moves into mobile homes, which is hardly likely despite their soaring popularity in recent years, the housing industry will not have the same advantage. Even prefabricated sections of housing cannot be trucked long distances without steep costs, as the manufacturers of housing made up of factory-assembled major components have found. Finally, the production of automobiles is unaffected by the weather, which is not the case with the housing production process. The variations in output—and thus income—caused by the weather discourages all but the most prosperous homebuilding concerns from investing in the kind of equipment necessary for large-scale operations.

Yet all of these realities, and any others arising from the necessities of the homebuilding process or from consumer tastes, do not explain the *extent* of the localization and fractionalization of the homebuilding business in the United States. It is not simply a matter of a builder's incapacity to produce for North Dakota what he is producing for Louisiana or to transport his product from Boston to Atlanta. For a builder is equally unable to produce for thirty-three localities immediately around Los Angeles what he is producing for Los Angeles itself because, as the Council of Housing Producers has noted, thirty-four of the seventy-seven municipalities in Los Angeles County have different and inconsistent building regulations. Housing producers face this kind of building-code morass in every part of the country, as well as a multitude of zoning ordinances that place vast amounts of land off limits to their output, so that even those with the desire and resources to produce on a larger and more economical scale are discouraged from doing so.

The result is fragmentation far beyond what technology or taste dictate. "Would General Motors be able to produce on the scale and with the economies it does if it had to contend with thousands of inconsistent and idiosyncratic local requirements?" one homebuilding executive declared to me with frustration, echoing a question one hears time and again from many of his colleagues. The fragmented and unstable management end of the homebuilding business (as with construction generally, firms enter and leave homebuilding at a high rate, and failures are frequent) is reflected on the labor end of the business by a highly transitory and mobile work force that is still far more seasonal in nature than befits the housing production process in the final third of the twentieth century. The consequences of seasonality in helping to shape the cost of housing will soon be seen.

Not everything is unchanging on the American homebuilding scene. One-third of all the housing produced in the United States in 1969 was turned out largely or entirely in factories, rather than "on site," a sharp departure from pre–World War II days, when on-site construction accounted for nearly all housing built in the country. Out of a total of 1.9 million new housing units of all types in 1969, 250,000 were the output of "home manufacturers" producing "packages" of prefabricated major components for rapid assembly on the site; 400,000 more were mobile homes, the fastest-growing subsector of the homebuilding business.

Even the conventional on-site builders, who still produce two-thirds of all American housing, have increased their use of prefabricated elements by employing such items (where building codes permit) as prehung doors, shop-fabricated roof trusses, and shop-assembled sections of plumbing systems. In fact, some of the largest conventional homebuilders use fabricated components and streamlined technics to such an extent that their operations, in effect, often amount to on-site "portable factories."

The "package" of preassembled elements turned out by the home manufacturers, who became a significant part of the American housing scene after World War II, is designed for assembly on the site in a matter of days. Separate on-site work is still needed for foundations and utility connections, but even with these, the total time for erecting a manufactured single-family home is still only a matter of weeks at most, as opposed to the four or five months it might take to build a single-family house without prefabricated major elements. Depending on the extent of prefabrication, the price of a home manufacturer's house—many produce garden apartment clusters as well as single-family homes—is lower than that of a house of the same size and amenities built by a conventional on-site builder using less prefabrication.

Most home manufacturers limit themselves to prefabricating such elements as floor, roof, and wall panels. The latter, for example, often contain in their factory-finished state the windows, siding, framing, and sometimes the electrical wiring. Some factory producers actually join together wall and floor panels in the plant and ship the three-dimensional results as sections of the finished product (so-called "sectionalized houses"), which are formed of several factory-assembled sections joined at the site.

Although home manufacturers represent a move toward the kind of mass production housing industry being sought in the nation, they are a long way in the early 1970's from what is needed. Of approximately 600 home manufacturers, only about one-quarter produced more than 500 dwelling units a year in the late 1960's, and only about a dozen turned out more than a thousand each. (The largest home manufacturer, National Homes, did sell some 28,000 in 1970, its best year ever.)

The reasons for the generally small scale of operations have already been referred to. Transportation costs have usually limited distribution of the housing "packages," which are generally sold through local builder-dealers, to within 300 or 400 miles of the factories. The maze of restrictive and inconsistent building codes, even within these few hundred miles, severely deters use of the prefabricated components. National Homes was the company that was forced by local plumbing and electrical inspectors to rip out the plumbing and wiring it had factory-installed in units for the previously mentioned Thomasville urban renewal project in Atlanta.

In addition, many Americans still have a lingering skepticism about prefabricated construction, believing that it is structurally inferior to on-site construction and synonymous with monotonous standardization. Housing experts agree that neither is necessarily the case: Structural quality can be high or low regardless of the method of construction, and prefabrication of structural components does not preclude design variation. In fact, as one government survey noted, "almost all sectionalized houses and manufactured homes in this country are built with exactly the same materials, used in the same way, as in conventional building." Moreover, the American landscape offers abundant testimony that more than a few on-site builders have been responsible for acre after acre of stupifying monotony that is no less esthetically deadening for its having been slowly fashioned on the spot rather than prefabricated in a factory.

In any case, there is one steadily growing group of Americans who have not been put off by fears of factory fabrication. These are the mobile-home dwellers, estimated to number nearly 6 million as the 1970's began. The approximately 400,000 mobile homes produced in 1969 represented a fourfold increase over the number produced annually in the early 1960's. With the Federal Housing Administration empowered in 1969 to insure loans made for the purchase of mobile homes, and with the Veterans Administration guaranty program extended to them in 1970, production of these units was expected to rise still further in the 1970's.

The authorization for the FHA and VA to extend their mortgage programs to mobile homes reflected official recognition of this type of housing as a major source of decent primary (as opposed to vacation) homes for the American people and testified to how far mobile homes had come from the trailers out of which they developed—and with which many Americans still scornfully identify them. Further recognition was accorded them by the Nixon Administration when it decided to count mobile homes toward the goals set by the 1968 Housing Act.

Produced entirely in the factory, mobile homes are designed to be transported from one location to another, though as a rule their occupants are no more mobile than those living in homes with permanent foundations. The average stay in one place among mobile home owners has been just short of five years, according to the Mobile Home Manufacturers Association. This is roughly the same as for those who own conventional homes. The association has estimated that three-fifths of all mobile home owners in the late 1960's had never moved their units.

The typical mobile home comes furnished by its manufacturer and has an aluminum-sheathed wooden frame resting on a steel undercarriage that stands on its wheels and trailer-hitch attachment. To be classified as a mobile home, a unit must be at least 30 feet long and 8 feet wide and must weigh 4,500 pounds. At this time, more than four-fifths of the mobile homes being turned out are at least 12 feet by 60 feet with some as big as 12 by 75—providing about as many square feet as the average new conventional single-family house that the FHA was granting mortgage insurance on two decades ago. Depending on size and furnishings, mobile homes are generally selling for from $4,000 to $18,000, the result, in great part, of the economies of factory fabrication.

The principal buyers of mobile homes have been older people whose children have grown up and who no longer feel the need for a large house, and young families, especially newly married couples. Most of today's more than 2 million mobile homes are outside the cities, and most are in mobile home "parks," where the mobile home owner rents space. The newer of these parks are in striking contrast to the transient trailer camps of the early post-World War II days. Today's mobile home parks are paved and landscaped, and a number offer community and recreational facilities in addition to basic sewage and utility lines to "plug into."

Nevertheless, mobile homes are still anathema in many established suburban communities, which zone them out altogether or relegate them to less desirable industrial areas. At worst, mobile home dwellers are scorned by many suburbanites as "trailer gypsies" who have no place among solidly grounded property owners; at best, they are lumped with apartment dwellers, which doesn't help their case much either.

Many housing analysts look to the mobile home sector to make an important contribution to the effort to provide decent low-cost housing for Americans. In some places mobile homes are already being used as temporary relocation housing while new construction or rehabilitation is carried out. Their use keeps slum dwellers from being scattered while their houses are renovated or replaced and permits families to remain in their areas and retain community ties while work is in progress. When units have finished serving this function at one site, they have been moved elsewhere for the same purpose.

Whether mobile homes will themselves become a large source of decent housing for the poor depends to a large extent on whether major technological problems in the production of these units can be overcome. It is common for those in search of a low-cost-housing panacea to point out that in the late 1960's mobile homes totaled 90 per cent of all single-unit housing sold in the nation for less than $15,000. But it is usually forgotten that a mobile home has a much shorter life expectancy than a conventional house, and this is reflected in financing terms that are far shorter in duration (usually seven to ten years) than the typical mortgage of twenty-five or thirty years on a conventional single-family home. The shorter the term of the loan, the higher the monthly repayment. When this is combined with additional payments for site rental, the cost of owning a mobile home is generally not much less, and can be more, than the cost of owning a $15,000 conventional house. Moreover, inadequate insulation and undersize structural members have meant higher heating and repair costs in some cases. Technological advances to extend the lives of mobile homes and improve their construction further without a significant increase in production costs will have to be made before mobile homes can take on, to any meaningful degree, the role many foresee for them.

"Bits and Pieces"

So far as the housing industry is concerned over all, efforts to lower costs face a vast and complex array of hurdles. The elements that determine the cost of producing and operating housing are so numerous, and the influences on them so far-reaching, that any attempt to lower the costs must be carried out on a sustained, massive, and highly coordinated basis that reaches into every corner of the nation's economic, political, and social life. As the President's Committee on Urban Housing put it, any such attempt "must work on all the bits and pieces which make up the initial costs of a housing unit and its subsequent operating and maintenance costs."

The "bits and pieces"—the costs of land, financing, materials, labor, and operation of the finished product, including property taxes—vary in how they are represented in the total costs of different houses or apartments. The proportions that the items form of over-all costs depend on such factors as the type of housing, the locality, the amenities built in, and the scale and efficiency of the builder's operation. One indication of what the cost components of housing production can be is provided by the President's committee in a "rough breakdown" of development and construction costs for conventionally built single-family homes and for apartments in apartment buildings with elevators. In both cases, the housing on which the figures are based is housing designed for lower-income families in northeastern metropolitan areas. The percentage breakdown of total costs is given by the committee's researchers as follows:

	Single-family homes	Apartments
Developed land	25	13
Materials	36	38
On-site labor	19	22
Overhead and profit	14	15
Miscellaneous	6	12[a]
	100	100

[a] The higher miscellaneous cost for the apartments is accounted for partly by architectural expenses, often dispensed with in single-family construction.

Whatever the breakdown in any given house or apartment, the elements that form the initial development and construction cost are not the only important determinants of the ultimate expense to the housing consumer. The cost of the money borrowed to finance the housing is a substantial part of the ultimate cost —directly to the homeowner as he pays the interest on the mortgage, indirectly to the apartment dweller as a component of his rent. The "operating costs"—property taxes, maintenance and repairs, utilities, and, where the unit is a rented apartment, various management expenses—also play a sizable role, accounting usually for 40 to 50 per cent of the homeowner's or tenant's monthly outlay for housing.

Given this fractionalization of the housing dollar, there is no question that economies will have to be achieved in a number of areas if the cost of housing is to be reduced significantly. Lower construction costs will be meaningless if land and financing costs increase sharply, and vice versa. Lowering all of these costs will also mean little if maintenance expenses, residential property taxes, and the various other components of operating cost, which can add up to half of the consumer's expenditure for housing, are not also lessened. *If this point is being made more than once, it is because it is one of the basic realities of the national housing picture, a reality that makes a pipe dream of the hope for some dramatic "breakthrough" that, by itself, will significantly lower the cost of housing in the United States.*

In fact, it will be a massive challenge just to keep housing costs from rising still further. In most component-cost areas in recent years, the trend has been sharply upward. Land costs, powerfully influenced by the intricate web of zoning and property-tax policies, have spiraled. In the major metropolitan areas the price of raw land, over all, was more than twice as high in 1970 as twenty years before. Costs for residential land have been rising even more rapidly than construction costs. For new FHA-insured single-family homes, the land proportion of total value, 12 per cent in 1950, had risen to 20 per cent in the late 1960's.

The cost of mortgage money, swollen as much by attempts to curb inflation as by inflation itself, was at one of the highest levels in the nation's history in 1970, not beginning to drop until the end of the year. It was not unusual in some areas for borrowers to be paying 10 per cent interest, or its equivalent in the form of interest plus "points"—the latter being additional charges by lenders to get around interest maximums on FHA-insured loans or maximums set by usury laws in some states. The FHA itself, recognizing the realities of the money market, reluctantly raised its interest ceiling three times in 1968 and 1969. Whereas the ceiling was 6 per cent in early 1968, it was 8.5 per cent as 1970 began.

What all this means to the apartment renter or home buyer, or to the government if it is subsidizing his housing, is measured more importantly in hard dollars than in abstract percentages. A rise of just one percentage point in interest can mean $15 a month more in rent on a five-room apartment that cost $20,000 to build. For the homeowner, monthly payments on a twenty-five-year, $10,000 mortgage (to take again a handy if somewhat wishful figure these days) are 15 per cent higher at 7.25 per cent than at 5.75 per cent. Thus, the National Commission on Urban Problems concluded, "The increase in the cost of money has added more to the ultimate cost of a home than has any other single item."*

Construction costs themselves have been up sharply. The cost of building materials, over all, rose 6 per cent in 1969 and just under that in 1968—a "two-year jump [that] equalled the cumulative increase for the entire twelve-year period of 1956–68," according to the Department of Housing and Urban Development. Moreover, cost increases for some materials were much steeper than the over-all figure. During one period from the late 1950's to the late 1960's, while the cost of construction materials was going up only 10 per cent generally, lumber costs, especially vital in home building, were increasing by 25 per cent. Union hourly wages in the building trades, exclusive of fringe benefits, went up an average of about 50 per cent from the late 1950's to the late 1960's. A spate of even sharper annual increases characterized two-year and three-year contracts signed as the 1970's began.

Some observers caution that construction cost increases are sometimes interpreted to give an exaggerated impression of the rise in housing costs. The construction cost indexes, they argue, don't take into account gains in labor productivity, besides which construction costs form only a fraction, even if a sizable one, of ultimate housing costs. They urge that the focus instead be on consumer price indexes, which indicate that increases in housing

* An even more striking view of the consequences of higher interest rates can be had from a long-term look. The same homeowner paying off his $10,000 mortgage over twenty-five years will pay a total of $7,979 in interest over that period if he gets his mortgage at 5 per cent interest. At 6 per cent, his total interest payments over the twenty-five years will be $9,332. At 7 per cent, it will be $11,204, and at 8 per cent $13,157, more than the amount of the loan itself.

costs for the most part have been in line with consumer price increases generally over the past two decades.

For economists, this is undoubtedly an interesting point of discussion. But for the occupants of the decaying, reeking tenements of the nation's cities, or the crumbling shacks of its countryside, all it adds up to, at best, is that they are about as far away as ever from a decent place to live. And "at best" does not always prevail.

More important, the point is not whether housing costs have or have not risen in line with consumer costs generally. The point is whether housing costs can be *reduced* from their present levels so that they take less of a bite out of the low-, moderate-, and middle-income consumer dollar and less of a bite out of the public treasury when government has to subsidize housing costs.

As for labor costs, the argument is similarly made that wage rises are given more blame than they deserve for increases in housing prices. The cost of labor in conventional homebuilding, union leaders point out, forms today only about one-fifth of initial development and construction costs, which themselves may make up only about 40 or 50 per cent of over-all monthly housing expenses (the latter, again, comprising operating costs as well as amortization of the initial development and construction costs). Thus, the argument goes, a 20 per cent cut in labor costs during the construction process might ultimately mean no more to the housing consumer than a 2 per cent decrease in his monthly housing expenditure.

No doubt this is so. But, aside from the fact that every "bit and piece" counts in the effort to lower housing costs, the effects of labor on the price of housing are not confined to the issue of wages paid per hour. The unions' sizable influence in preserving cost-heightening restrictions in building codes adds not only to the cost of the labor component itself but often to the cost of the materials component as well, because the use of cheaper materials is precluded by many of these restrictions. In short, the interrelationships of housing cost components are such that the actual cost-enhancing influence of labor extends beyond the relatively small proportion of housing costs that labor accounts for on the surface.

Two other aspects of the relationship between labor and housing are critical. One is the capacity of the ten-year program for meeting the nation's housing needs, set forth in the 1968 Housing Act, to serve also as a program to meet some of the drastic employment needs of America's blacks and other economically beset minorities. The other aspect, equally controversial, is the relationship of the building unions to prefabrication and to technological advances in homebuilding generally.

The view that the black and Spanish-speaking minorities should have a large share in the work required to build or rehabilitate 26 million houses and apartments is based not only on the need to increase employment opportunities for these groups but also on estimates that, if the goals of the 1968 act are to be met, at least 1 million more men will be needed in the construction trades by the mid-1970's.

Critics of the building unions see them as the major barrier to increasing black representation in the skilled and better-paying construction trades—and, in fact, as the force responsible for "artificial" manpower shortages in construction. Defenders reply that the building unions have been no more racially discriminatory than American industry and society generally. The unions reject the charge that they have willfully sought to keep the manpower force shrunk.

There is truth on both sides in this emotional debate. The percentage of blacks in other than low-paying jobs has been negligible in many industries and professions besides construction (in which lack of a union card often shuts off all possibilities of employment in many areas of the country). It was with more than a trace of scorn for editorial critics of the building trades that the Building and Construction Trades Department of the AFL-CIO cited a 1967 Associated Press survey of 300 daily newspapers across the country. The survey had found no black editors and only 119 black reporters on the papers.

At the same time, there is no question that in numerous areas of the country—outside the South as much as in it—resistance to increasing the number of blacks in the better-paying construction crafts is far more intense than resistance in other industries. The rising tensions between blacks seeking an end to what they consider unfair obstacles to their entry into these crafts and whites already in them was vividly illustrated as the 1960's ended in Chicago and Pittsburgh, where black demonstrations and white counterdemonstrations threatened to explode into violence. On one occasion, white construction workers who were massed before Pittsburgh's city hall chanted, "Wallace, Wallace, Wallace," making clear the context in which they viewed the push by blacks for greater opportunities on the building scene.

This is not to imply that every white construction worker sees George C. Wallace as the answer to the black drive. Nor is it to say that the building unions are monolithically resistant to increased opportunities for blacks in the higher-skilled and better-paying crafts. The unions' outlook and practices in this matter vary from locality to locality, because local unions and local interunion councils are to a great extent autonomous. From a national perspective, there is little doubt that things have begun to change for the better in recent years, but the change is only the merest beginning and hardly warrants self-congratulation by the unions.

The 1968 reports of the National Commission on Urban Problems and the President's Committee on Urban Housing reached basically the same conclusion. "It is only simple justice to say that conditions have improved greatly during the last two years. An estimated 8,100 Negroes are registered in current apprenticeship programs—nearly twice the number in 1966," the Douglas commission said. "The construction skilled trades, in fact, have better records, particularly in the last two to three years, than the skilled crafts in other industries—but there is still room for much more improvement," concluded the Kaiser committee. Some of the gains have stemmed from participation by the building unions in apprenticeship-recruiting programs among minority youths in a number of cities.

As far as the Nixon Administration is concerned, minority employment in the construction trades is one area where it has indicated movement in the right direction, in the view of some civil rights leaders. The Administration's "Philadelphia plan," setting minority hiring guidelines in that city for a half-dozen skilled construction crafts involved in federally aided projects, marked what these leaders hoped would be the beginning of a much larger government effort to help make a reality of the equal job opportunities embodied in civil rights legislation and in the officially voiced policies of the building unions' national leadership. This leadership, however, has vigorously opposed the Philadelphia plan, contending that it establishes racial hiring "quotas" insupportable in a democratic society.

The second controversy involving the unions stems from the effects of union-enforced work rules and practices on technological innovations in homebuilding. To some critics of the building unions, their policies on prefabrication and other construction advances make them look like medieval guilds thrust by a time machine into the twentieth century. The unions and their defenders find such a view a gross exaggeration by people who are "ignorant of construction work" and who choose to ignore instances where unions have cooperated in technological innovations.

Here again, there is truth on both sides. The National Commission on Urban Problems made a special effort to get behind the claims and counterclaims. After comparing examples of restrictive work rules and practices with the unions' explanations for them, the commission concluded:

> While there are honest differences of opinion about the seriousness or cost impact of any specific example of such practices on any particular construction project, the existence of them in many forms and variations is beyond question. They are embedded in custom and contract. It strains belief to think that the totality of these practices would not increase the cost, impair the quality, or decrease the supply of housing. However, the conclusion that these practices are completely without justification, or that they can be remedied in some simple fashion, is not supported by the facts. . . . What one man sees as a wasteful procedure or use of manpower, for example, may turn out to be a genuine, necessary safety feature in the light of experience. . . . But this may be abused. Everything called a safety rule is not necessarily that.

The commission also found that while many restrictive practices "retard the adoption of new materials and improved systems of handling old materials," unions have also been "active partners in a number of breakthroughs involving new products and methods."

Moreover, advances in prefabrication and technology do not loom as threats to all the construction unions. A survey that the Battelle Memorial Institute, a private research organization, conducted for the AFL-CIO building trades department found that while such advances posed threats to such groups as the painters' union, they offered opportunities for growth to other unions, such as the operating engineers', whose membership operates the heavy construction equipment. Finally, the homebuilding sector of the construction industry is less subject to union influence than the construction business over all, because many homebuilders, especially outside the big cities, use nonunion labor. Such labor was employed in residential construction by two-thirds of the builders belonging to the National Association of Home Builders, according to a 1968 survey by that group.

Nevertheless, the truth-on-both-sides conclusion holds up only for the national perspective. In many areas, technology-stifling, cost-heightening restrictions are highly conspicuous features of local union behavior. In New York City, building union practices are "among the country's most old-fashioned," according to the Institute of Public Administration. The nonprofit institute made this charge in a report evaluating a highly publicized experiment in "instant rehabilitation" that it conducted for the federal government on New York's Lower East Side in 1967. In the project, a decayed nineteenth-century tenement was completely renovated within forty-eight hours. A key aspect of the experiment was installation of preassembled kitchen-bathroom "core units" that were lowered through a shaft that had been cut through the roof and down to the first floor.

In carrying out the project while adhering to local union practices, costly concessions and compromises had to be made, according to the institute. To satisfy the unions, ironworkers and carpenters shared emplacement of the kitchen-bathroom cores, resulting in a larger crew. A plumbers' local in Manhattan refused to assemble and hook up cores that had been developed in Queens with labor from that borough; a second prototype had to be fashioned using Manhattan labor. These were among the factors that made the experiment more expensive than the results warranted, the institute said.

Such restrictions are deplorable, but at the same time they must be seen in perspective. They differ little from attempts by skilled workers generally to resist technological changes threatening their jobs. Industries as diverse as railroads and newspaper publishing have been wracked by similar controversies, in the one case over attempts to reduce the size of train crews, in the other over efforts to introduce automatic typesetting equipment. One need only visit a newspaper composing room to become keenly aware that construction sites are not the only places where craftsmen are zealously on guard lest a nonmember of a specific craft union perform even the most trivial task within the province of that union.

In construction, there are added pressures stemming from the instability and seasonality that are still conspicuous characteristics of the industry. From the time a construction man finishes work on one job until he begins on another, several days, and thus several days' pay, may be lost. During the 1960's, the number of men employed in construction jobs nationwide was about one-third higher in August than in February; in many northern states the disparity was far greater. Seasonality, while less of a problem than in past decades, remains a serious one. What outsiders consider excessively high hourly rates in skilled construction are seen by the unions as compensation for the lower number of hours worked yearly by many construction workers.

Yet the construction work force, precisely because of the nation's massive housing needs, need not feel so threatened by technology. Meeting the goals of the 1968 Housing Act would entail housing production in America far surpassing that of past years—an average of 2.6 million units annually instead of the 1.5 million yearly average since World War II—and would provide sufficient employment not only for those in building occupations today but for a projected minimum of 1 million more workers. If the nation were to keep the commitment proclaimed in the 1968 Housing Act, some of the fears that lead unionized labor to insist on technology-inhibiting practices would be assuaged, for the sheer volume of work available would make up for reductions in manpower resulting from increased use of prefabrication.

"GEE WHIZ!" AND "YAWN"

Again, an increase in prefabrication to lower construction costs is but one task in the over-all battle to reduce the consumer expenditure for housing. Yet because technology is far more fascinating to most people than the intricacies of zoning and mortgage financing and government fiscal policies—all just as important in determining the ultimate expense for housing—proposals for radically changing the housing construction process have traditionally been given the lion's share of public attention. Hundreds of thousands of people flocked to see Habitat '67 at the Expo fair in Montreal in 1967; how popular would a pavilion have been that featured the latest suggestions for model zoning and land-tax laws? Whenever I have written a newspaper article describing a proposal for some radical innovation in the housing construction process, I've invariably received comments from colleagues and friends about how fascinating it all is, and "do they really think it can work?" When I have written about suggestions for more economical land-use patterns or for fiscal policies that would not penalize housing, the reaction has been confined to letters from accountants pointing out misplaced decimal points.

Given the "gee whiz" fascination with technology and the yawning boredom with the other major elements of housing cost, it is no wonder that so many Americans have come to think of the effort to lower the cost of housing as synonymous with the pursuit of some dazzling technological breakthrough. By itself, this attitude is no cause for worry. However, it is potentially dangerous if it causes public officials to refrain from mounting the kind of intensive campaign needed to bring down the nonconstruction costs of housing. The illusory hope that a technological breakthrough is just around the corner and will render unnecessary all other efforts to lower housing costs will itself guarantee that the nation will not solve its housing problems.

To emphasize the reason for this: Construction costs may form 50 to 75 per cent of the initial development costs of a single-family home or an apartment but may account for only 25 or possibly 35 per cent of the consumer's housing dollar when the share of this dollar for maintenance, property taxes, and the other operating costs is taken into account. Assuming that construction costs account for roughly 30 per cent of a family's housing dollar, a 20 per cent reduction in such costs, which would certainly be an achievement of major proportions (we're assuming also no reduction in the quality, size, and amenities) would mean in the end only about a 6 per cent reduction in the family's monthly housing expense.

Granted, such calculations are rough at best; they do not, for example, reflect the additional savings in financing and other costs that would flow from the construction cost reductions. Nevertheless, they illustrate that the ultimate reduction in a family's housing costs are only a fraction of any economies in the construction phase.

None of this is to belittle the search for lower construction costs or to imply that the search should not be pursued with vigor. As one of the "bits and pieces" of housing costs, the construction element must occasion as great a search for savings as any other. But the point is to retain perspective, to keep in mind that the most impressive economies achieved in this phase will be negligible if economies are not achieved in the other phases as well, and that construction economies could be easily wiped out by continually rising costs in the other areas. So long as one retains this perspective, a "gee whiz" appreciation of innovation and experimentation in the pursuit of lower-cost construction is not out of order.

Examples of such innovation can be found throughout the country. In Phoenix, Arizona, there are the Ben-Jo Estates, a development of "mini-houses" whose two-bedroom model was selling in 1969 for $6,850 and whose three-bedroom model went for about $1,000 more. Based on a prototype built as a part of an experimental housing research project sponsored by the Department of Housing and Urban Development and the University of Texas, the mini-house was developed by National Housing Industries, an organization formed specifically to produce homes for the low-income market. A family not receiving a government subsidy could finance a mini-house in 1969 with monthly payments of only $65. This amount not only covered principal and interest on an FHA-insured thirty-year mortgage at 7.5 per cent (the FHA interest ceiling at the time), but also taxes and insurance. But Ben-Jo Estates was built under the federal government's new Section 235 program, and so, with the maximum subsidy under that program reducing a family's interest payment to 1 per cent, some families were paying only about $40 a month.

The mini-houses (the two-bedroom model has 720 square feet of floor space, the equivalent of a 60-by-12-foot mobile home) are of concrete-block-and-slab construction with conventional building materials throughout: half-inch gypsum board over two-by-four studs forming the interior walls; shingled, wood-trussed roofs; asphalt tile floors; and simulated acoustical plaster ceilings. Materials and equipment of standard lengths and widths were used, helping to reduce costs, and mini-houses were being built, employing conventional on-site methods, in as little as three weeks.

On Locust Street in Lancaster, Pennsylvania, three boxlike houses were offered in 1968 as another of the many suggested solutions for bringing down housing construction costs. The houses are of cellular concrete, a type in which protein substances added during the mixing form microscopic air bubbles that give the finished product a strong but lightweight quality. Clad in siding of sandblasted, cedar-veneer plywood, the attached dwellings are a three-story, five-bedroom model built for about $14,000; a two-story, three-bedroom model completed at a cost of about $12,000; and a one-story, one-bedroom unit (615 square feet of floor space) built for about $5,000. The cellular-concrete framing system was designed by Neal Mitchell, an architect and Professor of Construction at Harvard's Graduate School of Design, with the aid of a $50,000 grant from the cement and lime division of the Martin Marietta Corporation.

In Boston, more than a thousand low- and moderate-income apartments have been built using another innovative construction method called Techcrete. This system employs precast-concrete load-bearing walls and precast-concrete plank floors erected in a stacked "house of cards" fashion, with the open ends, or side walls, filled in with brick or siding. It was devised by the architectural firm of Carl Koch and Associates of Boston, with structural engineering by Sepp Firnkas.

With the stimulus provided by the Nixon Administration's Operation Breakthrough, innovation in the search for reduced housing construction costs sharply increased as the 1970's began. To lay the foundation for the research and development aspect of Breakthrough, the Department of Housing and Urban Development sponsored a prototype-design competition that drew more than 200 entries. Twenty-two of them were selected by the department for prototype construction as part of Breakthrough on nine sites across the country.

The twenty-two designs run the gamut of proposals for increasing the efficiency of housing construction in the United States. There are one-dimensional "panel systems," using concrete, wood, and even plastic, that combine the technology already used by the nation's home manufacturers with ideas, some European-influenced, for advancing this technology much further. There are the three-dimensional "box systems" whose various incarnations, like Habitat in Montreal and the "sectionalized" houses produced by some American home manufacturers, involve the precasting or prefabrication of "boxes," "cubes," or "modules" that are stacked atop and around each other at the site to form the finished dwelling.

The twenty-two also run the gamut of design and, to hear the critics tell it, of architectural quality as well. Like conventional on-site construction, they come in high-rise, low-rise, townhouse, row-house, garden-apartment, and detached single-family arrangements. Their various designs, according to one critic, include "attractive versions that suggest the famous California house style . . . pseudo-Franco-American colonial, [and] the lowest common denominator speculator ranch house."

But whatever the specific criticisms of specific designs, the competition clearly illustrates the basic point that industrializing the American housing industry need not mean deadening standardization any more than the automobile assembly line today means the black Model T Ford. Industrialized housing, as much or as little as conventional on-site housing, can cover a wide range in design and aesthetic quality.

Although the term "industrialized housing" is used by the layman to mean any housing whose major components are constructed off the site, the phrase actually signifies something more specific to housing professionals. In the words of Robert Borg, president of the Kreisler Borg Florman Construction Company:

> Industrialized housing is not just another name for prefabrication or modular construction or precasting of concrete. It is a technique of comprehensive application of a scientifically managed marshalling of all possible control of the entire process of building in one centralized organization, using the best available engineering and management techniques to govern the output of the building process from start to finish. Thus, while prefabrication, precasting and modular construction may be a part of the process, more importantly these will be integrated with such tools as optimum cost design using computerized information retrieval for apartment distribution; standardization of specification, and, of course, the new technologies for as much of the building as possible.

In short, "mechanization and programming are the basic elements," as another expert put it. He explained: "[Industrialized] system building comprises both the 'hardware' [and] the 'software,' the latter including such management techniques as time and motion studies of all tasks involved in prefabricating, shipping and erecting structures."

What the experts have in mind when they speak in these terms is not the typical factory producer of housing in the United States, but the mass producers of multifamily housing in Western Europe and the Soviet Union. It is common today for Europe's industrialized housing methods to be cited in discussions of the search for solutions to the housing problems of the United States. Sometimes they are cited as an example of what this country must do if it is to produce all the low-cost housing that it needs. At other times, the European way is pointed to as what this country should *not* do.

Europe's industrialized building systems make extensive use of high-precision casting machinery that turns out prefabricated housing components under highly advanced programming methods, which often schedule in advance, sometimes to the minute, when every major component of the finished product is to be produced in the factory, transported to the site, and installed. "Portable factories" that can be moved from one site to another are part of a number of systems, and some systems use as much as 85 per cent unskilled labor. Concrete is the most widely employed structural material, with precast, load-bearing wall panels a basic element of many of the European systems. In some of the systems, networks of factory-fabricated elements such as radiant heat pipes and structurally reinforcing steel are incorporated in the concrete floor slabs, just as insulation, electrical wiring, exterior finishing, and doors and windows are included in the prefabricated wall panels.

In the Soviet Union as the 1970's began, about 85 per cent of all multifamily housing was the product of industrialized building systems. In France it was about 50 per cent, and in England about 40 per cent. Italy, West Germany, and Denmark were also among the countries in which housing produced by highly sophisticated industrial techniques was prominent.

These techniques, developed over the past two decades, were born of the staggering housing needs that confronted Europe at the end of World War II. First the Depression and then the war itself had severely cut or halted housing production. In addition, the war had inflicted wholesale devastation on the housing stock of many countries. West European governments had already had a tradition of playing an active role in housing production long before the war, and when it was time to pick up the pieces after the second conflagration to ravage the continent in a quarter of a century, there was little hesitancy about the part that government was to play.

This is not to say that there were no obstacles to the industrialization of European housing production. Organized labor had its restrictive practices in some countries, and there were often building codes to contend with, too. But the sizable and sustained subsidies that West European governments provided to private housing producers made possible extensive research and development activities that provided a major boost to the creation of mass production housing industries—a stimulus in sharp contrast to the American Government's virtual abandonment in the 1950's of its 1949 commitment in behalf of a decent home and suitable living environment for every American family. In the Soviet Union and its East European satellites, of course, the government itself directly undertook the industrialization process.

If the most advanced industrialized systems of European housing production were adopted for multifamily construction in the United States, American advocates of these systems say, sizable construction cost savings would be realized—as much as 27 per cent in comparison with costs under conventional multifamily construction here, according to some estimates. Some American proponents of European methods further contend that *only* the highly mechanized and programmed approach of these methods will permit the United States to meet the housing goals, unsubsidized as well as subsidized, of the 1968 Housing Act.

On the other hand, some analysts recommend great caution in attempting to compare costs under European and American building techniques. "Evaluating the cost savings of [the European] experiences is extremely difficult," the National Commission on Urban Problems said. "Even where relatively comparable systems exist for collecting data and assigning costs, enormous problems are encountered in evaluating levels of amenity and durability," The President's Committee on Urban Housing contended: "It is not wholly evident that the highly industrialized multifamily systems are more efficient than sophisticated on-site assembly methods. . . . Conjecture plays too large a part in estimates often thrown about." At the same time, the committee said of the European systems: "A final verdict will have to await their full trial in this country. They clearly deserve to be tried."

There is also debate among American housing analysts over functional and aesthetic consequences of the European methods. Some Americans point to comments such as that by Gunnar Myrdal, the Swedish sociologist and economist, who noted that in the countries where a large portion of the housing is the product of the highly industrialized methods, the recognition was setting in "that standardization has in some cases even been driven too far, so that functional requirements and the characteristics of the products do not harmonize. It has also led to monotony in architecture. A more flexible approach is now searched for in these countries."

In part, the extremes of standardization can be attributed to the pressure that European countries felt to meet the vast and desperate shelter needs confronting them after World War II. This pressure often left little room for consideration of aesthetic qualities or the "dangers of overstandardization." In the Soviet Union, the concern for putting up the most housing the quickest way at the least cost, with little or no regard for aesthetics and nonessential amenities, is epitomized by the massive, monotonous blocks that continue to sprout everywhere on Russia's urban landscape. While most often a substantial improvement over the previous accommodations of its occupants, "most Soviet housing would not only be unmarketable in the United States, it would even be unacceptable from a policy standpoint for low-income families," the President's Committee on Urban Housing said. "Small room sizes, poor thermal insulation, and high site densities are among its drawbacks."

The fact that some West European countries have begun in recent years to seek more flexibility in their housing production can be interpreted as a healthy sign that the desperation that contributed to overstandardization has waned and that less immediate considerations are now important, American proponents of European industrialized housing systems argue. In any case, they say, the aesthetic and functional weaknesses in housing produced by these systems are not inevitable in housing created by industrialized methods—any more than massive monotony is inherent in conventional building techniques, which, after all, produced communities of suburban boxes that sometimes appear to have been spawned by a cookie-cutter.

Moreover, proponents of industrialization point out, while European building systems have turned out aesthetically deplorable results, they have also produced housing lauded for its aesthetic qualities. One example is the housing at Thamesmead, a new town near London where a precast concrete panel system has been employed with what some architectural critics regard as brilliant aesthetic success. This system was among the twenty-two winning proposals in the prototype design contest sponsored by the Department of Housing and Urban Development as part of Operation Breakthrough.

Just what influence European building systems will have ultimately on housing construction techniques in the United States is hardly predictable in the early 1970's. No more predictable is whether homebuilding methods in this country will change in *any* way that will result in truly significant construction cost savings, given the artificial barriers, such as building codes and restrictive union practices, that continue to form pervasive and deeply rooted constraints on construction technology.

One thing is certain: Experimentation to test potentially cheaper building techniques dependent for success on widespread application cannot be meaningful if performed on a small scale. It should be no surprise that a number of small demonstration projects to test the economies of proposed mass production or prefabrication methods have often ended up with costs not significantly lower than those of conventional methods, and sometimes even higher. When this has happened the proposals have been branded failures and people prejudiced against them from the start have not hesitated to gloat.

A proposed method may indeed be a failure. But inability to achieve lower costs in a small demonstration project is hardly a fair test where the success of a method is contingent on large-volume operation. In a one-time or small-scale demonstration project materials are not purchased in the same bulk as they would be if the method were functioning at its full scale, precluding the sizable discounts available for large-volume buying. Overhead costs cannot be spread over the large number of units that they would be at full-scale functioning.

The framers of the 1968 Housing Act recognized these realities and authorized a federal program of large-scale housing experimentation. The prototype construction portion of Operation Breakthrough is one aspect of implementing the program. The recent awakening in Washington to the proposition that the federal government must take the lead in promoting the large-scale experimentation needed to develop lower-cost homebuilding technologies is certainly a welcome move in the right direction. But it is only a half-step. Just as important as developing the new technologies is abolishing the institutional barriers—especially the maze of excessively restrictive and outmoded building code provisions—that would keep these technologies from being implemented on the scale necessary for maximum success and that would make cost-cutting techniques irrelevant to millions of the wretchedly housed whose misfortune is to live in cities with backward-looking construction codes.

On paper, Operation Breakthrough indicates that the Nixon Administration is fully aware of this, for the so-called "market aggregation" aspect of Breakthrough calls for review and revision of local laws and codes that impede the use of new and cheaper housing technologies. But aside from stating this obvious need, Breakthrough does little more than call on state and local government to undertake the needed reviews and revisions. By itself, such an appeal is as little likely to evoke the movement needed regarding building codes as it is regarding discriminatory suburban zoning laws. The states have only begun to stir in this area, and most cities and towns with excessively restrictive building laws have not even shown an inclination to stir. As a result, much more than appeals is needed from Washington if significant change is to come about in the next decade.

One course suggested by those who advocate federal *muscle* to get state and local movement on building code reform is amendment of federal urban renewal and model cities laws to make aid under these measures contingent on revision of excessively restrictive codes. In the case of smaller communities, where the threat of losing urban renewal or model cities aid might be considered no great tragedy and even a blessing, the same condition might be set for aid involving water and sewer facilities, often highly desired in such places. Excessive building code restrictions could be defined as those exceeding the requirements of the various model building codes devised by organizations of building officials or insurance industry associations, or exceeding the requirements of state model codes where these exist, or exceeding model standards that could be devised by the federal government itself. Local governments would still be permitted to adopt restrictions necessitated by local climate or geology, but at least the worst excesses of restrictive codes would be done away with.

However, these proposals are not likely to see the light of day as legislation. Congress can hardly be counted on to take up a cause against which manufacturing, labor, and local government interests can be expected to mount an intensive fight, and the Nixon Administration seems about as likely to press for such action as it is to take vigorous steps against communities that zone out low-income housing. Thus Operation Breakthrough, an incontestable reminder of what the nation has to do if the cost of producing housing is to be lowered, is also a reminder of what the federal government is failing to do to achieve a breakthrough other than on paper.

Roles and Responsibilities

Until the distant day when victory is proclaimed over the many economic, social, and political influences that militate against drastic reductions in housing costs, government in America will have to play a substantial role in housing, providing substantial subsidies, if all Americans are to be decently sheltered. To believe that private enterprise alone can do the job, at least until that faraway if not fanciful day, is to believe that a house can stand on water.

This statement is not necessarily an aspersion on the capabilities and efficiency of American private enterprise. Too often among proponents of a past and purer America, the reaction to such a statement is a flush-faced declamation that "American private enterprise has provided the greatest standard of living the world has ever known."

However, the private enterprise system that has provided the greatest standard of living the world has ever known has in one respect done little better than private enterprise systems that have provided less than the greatest standard of living the world has ever known. Specifically, American private enterprise, like all the world's private enterprise, has been unable to provide decent housing for those on the lower end of the economic ladder. Assuming that the poor of any country are to be considered inhabitants of that country just as fully as the middle and upper classes, then, to cite again the words of the Massachusetts Homestead Commission of 1913, "in no country has private enterprise been equal to the task of properly housing the inhabitants."

The reasons for this do not necessarily reflect any lack of ingenuity (Yankee or otherwise) on the part of private enterprise. They reflect the basic fact, as Edith Elmer Wood wrote in her study of the American housing picture in 1931, that "the crux of the housing problem is economic. Under the ordinary laws of supply and demand it is insoluble. In our modern industrial civilization, the distribution of income is such that a substantial portion of the population cannot pay a commercial rent, much less a commercial purchase price, for a home fulfilling the minimum health and decency requirements." She scolded: "The sooner we in the United States recognize these facts, as most thinking people in the rest of the civilized world have already done, the sooner we shall find a remedy."

To the captains of industry and finance in Mrs. Wood's day, such observations were Marxist rot. Four decades later, some very prominent corporate descendants of these captains met her definition of "thinking people." The President's Committee on Urban Housing concluded in 1968 that

> new and foreseeable technological breakthroughs in housing production will not by themselves bring decent shelter within economic reach of the millions of house-poor families in the predictable future. To bridge the gap between the marketplace costs for standard housing and the price that lower-income families can afford to pay, appropriations of federal subsidies are essential and must be substantially increased.

The committee that presented this view could hardly be accused of New Left tendencies. As previously noted, twelve of the eighteen members were presidents or chairmen of corporations or banks, one of them a former head of the Central Intelligence Agency. Besides Edgar F. Kaiser, chairman of the committee and chairman and chief executive officer of the Kaiser Industries Corporation, the committee included John A. McCone, former

CIA director and chairman of the board of the Joshua Hendy Corporation of Los Angeles; Graham J. Morgan, president and chief executive officer of the United States Gypsum Company; and Gaylord A. Freeman, Jr., vice chairman of the board of the First National Bank of Chicago.

Thus, the question of whether or not government should provide major subsidies for housing would seem to be settled by now, even in America. The notion of a substantial government role, based on the awareness that "the ordinary laws of supply and demand" do not work to provide decent housing for the poor (and at some times and in some places for those who are somewhat better off than poor) is fully embraced by men in the nation's highest corporate and financial circles. Seconding the views of Edgar Kaiser and John McCone is hardly likely to lead one to Bolshevik perdition.

At the same time, there is still plenty of room for private enterprise in providing decent housing for the millions who now lack it (assuming that private enterprise has any desire for such a role). Some Americans feel otherwise, of course. There are those whose socialistic ideology leaves no room for private producers generally. Many others simply feel the private sector long ago established that it was largely uninterested in helping to remedy conditions of wretched housing, and rather than waste time and energy trying to change this indifference, government would do better just to get on with the job itself.

On the other hand, the realities of national life being what they are, participation by the private sector would undoubtedly make a great difference in the extent to which the nation's low- and moderate-income housing needs were met. Even if the federal government reordered its budget to provide significantly more for the American people's massive housing needs—an unlikely prospect in the immediate future, Nixonian rhetoric notwithstanding—it is doubtful that any such reordering in today's world would provide sufficient public resources for the entire magnitude of tasks confronting the nation in housing and urban and rural redevelopment. Those who believe that providing desperately needed decent housing is more important than indulging probable pipe dreams recognize the value of the economic and managerial resources that private enterprise can contribute. They feel that these more than make up for the profit entailed by private participation.

Such participation in producing lower-income housing has been envisioned as involving more than just the homebuilding sector. Corporations whose businesses have little or nothing to do with construction have been urged to invest in the production of this type of housing by participation as sponsors in the various publicly aided federal programs. The prospect of depreciation and other income-offsetting tax benefits, over and above the limited direct return from the housing itself, has been held out as an inducement to these corporations, as in the previously discussed housing partnerships program established by the 1968 Housing Act.

Such inducements, most housing experts agree, are far more likely to succeed than appeals to the social conscience of corporate America. A rash of such appeals were made after the urban racial explosions of the 1960's, among the most prominent being the "give-a-damn" campaign in which the Urban Coalition, formed of business, labor, religious, and civil rights leaders, sought to stir business and other interests to work for the eradication of urban blight and poverty.

While the pictures of flames against the night skies of the nation's black slums were still freshly etched in memory, an encouraging number of big business organizations responded by reversing the indifference they had exhibited in the past toward programs to alleviate slums and poverty. Too often, however, they gave a damn for only a brief time and then went back to investments-as-usual. In some cases, though, the commitments have been for the long term, and while those involving housing represent only a spit in the cement bucket, given the nation's need and the financial resources of corporate America, they have to be welcomed.

The corporate involvement in lower-income housing has taken various forms. In some cities, business organizations have formed coalitions to spearhead or fund the construction of such housing. This was the case in Syracuse, New York, where most of the city's major industries have joined together to form the Syracuse Housing Development Corporation, which in 1970 was planning to sponsor projects under publicly aided programs of both the federal government and New York State. In Detroit, leading corporations have joined with labor and other organizations in the New Detroit Committee, which, among other things, is a major funding source for the Metropolitan Detroit Citizens Development Authority, an organization that has provided aid to community groups undertaking low- and moderate-income housing projects.

Other corporations have gone directly into the sponsorship of lower-income housing individually or in partnerships. The Celanese Corporation, a diversified chemical company, has joined American Standard, Inc., which produces a wide line of building and industrial products, to form an organization called Construction for Progress; as the 1970's began, it was building low-income public housing in New York City's slums for sale on a turnkey basis to the local housing authority. Several large utility companies across the country were newly involved in the construction or rehabilitation of low- and moderate-income housing at about the same time, among them the Michigan Consolidated Gas Company, the Niagara Mohawk Power Corporation in upstate New York, the Elizabethtown Gas Company in New Jersey, and Eastern Gas and Fuel Associates, parent organization of the Boston Gas Company.

The banking and insurance worlds, justly accused by critics of having been major contributors to the growth of slums over the years, have also begun to involve themselves in the effort to replace decrepit housing with decent places to live. With no little publicity, the nation's leading life insurance companies undertook in the late 1960's a commitment to provide $2 billion to finance the construction, rehabilitation, and purchase of decent low- and moderate-rent housing in slum areas across the country and the creation of job and business opportunities for residents of these areas. Of the first $1.2 billion provided, $878 million has gone for housing in slum areas of 240 cities. Some 80,000 housing units are being built, renovated or purchased with the money. In several places banks have joined together to provide financing for low- and moderate-income housing on a shared risk basis, and here and there a bank has by itself undertaken the sponsorship of such housing.

In the case of the banks and the insurance companies—the latter too are a traditional source of mortgage funds in the United

States—many argue that it will take long years of participation in the battle against slum conditions before these institutions even *begin* to atone for their role in the spread of these conditions. Over the years, both types of institutions for the most part consistently avoided making housing loans not only in blighted areas but also often in neighborhoods that they expected to "go under." Such "red-lining" was also practiced by fire insurance companies in their refusal to insure in these areas.

As with a landlord who fears that his neighborhood is threatened with decline, and who therefore is reluctant to put any more money into his building for maintenance, these actions by the banks and insurance companies were perfect examples of self-fulfilling prophesies. Without mortgage loans, no new housing could be built or old housing rehabilitated. Without the possibility of fire insurance, the rare mortgage lender who might otherwise have gone into a construction or rehabilitation project in such an area would feel compelled to withdraw.

From the point of view of the banks and insurance companies, their mortgage activities were dictated by the prudence necessary in safeguarding the money entrusted to them by depositors and policy-holders. Their approach on mortgage commitments, the institutions argue, were no different from policies of the Federal Housing Administration in its mortgage insurance program—which, of course, is unfortunately true. The fire insurance companies defend their actions by also invoking the need for prudently avoiding high-risk commitments.

In the short run, these excuses are valid. In the long run, they have contributed to the spread of blight eating away at the nation's cities and threatening to transform them into centers of decay and demoralization that can hardly provide a flourishing atmosphere for the worlds of business and commerce. As a result of the urban eruptions of the 1960's, the long-run perspective began to dawn on inhabitants of these worlds. But it was only a beginning. In the early 1970's, only a minuscule portion of American private enterprise was acting on the recognition that, in a society where such a basic commodity as a decent place to live was far scarcer than it should be, business as usual would have to include efforts to help rectify this deficiency.

7. Ignorance and the Crisis

The Statistical Narcotic

Just how great the deficit of decent housing in the United States actually is is not known. The figure of 11 million badly housed American families is a very crude and possibly very conservative estimate. To those who have seen the statistics-studded volumes of the United States Census Bureau's census of housing, this may come as a surprise. The 1,047 final reports of the 1960 housing census—which in some ways was designed to be far more comprehensive than its 1970 counterpart—contain more than 40,000 eye-wearying pages of charts, tables, and figures that seem, to the layman, to provide the most detailed picture possible of the nation's housing stock. But, as those familiar with the census housing data know, while they offer the most comprehensive picture available, they also are woefully inadequate, unreliable, and dangerously misleading.

Perhaps no man is more keenly aware of this than the chief of the Census Bureau's housing division himself, Arthur F. Young. The census housing data, Young told me, provides "only a very rough indicator" of the condition of the country's housing supply.

"My personal view is that if you try to use the census housing statistics to measure our urban problems, you will have a gross understatement. The statistics do not indicate the magnitude of urban blight," he said.

This evaluation has been echoed time and again. The National Commission on Urban Problems complained: "The hard job of estimating and projecting housing needs is made all but impossible by the ridiculously inadequate data now at hand. Nearly everyone concerned with the subject has known and said this since the first census of housing was published in 1940." Frank Kristof, a prominent housing economist and former assistant chief of the Census Bureau's housing division, put it this way: "No one who has dealt with the subject even casually can be satisfied with existing measures of housing quality. There is little doubt that the number of substandard units in older central cities is understated." Others have noted that, though perhaps to a lesser degree, the same can be said of inferior housing outside the cities.

The Census Bureau itself decided that its 1960 housing statistics were so unreliable that, in the 1970 census, it sharply altered its procedures for gathering housing data. In Young's words, "We did not want to perpetuate the errors we made in the past." Because the 1960 statistics served as the basis for projecting housing needs and fashioning governmental responses through the late 1970's, and because the 1960 census was the last to include a comprehensive, unit by unit evaluation of the structural condition of the nation's housing, it is important to see what these errors were and how they were made.

The reasons for the errors were twofold: the way in which the housing information was gathered, and, more important, the definitions that the Census Bureau used in rating the nation's housing stock.

Regarding the methodological element, in 1960 the typical census-taker—"enumerator" in the bureau's jargon—was a housewife in her 30's or 40's with a high school education and, in the Census Bureau's own words, "with no particular experience in architecture, building construction, or any other line of endeavor relevant to the rating process." To prepare the census-takers for the task of evaluating structural condition, the Census Bureau provided them with thirty minutes of training (part of an over-all nine-hour training session) and an illustrated eighteen-page booklet containing definitions of the census categories of housing quality. Most enumerators were paid a rate that permitted them to earn about $1.60 an hour and that, given the array of information to be gathered from each household, resulted in a very brief time spent in evaluating the structural condition of an individual dwelling unit. "For most units the amount of time taken to make a rating was probably less than one minute," the Census Bureau said in a post-census assessment of its own housing-evaluation methods.

The fruits of such a system—is anyone surprised?—turned out to be "unreliable" and "inaccurate," the Census Bureau later declared in the unpublicized self-assessment of its housing-evaluation effort. The bureau made the following points in its critique:

> Our best estimate is that if another group of enumerators had been sent back to rate the housing units of the United States, only about one-third of the units rated as dilapidated or deteriorating by either group of enumerators would have been rated the same by both groups of enumerators.
>
> There is evidence that about one-fourth of the units which could be classified as substandard from the findings of one group of enumerators, would have been differently classified according to the findings of another group of enumerators.
>
> The 1960 census evaluation program indicates that dilapidated housing in the United States, as determined by the 1960 census, is understated by at least one-third.

At the same time, the bureau expressed doubt that more reliable results would have been obtained had more highly skilled and motivated people been employed to rate housing conditions. The primary difficulty, according to experts both inside and outside the Census Bureau, lay not in the census-takers but in the deficiency of the definitions and the criteria for applying them that the enumerators had to work with.

In 1960, the nation's housing stock was divided by the census agency into the three categories "sound," "deteriorating," and "dilapidated." Sound housing was defined as housing with no defects or with "some slight defects," including such things as small cracks in the walls or chimney, lack of paint, and cracked windows. Deteriorating housing was said to be housing that "needs more repair than would be provided in the course of regular maintenance"; specifically, "one defect serious enough to be listed as intermediate is enough to classify a house as deteriorating," the census-takers were instructed. Examples of intermediate defects were given as holes, open cracks, and rotted, loose, or missing materials in the foundation or in the walls, roofs, floors, or ceilings, "but not over a large area"; shaky or unsafe steps, porches, or railings; several broken or missing window panes; and rotted or loose window frames that no longer kept out rain or wind.

The last category, dilapidated housing, was described as housing that "endangers the health or well-being of its occupants"—specifically, housing that was characterized by either "a combination of intermediate defects," "one or more critical defects," or "inadequate original construction." Critical defects were things like holes, open cracks, or rotted, loose, or missing materials "over a large area"; "substantial sagging" of the floors, walls, or roof, and "extensive damage" from fire, flood, or storm. As for inadequate original construction, the census-takers were to look for dirt floors, the lack of a foundation, and "makeshift walls or roofs." If they found anyone living in a packing box or a barn where goats and pigs also lived, they need not hesitate to put that down as inadequate original construction, they were also informed.

Following the three-way classification of structural condition developed by the Census Bureau on the basis of these definitions, the classification was combined, by government housing agencies, with the census findings on plumbing facilities to develop the more widely utilized categories of "standard" and "substandard" housing. A standard housing unit, based on the 1960 census, was defined as a sound or deteriorating unit that had all required plumbing facilities.* A substandard unit was defined as a dilapidated unit, as well as any other unit, regardless of its structural rating, that lacked either hot running water in the structure, a flush toilet for the household's private use, or a bathtub or shower for its private use.

Given these breakdowns, this was the state of the American housing inventory as determined by the 1960 census:

	Number of Units (in millions)	Per Cent of Total
Sound	47.3	81.1
Deteriorating	8.1	13.9
Dilapidated	2.9	5.0
Totals	58.3	100.0
Standard	47.7	81.8
a) Sound, with all plumbing facilities	43.1	
b) Deteriorating, with all plumbing facilities	4.6	
Substandard	10.6	18.2
a) Sound, with inadequate plumbing facilities	4.2	
b) Deteriorating, with inadequate plumbing facilities	3.5	
c) Dilapidated	2.9	

Source: Frank Kristof, *Urban Housing Needs Through the 1980's: An Analysis and Projection: Prepared for the Consideration of the National Commission on Urban Problems,* Research Report No. 10 (Washington, D.C., 1968), p. 89.

* Inclusion of "deteriorating, with all plumbing facilities" in the standard category has been a subject of dispute. Those who favor including it in the standard classification hold that nothing in the census definition of "deteriorating" justifies considering this category as containing housing that is not fit for human habitation. Those who feel that the category should be included in the *sub*standard classification argue that the substandard concept should be broadened to include housing with many of the "intermediate" defects that, under the Census Bureau definitions, characterize deteriorating units. Frank Kristof says, "There can be no question that some proportion of the 'deteriorating, with all plumbing facilities' category belongs in the substandard group. What this proportion is, it would be almost hopeless to guess, although this writer would hazard the proportion at about one-third." Others have hazarded the proportion as one-half or two-thirds. If this debate means anything, it is testimony to the sophistication of housing-condition analysis in a nation whose computers have little difficulty pinpointing a landing site on a heavenly body 250,000 miles away.

The Census Bureau's 1960 classification of sound, deteriorating, and dilapidated was considered an improvement over the categories used in the first housing census, in 1940, and in the 1950 census. In 1940, the nation's housing had been divided into the two categories, "not needing major repairs" and "needing major repairs." This approach was later deemed inadequate because, as the Census Bureau itself put it, it "measured only the physical condition of the structure without indicating the level of quality: e.g., a tarpaper shack, or a cellar, may have been classified as not needing major repairs." The two-way classification of "not dilapidated" and "dilapidated" was therefore developed for use in the 1950 census, and these ratings were refined in 1960 by the addition of the "deteriorating" category, partly at the urging of housing and urban renewal officials who felt the need for an intermediate level of classification.

Despite this evolution, the 1960 housing census remained a crude and unreliable measure of housing conditions. And the reason was simply that the definitions used, and the criteria for applying them, were deficient. The criteria still left room for a good deal of subjective judgment in evaluating a home, as the instructions to the enumerators clearly indicate. In addition to those cited, there were such guidelines as this: In noting that a unit should be considered dilapidated if it had a "combination of intermediate defects," the enumerators' instruction booklet explained that "no set number of defects is required. It may be two or three, or it may be five or six, depending on whether in combination they extend over a large area, or whether when taken together they indicate that the house no longer provides safe and adequate shelter."

One is hardly surprised that the average census-taker, whose knowledge of structural engineering or public health is elementary at best, would apply such a directive with any degree of reliability. But as the Census Bureau later discovered, the reliability of far more qualified people in applying this and similar specifications appears to be not much better.

In one of several experiments carried out by the bureau to evaluate 1960 housing data techniques (this one conducted in Louisville in 1964), the work of a group of "experts" from Washington—largely employees of the bureau itself and of various housing agencies, and all with experience or training in statistics or housing—was compared with the work of locally recruited enumerators given training in the rating of structural condition that was nearly identical to the training of enumerators who had worked in the 1960 census. After comparing the frequency in the experiment with which a single housing unit was given two different ratings by two different experts to the frequency with which a single unit received two different ratings from two different nonprofessional enumerators, the Census Bureau concluded that the experts were "not any more reliable in their ratings than the enumerators." In one category, the bureau found, the experts were "significantly less reliable."

Beyond the human element, however, the 1960 census definitions were inadequate—and would have remained so no matter how reliably applied—simply because they did not take into account some of the most crucial components of housing quality. Rather, they embraced only the most rudimentary conditions of human shelter. A survey confined to measuring these conditions was hardly the instrument for rating a nation's housing needs at the dawning of the space age.

Among the factors that the census criteria omitted were such items as room size, ventilation, access to natural light, and the regularity of such services as heat and hot water—all of which are crucial in defining the quality of a given house or apartment and are governed by most local housing codes through the provision of minimum standards in these areas. The census approach also did not measure the vital neighborhood conditions—inadequate sanitation services or sewage facilities, the decay of surrounding buildings, foul odors or noxious fumes from nearby industrial plants—that also have a direct bearing on determining the quality of life in a given dwelling.

Noting the many elements not reflected in the statistical volumes that fill nearly 15 feet of shelf space in his office, Mr. Young, the census housing chief, summed up the significance of his 1960 figures as follows: "It is an oversimplified view to look at housing only in terms of structural condition. There is nothing in the census data that really measures the deterioration of our cities."

The National Commission on Urban Problems put it more picturesquely. The census statistics, it said, reflect criteria for acceptable housing that add up to "a nearly weathertight box with pipes in it." Moreover, the commission stated, the census approach "results in a lower estimate of the volume of substandard housing than most reasonable persons would arrive at on the basis of careful local studies."

The commission concluded that if the American people were to begin employing a definition of substandard housing based on the minimum standards set forth in local housing codes, "no one would have any realistic conception" of the extent of substandard housing in the United States, because "the magnitude has never been accurately measured."

Despite all the strictures regarding the census housing statistics, they have nevertheless been used time and again to justify the comforting view that the nation has been making rapid and steady strides in wiping out its inadequate housing. Typical is a statement in a book written in collaboration with a former director of the Census Bureau. After noting that 18 per cent of the nation's dwelling units were classified as either dilapidated or without all plumbing facilities in the 1960 census, as opposed to 37 per cent in the 1950 census, the authors declare:

> This, too, is a dazzling statistic. Its meaning? The chances were about twice as great that a typical American family would live in poor housing in 1950 as in 1960. That, briefly, is the slum story in America: we still have them today, but they are far fewer than they were just a few years ago, and they will be fewer still in the years to come. Despite all the talk about the inadequacy of urban-renewal and slum-clearance programs, this would seem to be a field where remarkably fast progress is occurring. That, at least, is what the statistics would indicate.

And that, indeed, is what the statistics do indicate—when glibly taken at face value. But, as those within the Census Bureau who have gone beneath the surface of the figures have concluded, "use of the 1960 census statistics grossly distorts estimates of trend in dilapidated housing from 1950 to 1960."

(To be fair, it should be pointed out that not all experts have been dismayed at the bureau's finding that it understated the number of dilapidated units in 1960 by at least one-third. Frank Kristof terms such dismay "a tempest in a teapot," reasoning that the tally of "substandard" housing was not affected to the same extent as the under-count of "dilapidated" units. He says that about half of the "dilapidated" units misclassified by census enumerators in making structural condition ratings were picked up in the housing agencies' "substandard" count anyway, because these units lacked all required plumbing facilities; thus, trends in "substandard" housing from 1950 to 1960 are not as unreliable as trends in "dilapidated" housing over the ten years.

On the other hand, his argument could well be offset by Census Bureau findings suggesting that "the single most important factor in the decline in the substandard inventory" in the 1950's was not a net improvement in the structural condition of the old inventory, or net additions provided by new construction, but rather the installation of required plumbing facilities where they had not previously existed. Many housing experts have cited a widespread installation of minimal-grade plumbing in old housing whose otherwise low quality remained the same. So there is good reason to question just how reliably the drop in "substandard" units, as indicated by the census measurements, reflects an actual decrease in inadequate housing during the 1950's.

In any event, such statisticians' debates are beside the point. The issue is not whether a half-million or so "dilapidated" units were recaptured for the "substandard" category or whether this should be weighed against the plumbing component. The issue is the over-all inadequacy of the census criteria and the data based on them, and the widely circulated but often unwarranted and dangerously misleading conclusions that superficial interpretations of these data give rise to.)

Because most Census Bureau officials became aware in the 1960's that their structural condition statistics were "dangerous data to work with" (census official Young's words), the bureau, in the 1970 census, did away with the unit-by-unit rating of structural condition. Instead, it collected from each household information about such things as property value and rent, the number of rooms in a home, the number of apartments in a building, and, as in the past, data about plumbing facilities. Based on this information, the bureau at this writing is making estimates of housing conditions in the nation's metropolitan areas and cities. But the old ratings of sound, deteriorating, and dilapidated have been restricted for the 1970's to use in a sampling survey designed to provide a basis for estimating 1970 housing quality in relation to the 1960 census findings. However, the Census Bureau warns, "it is unlikely that comparability will be achieved to any substantial degree" partly, again, because of the "unreliability of enumerator ratings."

The bureau's announcement of its 1970 plans evoked misgivings from a number of local housing and redevelopment officials over the abolition of the structural ratings on a house-by-house, and thus neighborhood-by-neighborhood, basis. The officials reasoned that, whatever the shortcomings of census statistics in the past, they nevertheless were all that many localities had to work with, and estimates of condition projected for an entire city or metropolitan area would leave their agencies at an even greater disadvantage.

Young's response, as he put it to me, hits the mark squarely: "If you withdraw a narcotic, are you depriving the patient? I've often thought of the condition-of-structure data as a narcotic—it gives you the impression of having something that's just not there." Along with other critics of the state of the nation's housing knowledge, he hopes that removal of the census ratings of structural condition will stimulate federal housing and health agencies to develop improved methods of housing quality measurement.

Granted, there will always be a large element of subjectivity in defining the quality of housing, and "one family's proud palace is another's veritable hovel," etc. But we are talking here about definitions of *minimum standards.* It is reasonable to expect that in space age America the determination of how many families live in substandard housing and how many do not will be based not on outhouse era standards but on standards that take into account such crucial and elementary conditions as ventilation, sewage facilities, garbage disposal services, and the provision of heat in winter.

One goal urged by many housing experts is the development of national rating standards that can be applied in intensive local surveys whose results, when taken together (and even if only a portion of the country's housing inventory is examined), will offer a far more meaningful and reliable picture of the American housing situation than the geographically broader but superficial and defective census surveys. Some urge that any new measuring standards be modeled on a system for rating housing quality that has been devised by the American Public Health Association. The system takes into account many of the determinants of housing quality that are not measured by the census criteria, including elements of neighborhood environment, and employs a rating scale, with graded penalty points for various types of housing defects, that permits the over-all condition of a house or apartment to be expressed by a single number on the scale.

The Best Guesses

No such system, however, is on the verge of widespread implementation, and in the meantime assessment of the nation's housing needs will have to remain based on the inadequate census data. Given these data, the President's Committee on Housing has projected a need of 26.7 million new and rehabilitated dwelling units—including 6 to 8 million government-subsidized units for families at the lower end of the economic scale who cannot afford decent housing on their own—in both urban and rural areas through 1978. The committee based its projection on a consultant's estimate that there were 6.7 million occupied substandard units at the time of the committee's 1968 report (with substandard defined as the federal housing agencies have usually defined it: The Census Bureau's dilapidated category, plus units lacking all required plumbing facilities).

In addition to the need to replace or substantially upgrade these units, the committee's consultant—TEMPO, the General Electric Company's Center for Advanced Studies—projected the following needs through 1978 to arrive at its 26.7 million total: 2 million units to replace additional units that are expected to become substandard by 1978; 3 million more to replace units expected to be purposefully demolished or accidentally destroyed; 13.4 million to provide housing for an anticipated increase in the number of American households, and 1.6 million units to maintain sufficient vacancies to accommodate an increasingly mobile population. The Kaiser committee's estimate of total need, and of specific need for the poor and those economically just above them, was typical of the analyses that led to the goals of the Housing and Urban Development Act of 1968.

But the Kaiser committee's figures underestimate the nation's true housing need, even aside from the inherent deficiency of the census data on which they are in great part based. The Kaiser committee itself noted that the definition of substandard used by its consultant was "fairly restricted; those who use more liberal definitions arrive at much larger figures." Specifically, TEMPO did not include in its definition the 4.6 million units that the census in 1960 described as "deteriorating, with all plumbing facilities," or the nearly 4 million standard units found then to be overcrowded by census standards—that is, to house more than one person per room. The National Commission on Urban Problems did attempt to allow for these categories, which overlap, and as a result it arrived at an estimate—still based, remember, on the inadequate census criteria—of 11 million units of physically deficient or overcrowded housing in the nation. If one substitutes this larger and more likely estimate, which represents 16 per cent of the existing housing stock, for the 6.7 million figure used by the Kaiser committee's consultant, and adds to it the other components of projected need, then there is a total national housing requirement through 1978 of at least 31 million units.

Whether 26.7 million or 31 million, this projection reflects a massive need that, as the previous discussion of the census criteria has made abundantly clear, still does not state the whole case. Nevertheless, this projection alone—and 26 million units over ten years is an average of 2.6 million a year—is certainly prodigious when measured against the size of the current housing inventory of approximately 70 million units, and against past production of housing in the United States, which has averaged some 1.5 million units annually since World War II, and about 50,000 government-subsidized units annually for low- and moderate-income families over the past three decades.

But the severity of America's housing needs is not to be defined in terms of aggregate national requirements alone, as extensive as these requirements are. To appreciate fully the dimensions of the housing crisis, one must look at it in more specific terms.

A Geographical View

Geographically, the nation's substandard housing is often estimated today to be about evenly divided between urban and rural areas (again, with the definition of substandard based on a conservative classification of the census categories). Some experts, however, maintain that the current breakdown is closer to that found when the Census Bureau last rated the structural condition of every dwelling in 1960: roughly three-fifths of the nation's substandard housing was found in rural areas at that time. Either way, the urban-rural division must be taken in conjunction with population data, and because nonurban areas contain less than a third of the country's population, rural America, proportionally speaking, has a much more extensive housing problem than urban America.

Just how big this problem may be in absolute terms was indicated at a conference of rural housing experts and concerned officials at Warrenton, Virginia, in 1969, where a goal of 7 million housing units built or rehabilitated with government aid was urged as necessary during the 1970's to overcome the housing deficits of the nation's rural regions. (To repeat some previously discussed statistics, two decades of federal rural housing programs have resulted in the construction, rehabilitation, and acquisition of some 300,000 units, as of 1970. The rural share of the goal of 6 million subsidized units under the 1968 Housing Act is projected as 1.5 million units.)

What all this signifies in *human* terms was described by Mrs. Willie Anderson, the wife of a migrant farm worker, as she told the Commission on Rural Poverty just what it means to live in a clump of shacks that is the typical lot of a major portion of the rural poor:

> The houses were raggedy. It would come a dust storm, the wind would blow, and everything in the house would shake, and the dust

> would blow in through all the cracks. . . . Most of the people . . . they don't know what it is to get up and turn a faucet on and get hot water, and they don't know what it is to get into a bathtub in a bathroom, you know, and take a bath. They have to heat their water on the stove and take a bath in a tin tub. They don't know what it is to have heat in their house.

Frequently, as numerous volunteers in VISTA (the domestic peace corps) and investigators for governmental commissions have learned, the shacks of the rural poor in today's America are often but a scant improvement over the crude log cabins, chinked with clay and straw and littered with a few rickety chairs, a dirty bed or two, and a few grease-crusted cooking utensils, that served as home to those on the bottom rungs of the nation's rural economic ladder a century ago.

Although in terms of population proportions there is a greater need for decent housing in America's rural regions, it is in the country's urban centers, as the explosions during the 1960's vividly demonstrated, where American society's failures in housing, among other basic areas, are coming home most convulsively to roost. In rural America the ill-housed are as scattered socially and politically as they are geographically. In the nation's cities, concentrated in slums that are often tightly compressed pockets of poverty, they form what is perhaps the most volatile element in the American social cauldron that Fourth of July orators still insist on fantasizing as a melting pot. From a moral standpoint, the housing failures of American society are unquestionably as serious outside the cities as they are in them. From a practical point of view—and most nondeprived Americans, if moved at all by the plight of the deprived minority among them, are moved by practical considerations—the American housing crisis is today an urban crisis.

By Race and Origin

Racially and ethnically, the extent to which the burden of the nation's shortcomings in housing are being disproportionately borne by the nonwhite and Latin-American minority groups is readily seen in government statistics. A joint report by the United States Department of Labor and Department of Commerce cites figures showing that, in 1968, one out of every four nonwhite households was living in housing that was either dilapidated or lacked basic plumbing facilities, while only one in every sixteen white households was living in such conditions. TEMPO, the General Electric studies center, measured the situation for the President's Committee on Urban Housing by developing statistics on "house-poor" families—those unable to afford decent housing without a governmental subsidy. TEMPO found that not only were house-poor families disproportionately nonwhite today but also, assuming no significant changes in economic patterns and national policies affecting the over-all housing situation, they were likely to remain so through the 1970's.

By way of illustration, TEMPO estimated that 23.4 per cent of nonwhite families living in metropolitan areas in 1968 were house-poor, while only 9.6 per cent of white families in these areas were in the same predicament. In 1978, the research unit projected, 18.3 per cent of nonwhite metropolitan-area families will be house-poor, as opposed to 7.7 per cent of their white counterparts. In both urban and rural regions of the country in 1978, TEMPO estimated, one in every four nonwhite families will need a housing subsidy, compared to one in every twelve white families.

Regarding Mexican-Americans and Puerto Ricans, there is no disagreement among housing experts that deficient living quarters are found in far greater proportion within these groups than within the over-all white population of non-Spanish derivation. Summing up the situation of the estimated 5 million Mexican-Americans, Frank G. Mittelbach, associate professor in residence housing, real estate, and urban land studies at the University of California at Los Angeles, said, "The over-all quality of their housing is poor, as measured by the incidence of substandardness, dilapidation, or overcrowding. Especially in Texas and California, their housing is inferior not only to [that of] the Anglo majority but also that of the nonwhite population."

Other indications of the quality of Mexican-American housing have been obtained in local surveys. In the predominantly Mexican-American community of East Los Angeles, 35 per cent of the dwellings are considered substandard, while in Guadalupe, Arizona, 500 of 677 dwellings in the Mexican-American area are in a similar state. "Substandard," the betterment group Urban America said, "is a polite phrase for wooden shacks with metal roofs and outside toilets."

For the 1.5 million Puerto Ricans who have migrated to the mainland, the situation is hardly better. In New York City, one-ninth of whose population is made up of the former territorial islanders and their children, estimates of the proportion of Puerto Ricans in substandard or deteriorating housing range up to 50 per cent and more. What this means in terms of stark reality becomes swiftly and vividly clear on a visit to such neighborhoods as Spanish Harlem, the Lower East Side, the South Bronx, and the Williamsburg section of Brooklyn, in whose crumbling tenements and cramped apartments the city's heaviest concentrations of Puerto Ricans are crowded.

But perhaps the minority for which miserable housing is most extensive, though least publicized, is the nation's 450,000 reservation Indians. The Bureau of Indian Affairs in the United States Interior Department reports that of the 80,268 reservation homes standing in 1969, 53,872—*nearly 68 per cent*—were considered substandard, while 14,189 more were overcrowded. Thus, only 15 per cent of the reservation dwellings were considered structurally adequate or not overcrowded. Of the nearly 54,000 substandard homes, 36,993 were found to be "inadequate and unrepairable—they should be razed," according to a spokesman for the bureau, and the 16,879 others were held to be "inadequate but repairable." Some students of reservation life contend that the official figures, as shocking as they are, still understate the situation. The Bureau of Indian Affairs spokesman conceded as much when he cautioned that "a middle-class family would not always agree" with his agency's concept of "adequate."

Just how wretched much of the reservation housing is cannot be appreciated until one visits some of these tracts and does a bit more scouting than is usually required to purchase a string of beads or a fringed vest at a roadside stand. On the Blackfoot reservation in north central Montana, for example, a visitor in 1969 found many families sheltered in squalid, flimsy shacks that appeared to have been plucked from the dust bowl of the Depression and left to fester in neglect for another generation. In Pine Ridge, South Dakota, possibly half of the families on the Oglala Sioux preserve were found living at the end of 1969 in tiny, dingy, dirt-floored huts—and these accommodations were luxurious compared with some of the other facilities called home on the reservation: tents, discarded automobile bodies, abandoned chicken coops. At least three-quarters of the reservation's families lacked indoor plumbing.

None of this is to say that the American housing crisis today is a crisis only for the nation's black, red, and Spanish-speaking minorities. In absolute numbers, the housing needs of white families who are not of Latin-American derivation are greater than those of nonwhites and Spanish-Americans. A consultant to the President's Committee on Urban Housing reported that of the 7.8 million urban and rural families currently estimated to be unable to afford decent housing on their own, 5.6 million are white and 2.2 million are nonwhite. Even taking into account the Mexican-Americans and Puerto Ricans in the white population, it is clear that the majority of house-poor American families are white and not of Latin-American origin. Moreover, in the last complete structural condition census, in 1960, it was found that white households resided in two-thirds of the country's substandard rental housing and in four-fifths of its substandard owner-occupied housing. It is unlikely that these fractions have substantially changed since.

But the fact remains that, *in terms of their share of the American population*, the black, red, and Spanish-speaking minorities are carrying the heaviest share of the burden of inadequate housing, and it is in this sense that the need for these groups is most severe.

Housing and Health

At this point in medical history, it is hardly necessary to discuss in detail the hazards to health implicit in all of the foregoing statistics. An extensive body of literature has been developed by public health experts that traces the contributions of decayed, unsanitary, overcrowded, or inadequately ventilated, heated, and lighted housing to a number of physical illnesses, including tuberculosis and rickets, and to the frustrations and tensions that often contribute to emotional depression and the breakdown of family life. Moreover, one need not be a public health expert—a teacher in a slum-area elementary school will do—to know what decrepit or badly overcrowded housing means to young children. It is written in the school attendance records that plummet in winter as the youngsters are regularly brought down by illnesses readily developed and rapidly spread in unheated or poorly heated apartments and in rooms made drafty by crumbling walls and cracked windows. It is written in the faces of the children who fall asleep in class because sleeping three or more in a room—or in a bed—rarely affords a decent night's rest at home, just as living seven or more in three rooms rarely allows for a quiet spot for homework.

In this connection, it is interesting to note what, as long ago as 1950, the American Public Health Association's Committee on the Hygiene of Housing recommended as the "essential space requirements of a dwelling which, without extravagance, will make physical and emotional health possible." For a single-person household, the committee said, 400 square feet of floor area is required; for a family of two, 750 square feet is necessary; for three people, 1,000 square feet; for four, 1,150 square feet; for five, 1,400 square feet; and for six, 1,550 square feet. Even many middle-income families lack these amounts of space; in the slums, it is safe to assume, there is an even wider gap between recommendation and reality.

One health hazard of poor housing that warrants discussion, largely because the general public has mistakenly come to regard it as a thing of the past, is the widespread menace of lead poisoning to small children. As much a scourge of slum life as the more easily recognized peril of fire, lead poisoning, caused primarily when youngsters swallow bits and pieces of paint and plaster that drop from decayed walls and ceilings, is today a silent epidemic among the nation's poorly housed. Lead-based paints stopped being used on interior walls in most areas of the country in the 1940's and 1950's. In many communities their inside use was outlawed when their danger became clear. In others, such use gradually ended as the paint industry developed safer substitutes. But despite the general belief that these steps marked an end of the problem, lead poisoning has remained a widespread affliction. This is because lead from the old coats of paint, although covered up by the more recent and safer coats, is still present in large quantities in the chips of paint and plaster that peel and flake from walls and ceilings in deteriorated apartments. Thus pica, the craving for nonfood items that widely characterizes small children of all economic and social classes, is a far deadlier trait for youngsters in poor housing.

The New York Scientists' Committee for Public Information, whose board of advisers includes such eminent scientific and medical men as René Dubos, the expert in environmental biomedicine, and Alan Guttmacher, president of Planned Parenthood–World Population, estimates that between 5 and 10 per cent of the nation's slum children between the ages of one and six—perhaps several hundred thousand youngsters in all—are afflicted with lead poisoning today to one degree or another. But, because few communities consider it important enough to establish programs to screen slum children routinely for this common legacy of decayed housing, only a small fraction of the cases are ever detected. These are usually found when the sickness has reached an acute stage requiring hospitalization; yet serious damage can also be done to lead-poisoned young bodies in which the illness does not reach this stage and thus remains undetected.

Just how extensive the problem may be is indicated by the situation in New York. No more than several hundred lead poisoning cases were reported annually in that city in the 1960's, but the scientists' committee, based on testing programs carried out in various slum neighborhoods, estimated that as many as *18,000* of the city's small children were going around with lead poisoning in their systems in various stages—and even this was held to be a conservative projection by some medical experts. For their part, city health officials agreed that the reported cases represented what one called "the tip of an iceberg."

The implications of the tragic statistics may well extend beyond the immediate medical perils of damage to the nervous system, blood, and kidneys that may mark the early stages of lead poisoning. (Permanent mental retardation, cerebral palsey, and sometimes death are the results of the more advanced stages.) For damage to the nervous system that might be caused by undetected lead poisoning in the pre-school years could well be related to some of the learning difficulties and behavioral problems that show up in the early grades of school, and that later mushroom into full-fledged academic failure or antisocial behavior.

In the early 1970's, there are encouraging signs that the extent of the lead poisoning menace is beginning to be appreciated. Some cities, including New York, have begun screening programs among slum area children in an attempt to detect the poisoning. In some places—Chicago, Baltimore, Washington, and New York among them—these efforts have been tied in with steps to remove the lead danger where poisoned children have been discovered. Congress in 1970 authorized use of federal funds to aid localities in carrying out such programs. In most cases the official actions have followed campaigns by community groups and concerned scientists and medical people to publicize the extent of the lead poisoning problem. But while this awareness is encouraging, it is only a beginning. Fewer than a dozen major cities and not more than the same number of states even keep statistics on the number of lead-poisoned children, and governmental moves to combat the problem are still the rare exception across the country.

Besides all the foregoing hazards to health presented by bad housing, there is also a more subtle, psychological one. The President's Committee on Urban Housing summed up this aspect most succinctly when it noted: "The place a man lives is more than just another commodity, service, or possession; it is a symbol of his status, an extension of his personality, a part of his identity, a determinant of many of the benefits—and disadvantages—of society that will come to him and his family." When so fundamental an aspect of life is squalid and shabby, and when there appears to be no hope of improving it, is it any surprise that many inhabitants of rotten housing exhibit despair, hostility, or a feeling that they have little stake in American society?

This is not to say, it should be made clear, that American society's housing failures are the only causes of the personal miseries and social ills found in the nation today, or that if all

Americans were decently housed most of the miseries and ills would disappear. Overzealous advocates of government housing programs may well have implied this view three decades ago, when efforts to get such programs started had to overcome vigorous opposition. Clearly, though, there is much more to America's deeply troubled domestic life than can be cured by solving its housing problems alone. The lack of equal opportunity in jobs and education, the absence of equal municipal and medical services for all segments of the population, the hostility and fear so often evoked by racial and ethnic differences—all these and more would have to be overcome before the clichés about American democracy could begin to be more than pretensions.

At the same time, though, there is no question that decent housing is so basic a human need that a society's serious failures in fulfilling it must inevitably be a major contributing element to explosive social unrest, as it is to individual distress.

8. The Experts and the Crisis

BUILD UP OR BREAK UP THE SLUM?

Every war has its generals—armchair and actual—and every general (and every colonel, captain, sergeant, and private) has his own notion of how to win the war. American society's war against its housing deficiencies, assuming there is such a war in reality as well as rhetoric, is no different. In annual conferences of housing and redevelopment officials and interested friends; in government studies, academic theses, and professional journals; in the slick newsletters of industry associations and the crudely mimeographed policy statements of slum area community groups, torrents of proposals regularly pour forth for solving the problems of human shelter in America. Sometimes these proposals contradict each other hopelessly; sometimes they add up to what would be a comprehensive, rational approach to the stated goal of a decent home and a suitable living environment for every American family. Often they deal with very narrow technical aspects of the over-all housing scene and, though exciting keen debate among housing professionals, are highly abstruse to the layman. And often they deal with aspects that involve the broadest social, political, and economic issues of contemporary American life and are the subjects of bitter national controversy.

Among the most hotly debated proposals, as we've seen, are those addressed to the issue of where government-subsidized housing should be built. The views of those who don't want this housing in their own backyards is well known. But what are the views of those not directly involved, those who argue and propose from the perspective of the "big picture"?

Some housing experts argue that most of the limited resources available for low-cost housing should be devoted to improving housing in existing slums. This school of thought reasons as follows: Given the present social and political climate in America, it is futile to hope that the nation's black, Mexican-American, and Puerto Rican slum dwellers can be significantly integrated into the middle-class mainstream. While the illusion that they can is pursued, the big city slums continue to grow more miserable and more explosive. Increasingly, they are scarred with expanding stretches of abandoned buildings, foresaken by tenants and landlords and stripped of their plumbing and electrical fixtures by vandals and drug addicts who sell them for salvage. These ravaged hulks, hangouts for narcotics users and dumping sites for garbage, are sources of misery and fear to the residents of the buildings around them. This and the other miseries of slum life render obscene the view (expressed by some urban affairs analysts) that in the long run the increase in slum building abandonments may be for the best if it reflects and further spurs the breakup of the worst slums.

Proponents of the "build up the slums" concept also argue that the time and energy expended in trying to build low-income housing *outside* slum areas simply are not warranted by the results. Given the opposition to low-cost housing in suburbia and in middle-class in-city areas, gains are bound to be small and slow in coming, they insist. They add that trying to get around this by building low-cost housing in largely vacant outlying areas of the central cities is equally unwise. Such development entails the construction of a mass of public utilities—sewer, water, gas, and electrical lines—and expansion of health, police, fire, and transit services to the new areas, all of which vastly increase the expense of such an approach. These facilities and services already exist in the slums, and if they are frequently far less than they should be, the argument goes, it is still cheaper to improve them where they are than to provide them anew in undeveloped areas.

In short, as *American Builder* magazine summed it up, adherents of this position "believe it is more pragmatic to bring the ghetto and its residents up to a decent standard of living. Once that is accomplished the larger question of how—or whether—the ghetto should be broken up can be dealt with."

The pragmatism said to lie in this position has been reinforced in recent years by the growth of black pride and militancy. The frequently voiced rejection of integration into "Whitey's world" has been one side of a coin; the other has been demands that the major share of publicly financed efforts to better the lot of blacks be concentrated on improving their ghettos.

On the other side of the issue are those who hold that concentrating most low-cost-housing funds in the slums will accomplish little more in the end than the creation of "gilded ghettos" whose problems of poor schools, unemployment, crime, and drug addiction will be as extensive as before. Here the reasoning is as follows: The model cities approach of tackling the many nonhousing problems of the slum environment at the same time as it attempts to overcome deficiencies in housing will never be funded sufficiently enough to have significant impact, especially while the Nixon Administration is in office, so that new and rehabilitated low-cost housing in the slums will generally have little more influence on improving over-all conditions than have public housing projects of the past. In addition, because most existing city slums are already densely built up, construction of new housing must be accompanied by relocation, a painful and time-consuming process. And with the increase in the 1960's of delay-causing clashes with community groups over housing and renewal projects, subsidized housing can no longer be built in the slums with the dispatch once possible.

Thus, it is argued, the most expeditious way to deal with the decay of big city slums is to devote most low-cost-housing subsidies to the construction of projects outside of existing slums for a number of years. Then, after many of today's slum dwellers have left the blighted areas for these new accommodations, redevelopment of the decayed neighborhoods will be much more feasible.

The belief that low-cost-housing programs should be carried out to foster the dispersion of existing slums frequently is based also on a feeling that the perpetuation of existing ghettos of disadvantaged minority groups through government action implies tacit acknowledgment by the government that the ideal of an open society no longer makes sense for the United States. Even if this is not the government's position, it is argued, the battle for an open society is no less damaged. For example, government housing policies that contribute to strengthening racial concentration are seen to undermine the judicial victories the civil rights movement has achieved in the battle against racial segregation in the schools.

The opposition to concentrating on "fixing up the slums" was summed up by Gunnar Myrdal, whose writings on America and its black minority are as widely quoted as his findings on social trends in Europe. Testifying in 1969 before a congressional subcommittee on urban growth, the author of *An American Dilemma* said, "You cannot solve the slum problem just by amelioratory building in the slums. They have to be spread out. You have to look on it as a metropolitan problem if you want to have really good cities."

Between the two contending positions outlined above is a third: that the government's housing policies should travel a middle course, concentrating neither exclusively on improving the housing stock in existing slum areas nor exclusively on providing low-cost housing outside of them. "I think both of these are wrong," Robert Weaver, George Romney's predecessor as Secretary of Housing and Urban Development said. He explained:

> You have to do the two things simultaneously. You have to improve the living conditions where people are now concentrated. I don't believe this means gilding the ghetto; it means bringing it up to a standard of decency, involving the people in the decisions which affect their lives, and making these attractive and viable places to live. At the same time, you open up the other areas, so that the person now living in the ghetto can have some mobility. I say you can work both sides of the street.

To some, "working both sides of the street" is just a euphemism for traveling the middle of the road to escapism. To others, it is the soundest course strategically, undermined only by the unwillingness of the nation to apply itself as vigorously as it should to the housing challenge before it.

THE NEWEST VOICES

Weaver's statement touched on a second major issue whose prominence on the American housing scene has been the subject of bitterly contested proposals: "involving" the nation's slum dwellers "in the decisions which affect their lives."

The controversial and often emotional issue of slum residents' participation extends far beyond housing, of course. Bitter battles have been fought over the issue of "community control" of public schools; calls have been issued by militant blacks for neighborhood control over the police in the slums; hospitals have been occupied by local groups claiming that the "outsider-controlled" staffs are indifferent to the needs of the slum area residents. In housing, numerous community groups have acted as sponsors or cosponsors of low-income construction or rehabilitation projects. Others have had vigorous voices in planning such projects, not infrequently to the point of having a veto over plans failing to meet their approval.

The federal laws that have fostered this extensive slum neighborhood involvement have been the antipoverty and model cities legislation of the Johnson Administration. Those who applaud the concept of "citizen participation" and "community action" offer two basic rationales. (Cynics insist there is a third, important even if unvoiced.) One is that, as a matter of democratic principle, slum dwellers should be given every opportunity to influence the decision-making process in public programs that substantially and sometimes even drastically affect their lives. Other Americans, working through interest groups, have traditionally had this opportunity throughout American history, the argument goes, so why not the poor and ill-housed?

The second argument is based less on principle than on necessity. "If citizens are not involved, if they do not participate, they have discovered demonstrable techniques for stalemating an agency's program," Edmund M. Burke, chairman of the department of community organization and social planning in Boston College's Graduate School of Social Work, has said. Newspaper headlines across the country certainly testify to the validity of this argument. Sit-ins, threats of violence, and violence itself have delayed or caused the modification or cancellation of more than a few development projects in slum areas across the country since the mid-1960's.

The argument of necessity can also be stated in more general terms: The poor, especially the inner-city minority poor, have grown so alienated from, and hostile to, the established system that it is all-important to provide them with opportunities in such a way as to demonstrate that the system does indeed offer room for their influence to be felt.

For these reasons, proponents of community participation in public programs say, such participation should be extended as widely as possible among the nation's poor, in rural as well as urban areas, among poor whites and American Indians as fully as among blacks, Mexican-Americans, and Puerto Ricans, in housing programs as well as in programs involving education, health, and the fight against crime and drug addiction.

On the other hand, there are those who hold that the best thing that could happen to this country, next to the return of a good five-cent cigar, would be the dumping of the whole notion of community participation and action. Citizen involvement through community-action groups in the slums, they argue, has accomplished nothing more than the erection of one more obstacle to getting on with the necessary tasks of combating deprivation and blight. More than a few such opponents have voiced the cynical contention that the official fostering of community participation was fraudulent in intention, that it is a politicians' sop to the poor and the black, a way of building up the *illusion* of a vigorous fight against slums and poverty and of distracting attention from how meager the efforts have been when measured in the only terms that count—dollars.

So far as housing specifically is concerned, the opposition's argument is that community participation, with its disputes between housing agencies and neighborhood groups over what should be built where and for whom, and with its bickering among the groups themselves over the same questions, poses yet one more barrier in the way of the nation's achievement of its housing goals. "From a bureaucrat's viewpoint, there is always trouble in citizens' organizations, because leaderships change," M. Justin Herman, executive director of San Francisco's redevelopment agency, explained. "In good faith, we proceed to work with those whom we think are the leaders of the neighborhood or the community. We make agreements with them. We enter into partnership with them—only to discover that they have been deprived of leadership and some new leaders have come forward and frequently accuse us of not having worked with the community."

Even where shifting leadership and difficulties of determining who "speaks for the community" are not a problem, some housing professionals—government bureaucrats, private developers, housing experts affiliated with long-established civic groups—consider the community-participation concept a major obstacle because of the element of amateurism that it introduces into the housing-production process, where amateurism has no place, they insist, if the nation's housing goals are to be met. In the words of Eugene Morris, a New York lawyer and specialist in the development of publicly aided housing:

> Philosophically and socially [community participation in the planning of government-subsidized housing] is a sound concept, but from the practical point of view, the processing of a housing project is an incredibly complicated and difficult process. It requires a highly skilled team, a group of experts. . . . When you impose on this team a local group that dictates what kind of housing and what kind of design, layouts and setup should be used, that impedes and makes more difficult the job of the professional team. . . . You end up in a series of meetings where everyone gives his opinion; there are long oratorical contests, but no housing.

Because of an aversion to amateurism, other housing professionals have held that it is folly to advise community-action groups or other slum area organizations, such as churches and settlement houses, to undertake large-scale housing rehabilitation efforts, a step often suggested for upgrading the slums. Rehabilitation can be a complex and costly process, they argue, and community groups lack the expertise to supervise such work properly. Besides, most groups would lose interest in a renovated building after "the excitement of doing the work is over," the leader of one long-established "downtown" civic group asserted.

Among community activists in the slums, such a view is greeted with scorn. "Maybe some groups will lose interest when the job is done. But the cats who tell us this lost interest in our buildings fifty years ago and that's why we're where we're at," an official of a community group in New York's Harlem declared.

Still another perspective on community action in the slums was provided by the betterment group Urban America,* whose nonprofit housing center provided professional and technical aid to nonprofit organizations involved in housing programs. It saw the community-action groups as part of an important new force in the campaign to improve the nation's cities. As Urban America put it in 1969:

> Between public and private enterprise in the development of the cities is an emerging new force—what might be called community enterprise. The third force in development has grown out of the experience of nonprofit organizations—churches, labor unions, citizens groups, foundations, community-action agencies—who have produced more than 90,000 units of low- and moderate-income housing under federal mortgage assistance programs. The one characteristic which all of these organizations share is their motivation: they become housing sponsors to improve their community and the lives of its not-so-well-off residents.

Just what part government-funded community-action groups will continue to play as part of this new force is difficult to predict in the early 1970's. A large network of neighborhood organizations has arisen in the nation's urban slums, but the existence of such groups, dependent as they are on federal funding, is far from secure. Spiro Agnew, as Vice President-elect, long before he began taking on the "effete snobs" spreading their sedition throughout

* Since merged with the Urban Coalition to form the National Urban Coalition.

the land, had a go at the community-participation people. All too often, he declaimed, participation by the poor in the programs designed to aid them has been construed to mean "playing both patient and doctor."

Agnew was expressing a view widely held in the Middle America he speaks for; many of its citizens find it the last straw that slum dwellers should have the gall to be *choosy,* no less, about how they receive their handouts. Among the Nixon Administration's constituents, there would be few tears shed if the community participation programs in the slums were completely starved to death, and advocates of such programs had this constantly in mind in the early 1970's.

At the same time, one does not have to view America through Spiro Agnew's eyes to have reservations about aspects of the community participation trend among slum dwellers. Aside from the difficulty of dealing with community groups because of changing leadership and bickering among them, there is the feeling on the part of too many community activists that community participation means that every single group in a highly fractionalized neighborhood enjoys a veto over what is done in that neighborhood. This is a valid cause for concern among a number of people who basically support the concept that slum area residents should have a voice in the programs significantly affecting them.

While the future of government-financed community action remains uncertain, two other aspects of the community-action scene have taken on vigorous lives of their own in very recent years. And with them have come still new points of controversy. These are the "tenants' rights" and "squatter" movements.

The first is the swiftly growing movement across the country in which groups of tenants—in middle- and upper-income housing as well as low-income housing—are banding together for collective action against landlords, whether private owners or public housing authorities. On building-wide, neighborhood-wide, and even citywide scales, tenants are increasingly engaging in organized rent strikes, court suits, mass rallies, picketing, and sit-ins to force landlords to act on grievances over such matters as the size of rent increases, inadequate building maintenance and security, one-sided apartment leases that favor landlords, and lack of a tenants' voice in management policies. A study by the Chicago-based Urban Research Corporation found that during an eight-month period in 1969, tenants' organizations took collective action on sixty-seven occasions in twenty-nine cities.

Tenant militancy is not entirely new, having been a feature of the New York housing scene for a number of years. What is new is that such militancy is now spreading across the country and, just as significantly, is no longer confined to the ranks of the poor but is rapidly increasing among middle- and upper-income tenants. The Urban Research Corporation reported that middle- and upper-income tenant groups accounted for 26 per cent of tenant group activities in 1969 and for *40 per cent* in the first half of 1970.

In many if not most cases, especially among the middle- and upper-income tenant groups, the objectives of organized tenants' action are confined to seeking redress of the kinds of grievances noted above, with the most "far out" demand being a voice in housing management policies. In some cases, however, largely among low-income and campus area tenant groups, the ultimate objective is abolition of the landlord and the transfer of housing ownership to tenants.

Some of the most impressive successes of the tenants' rights drive have come in public housing. As a result of the activism of such recently formed groups as the National Tenants Organization, standard lease and grievance procedures have been granted in federally subsidized public housing to replace the wide array of practices by local housing authorities in such matters as evictions, the entry of management personnel into apartments without notification or permission of tenants, assessment of fines for damage, and tenants' participation in management policy-making. In St. Louis, through the previously discussed rent strike, and in Pittsburgh, collective action by tenants has led to the replacement of housing authority officials and the addition of tenants to the authorities' governing boards.

As might be expected, the tenants' rights movement has aroused sharp emotions regarding its merits and validity. Most landlords view tenants' rights activism—whether higher-income reformist or campus and slum neighborhood radical—with hostility and indignation. To them, as to many American tenants themselves, the notion that tenants should have a voice in the management of property in which they have no share of ownership is an alien notion indeed. As one landlord put it:

> It violates the entire concept of private property as we know it. No one forces a tenant to rent on terms he does not like. No one forces him to remain in a building whose management policies he does not like. If he has signed a lease and finds that he is not being provided with the services he is entitled to under the lease, or with services essential to his health and safety, there are judicial and administrative remedies—after all, that's what the courts and housing codes and building inspectors are all about. But if, beyond this, he wants a say in how the building he lives in is managed, then he ought to be living in a cooperative, where he has a share in the property and thus is justified in having a voice in how it's run. In a rental building he owns nothing, but is simply contracting to lease space on the terms offered by the owner.

This view, of course, is similar to the view of an earlier America that labor unions violated the concept of property inasmuch as workers had no share in the ownership of the companies that employed them, and thus no legal right to act collectively to force changes in the terms under which they were employed. "No one forces a man to work here if he does not like what I offer," many an employer snorted in the fledgling days of organized labor. But just as most Americans now discount the theory that an employer and an individual employee bargain from positions of equal strength, so someday may they acknowledge that, at least where housing is in short supply, a tenant's power in bargaining with a landlord is just as mythical.

In any case, most landlords see it otherwise, and their prevailing view, which predominates among Americans generally today, can be expected to motivate court challenges and other resistance to tenant-group activities. At the same time, some landlords and industry leaders, believing that practicality may be the better part of principle, are urging a soft line on tenant activism, or at least on reformist tenant activism. Rather than fight it, they counsel, a wiser course would be concentration on preventing the conditions that lead to organized tenants' action and, where tenants' groups have already been formed, cooperation with the "responsible" (usually translated as nonradical) ones.

This advice is based on the belief that a hard line toward reformist tenant organizations will simply make them more determined and unnecessarily hostile toward landlords, and possibly will strengthen the hand of the radicals in the tenants' rights movement by driving into their ranks many whose aim now is simply to improve the tenants' position in his dealings with the landlord and not to abolish the landlord.

As for the squatter movement—if it can yet be called a movement—the number of episodes in which slum families have moved illegally into vacant buildings scheduled for urban renewal or private demolition or for renovation into more expensive apartments has been growing in cities where, as in New York, decent low-rent housing is in acutely short supply. For the squatting families, the illegally occupied quarters, though often bad enough to be demolished, usually are better than the homes the families have come from. Many squatters are motivated by the desperate hope that once they are illegally occupying a building, plans to demolish it or convert it to apartments beyond their means will be scrapped and they will be permitted to remain at rents they can afford. Or, on urban renewal sites, they may hope that they will be offered decent apartments as an inducement to leave without a confrontation with the police, which might be embarrassing to the city administration.

For the individuals and groups organizing the squatting, the motives have been varied. Aside from helping specific families in severe straits, some activists see squatting as the most vivid and effective way to dramatize the starkness of the low-income housing shortage in their cities and to spur the authorities to act on the problem. Others see it as a means of promoting the view that housing is community property; still others place it in a context beyond housing, as a way to arouse the poor of a city or neighborhood to activism generally or to provoke confrontations with the authorities that sharpen urban conflict in the interests of revolution. Often more than one of these motivations are present in a squatting episode.

The reaction to squatting has ranged from the view that no time should be wasted in evicting squatters and arresting them as trespassers ("there can be no compromise with such a blatant violation of property rights and such anarchical disregard for orderly procedures," one businessman put it) to the position—much less widely held in America—that the moral justification for squatting by those trapped in squalid housing is unassailable ("the existing system has shat all over these people and it's sheer hypocrisy to ask them to respect the rules and values of that same system," one community organizer on New York's Upper West Side declared).

In between is a more anguished view. On the one hand, if every family housed in squalor sought to better its circumstances by squatting, there would be a jungle battle in which the strongest or wiliest emerged with the few prizes. Thus "orderly procedures" is hardly an empty phrase. On the other hand, given the gross failure of American society to make available decent housing opportunities to so many of the poor, the treatment of desperate squatting families as common criminals when they refuse to play by the rules is indeed "sheer hypocrisy."

In the end, one can say only that, as a method of providing the wretchedly housed with relatively decent quarters, squatting can hardly be the way. But as a method of dramatizing the housing plight of America's poor, and perhaps stimulating a massively indifferent nation to do something about it, squatting is fully acceptable and within the tradition of nonviolent civil disobedience. In any case, whatever the motivation, squatting is only a symptom of America's housing ills and would cease to be a problem if the nation met its twenty-year-old commitment of a decent home and suitable living environment for every American family.

Best the Subsidy?

Just as there are sharply differing opinions about where to build the fruits of government housing subsidies and how much of a voice slum dwellers should have in how these subsidies are used, so there are differing outlooks regarding the form in which these subsidies should originate.

Traditionally, government housing subsidies in the United States have been tied to specific housing units rather than to the families that have occupied those units. Thus, families have retained their subsidies under the various programs only as long as they have remained in subsidized dwellings; a change in residence has meant, for them, a loss of subsidy. This arrangement has frequently been criticized for the restraints and the massive bureaucracy that accompany it. The occupants of government-subsidized housing find their freedom of choice circumscribed, in that they have to "go where the project is," as one woman put it.

Far preferable to "going where the project is," some housing experts say, would be a system under which housing subsidies were given directly to the families in need so that the families could decide for themselves where and how they wanted to live and could compete for housing in the private market. Among other things, it is argued, such a system would remove the stigma that low-income families may feel when their subsidized housing is in the form of an apartment in a low-income public project, would avoid bitter controversies over where government-subsidized housing should be built, and would facilitate the integration of the poor into middle-class neighborhoods and suburban communities. Moreover, proponents say, so long as use of the subsidies were restricted to standard housing and prohibited in slum housing, they would, over the long run, stimulate an increase in the supply of decent housing as owners of substandard dwellings upgraded their properties in order to rent them and as the homebuilding business responded to the increased effective demand by building additional new housing.

Finally, administrative costs and bureaucracy for a direct housing subsidy to needy families are seen as probably being much less than under the present system, in which construction or rehabilitation of housing, if not undertaken by public agencies directly, is rigidly supervised and regulated by government agencies, as under the various programs providing for publicly assisted private development.

Others close to the housing scene say the arguments in favor of direct housing allowances are outweighed by the arguments against them—at least if the allowance system is urged as a complete substitute for the system of dwelling-attached subsidies. For one thing, the predictions that an allowance arrangement will stimulate widespread new construction and rehabilitation are valid, if at all, only for the long run. The nation's housing needs are too pressing to admit of an exclusively long-run approach, it is argued, while the system of subsidizing the housing itself, rather than boosting the incomes of needy families, is a far more direct and rapid way of stimulating the large amount of new and rehabilitated housing that the United States desperately needs.

The point is made also that, at least in the short run, a large-scale infusion of additional residential purchasing power into the economy, unaccompanied by an increase in the supply of decent housing, will result in inflated costs for existing decent housing (assuming that the allowances are restricted to standard-quality housing, as one would hope any such allowance would be).

After weighing all the arguments for and against the allowance approach, the President's Committee on Urban Housing recommended that a program of direct housing allowances "be introduced on an experimental basis, subject to full and careful analysis of its results."

Reservations expressed about allowances apply also to the view that the answer to the nation's low-cost-housing needs lie primarily in raising the incomes generally of the poor and near-poor. Some have implied, for example, that a guaranteed annual income would obviate the government's housing subsidy programs. Others have responded that, unless this guaranteed income were so high as to boost poor families into the moderate-income range in many high-cost areas—as politically likely in America's near future as victory in the next Presidential election for the Communist Party candidate—then a guaranteed income scheme would hardly permit its beneficiaries to afford the decent housing available on the private market in these areas.

And even if, miracle of miracles, every poverty-stricken American were guaranteed by the government whatever it might take to raise his income to, say, $6,500 a year in high-cost areas, such a step, unless accompanied by simultaneous steps to increase the housing supply, would inflate prices for existing housing before stimulating new construction and rehabilitation—which it is unlikely to do in any case at $6,500 a year in high-cost regions.

In short, as the National Commission on Urban Problems concluded, "no serious proposal made so far as to the amount of a guaranteed annual income, let alone one that would have any chance for adoption, would do away with the need for housing aids. Such an antipoverty measure would lighten the load on some housing programs, but they would still be needed."

And housing programs—explicitly designed to produce decent human shelter by the swiftest and most direct means—would also still be needed no matter how successful the drive for equal employment opportunities is. Officials of the Nixon Administration have expressed their belief that racial and ethnic discrimination in employment is the most important barrier for the federal government to concentrate on in the civil rights area. Of what value is the right to a good education, they ask, if one is kept by racial or ethnic discrimination from a job that the education would otherwise qualify him for? Of what value is the right to eat in a good downtown restaurant or move into a $30,000 suburban home if the incomes that might pay for these are denied because of job discrimination?

Of course, no civil rights advocate would deny the validity of such questions. But if they point up anything, it is that the quest for equal employment opportunities must be relentlessly pursued as an accompaniment to, rather than a replacement for, programs explicitly aimed at producing massive amounts of new and rehabilitated lower-cost housing.

There are two reasons for this. No matter how successful the drive for equal employment opportunities is (and in this bitterly divided nation, significant results will be agonizingly slow in coming regardless of what administration is in office), "house-poor" families—white and American Indian as well as black, Mexican-American, and Puerto Rican—will continue to be part of the American scene in sizable numbers. And, as with proposals for housing allowances and guaranteed annual incomes, any major increase in purchasing power flowing into the economy from gains in the drive for equal employment opportunities will push up prices for existing housing, including blighted housing, long before they stimulate new construction and rehabilitation.

Still another alternative to governmental subsidization of housing through existing programs is suggested: subsidies primarily in the form of income-tax concessions to encourage private builders and investors to put their efforts and money into low- and moderate-cost housing.

The question of whether or not private enterprise has a role to play in the effort to meet the nation's housing needs has already been discussed. In the present context, the issue is whether or not, given the stimulus of preferential income tax treatment, private enterprise should be relied on to play the *major* role, with direct governmental expenditures for housing subsidies relegated to a secondary place. More specifically, the question could be put as follows: Should most of the appropriations for subsidizing housing—whether for subsidizing all construction and development costs, as in public housing, or for subsidizing mortgage interest only, as in the programs adopted in the 1960's—be halted, and should equivalent amounts be permitted in tax reductions on income from investments in low- and moderate-priced housing?

The arguments on both sides of this question were also closely examined by the National Commission on Urban Problems. The commission noted that those in favor of a housing subsidy primarily in the form of income-tax concessions

> argue that, as compared with alternative types of subsidies: (1) This approach should be more feasible to enact, since any public costs involved would be indirect (in the form of revenue loss) rather than involving an increase in federal expenditures; (2) once built into the federal tax system, such subsidies would have far more chance of continuity than would subsidy programs subject to the usual process of specific statutory authorization and annual budgeting and appropriations; and (3) tax incentive subsidies could operate with far less detailed governmental control than direct subsidies, since most of the decisions about the tax-preferred housing to be provided would be left to private investors and builders.

But the arguments against primary reliance on the tax-incentive approach outweigh the arguments in favor of it, the commission concluded. Among other things, according to the Douglas commission,

> it seems clear that the indirect subsidy approach through tax preferences would be economically inefficient, since some—perhaps even

> a very large part—of the tax benefits would go for residential investment that would have occurred anyway. This approach may also be socially wasteful in stimulating residential construction of types, or in locations, that rank low in priority from the standpoint of the urban housing needs intended especially to be served. If an effort were made to minimize these problems by limiting the prospective tax benefits to rather narrowly defined categories or locations, the program would confront many of the problems of detailed specification and "bureaucratic" control which the tax-incentive approach is alleged to avoid. The claim for "cost invisibility" and political appeal can also be questioned, in view of the growing awareness by the Congress . . . that revenue-sacrificing tax concessions are similar in their budgetary and economic effect to federal expenditures involving similar sums.

The last point is especially stressed by opponents of dominant reliance on the tax-incentive approach. Tax reductions—revenue losses—cost the government money no less than appropriations do and "really amount to fiddling around with the arithmetic," as former Housing and Urban Development Secretary Weaver put it. Still others are deeply skeptical of the whole philosophy of tax concessions as the principal financial instrument for the nation's housing and redevelopment efforts. Clarence Mitchell, head of the Washington bureau of the National Association for the Advancement of Colored People, summed up this view when he asserted that the tax-incentive approach amounted to "government bonuses" for business to allow the money to "trickle down" to the poor.

Sometimes the form the governmental housing subsidy should take is discussed in terms of whether or not low- and moderate-income housing should be regarded as a public utility. Those who urge that it be so regarded advocate expansion of the dwelling-attached subsidy approach. Their opponents, on the other hand, argue that any governmental housing subsidy should take a form that strengthens the unrestricted functioning of the traditional private market, and for this reason they favor the approaches with "the fewest strings attached"—housing allowances for poor families, income tax incentives to builders and investors, or both.

The debate over lower-income housing as a public utility is semantic and secondary. If the nation is to build all the housing within the means of the poor and lower middle class that it so critically needs, and if it is to build it within the next decade or two rather than the next century, then it will have to do so under governmental programs aimed at achieving that goal swiftly and directly. If this involves the kind of guidance and regulation characteristic of a public utility, then the nation will hardly be the worse for it. In fact, the viewpoint is entirely valid that such a relationship between government and the private sector in low- and moderate-income housing embodies the same kind of partnership for production (if not always for progress) that supplies the Pentagon with weapons and sends men to the moon. Significantly, one rarely hears denunciations of the government-guided space and weapons production programs as socialistic schemes sapping the lifeblood of free enterprise.

Finally, there has arisen in recent years still another controversy over the funneling of government funds into programs dealing with matters such as housing and the effort to eliminate slums. This is the controversy over "revenue sharing"—turning over to state and local government, for use with minimal or no federal restrictions, a sizable share of the tax revenues collected by Washington. Revenue sharing affects far many more programs than those involving housing and redevelopment, of course. But government efforts in these areas would be profoundly affected by revenue sharing, so the debate over sharing is also a debate over how best to channel public moneys into housing and renewal efforts.

As vigorously championed by President Nixon, revenue sharing is the key to a "historical and massive reversal of the flow of power in America," a reversal necessary because the federal government supposedly has become too pervasive and unhealthy an influence in the nation's life. "Local government is the government closest to the people and more responsive to the individual person; it is people's government in a far more intimate way than the government in Washington can ever be," the President declared in presenting his revenue sharing proposals in 1971.

These words strike a responsive chord in many Americans, Middle and in some cases far from Middle. Distaste for that "distant dictator"—the vast bureaucracy in Washington—is shared by an incongruous combination of Nixon's "silent majority" and the anti-Nixon New Left. The first sees the national government as a too-powerful machine that sucks up revenue from a tax-squeezed nation and uses it for wasteful or ruinous social engineering; the latter demands "all power to the people" (though the people they have in mind are not the people that the Nixon constituency has in mind).

In urging revenue sharing, the President proposed the simultaneous adoption of two forms: "general" sharing, under which state and local governments could use certain moneys received from Washington in any way they chose, and "special" sharing, under which federal moneys previously channeled to state and local government through narrowly specified categorical programs such as model cities and urban renewal would instead be distributed to them under six broad headings—urban development, rural development, education, manpower training, transportation, and law enforcement. Within each broad area, the state and local jurisdictions could generally use the funds as they desired, with drastically reduced supervision by Washington, devoting as much or as little as they chose to the specific programs brought together under the broad headings. Thus, in the case of urban development, a local government could decide for itself how much it wanted to devote to urban renewal, model cities, and programs providing funds for property rehabilitation and water and sewer facilities—all combined under the urban development heading. If it wished, the local government could alter these programs or disband them altogether.

Whatever the case, the decision would be that of government close to home rather than in distant Washington, and thus it would be the decision of "government that truly is by the people," as the President saw it.

Not everyone was as enthusiastic. First, by itself, critics noted, revenue sharing means little unless it is accompanied by a major increase in the level of public funds for such critical domestic needs as the elimination of substandard housing. Without such an increase revenue sharing is simply a sleight-of-hand maneuver that distracts attention from the central issue—*how much* of the nation's resources is devoted to these needs—and focuses it on the secondary issue of how these resources are made available. The President assured the nation's mayors that under revenue sharing no city would get less federal money than it did under the categorical program system. But this is beside the point. The issue is not whether federal contributions will remain the same, or increase slightly, but whether they will be increased to the great extent necessary to deal with such problems as housing and urban and rural blight. And this is an issue basically apart from the merits or demerits of revenue sharing.

Even more important, however, are the questions arising from the mythology on which the revenue sharing concept is founded. State and local government may have been closest to the American people in theory, but they certainly have not been in fact—not to the nation's wretchedly housed or its racial minorities or its citizens beset by the problems of old age. It was to fill the gaps left by state and local neglect or inability to act in behalf of these Americans that the federal government undertook the programs—in housing and community development as well as scores of other areas—whose growth is now attacked by Middle America and the New Left. But the truth is, as Senator Jacob Javits of New York has pointed out, that "those who live in the ghettos, barrios, and rural poverty pockets of our nation are more distant from the mayor's office than from the federal establishment." Arthur Schlesinger, Jr., the historian, put it this way:

> Local government is characteristically the government of the locally powerful, not of the locally powerless; and the best way the locally powerless have found to sustain their rights against the locally powerful is through resort to the national government. . . . The growth of national power, far from producing government less "responsive to the individual person," has given a majority of Americans far more dignity and freedom than they could win in a century of localism.

So far as the nation's miserably housed are concerned, things have not changed sufficiently to warrant the federal government's abdication of its efforts, however insufficient they may have been, in behalf of a decent home and suitable living environment for every American. Revenue sharing, at least as put forward by President Nixon in 1971, embodies such an abdication.

However, this is not to say that vigorous federal efforts in behalf of decent housing must be accompanied by overwhelming complexity, confusion, and irrational legislative and bureaucratic fragmentation. The streamlining or consolidation of federal housing programs is certainly to be welcomed, and, as previously noted, moves toward this end were under way in 1971.

The Nixon Administration's efforts included proposals to reduce several dozen FHA programs to eight, and to provide common standards and definitions regarding income, rent to income ratios, and design and construction in all federally assisted housing. Housing program reform was also envisioned as part of the President's proposal to revamp the Cabinet and create, among other new departments, a Department of Community Development that would supercede the Department of Housing and Urban Development and also incorporate the rural housing programs administered by the Farmers Home Administration of the Agriculture Department, as well as federal community action, transportation, and other activities. A number of congressmen had their own ideas about reform, as did various groups such as the National Association of Housing and Redevelopment Officials, which made perhaps the most sweeping proposal: do away with the jungle of existing federal housing subsidy programs and replace it with a "single subsidy mechanism" that would apply to all rental, private, and cooperative housing built with federal aid.

Under this approach, any family certified as unable to afford decent housing in the private market would be eligible for federally subsidized housing. The difference between the total cost of building, operating, and maintaining such housing and the rent or purchase payments from the families living in it would be made up by the federal government. Sponsors could include limited-profit and nonprofit private organizations, local public authorities, and regional or state agencies. Their basic financing could come from government-insured mortgages obtained at market interest rates from savings institutions and other traditional mortgage sources; from bonds issued by the local public authorities, and from any other state and local mortgage programs. Full real estate taxes would be paid on the housing, so that local governments would not be deprived of badly needed revenues by its presence, and the families in each development would have a relatively broad range of incomes.

Perhaps the most controversial and far reaching element of the association's proposal was that if, after two years, the Secretary of Housing and Urban Development "determines that there are any areas of the country where a substantial number of families require housing assistance and no agency or sponsor is providing such assistance, he may act as sponsor, or designate a sponsor to develop housing to meet this need."

This suggestion—that the federal government move in *directly* to put up desperately needed housing if nobody else will—arouses bitter contention throughout the country. But the fact is that it may be the only solution if the United States is to make a reality, in the foreseeable future, of the goal of a decent home and suitable living environment for every American family. As the President's Committee on Urban Housing—the majority of whose members, it should be recalled, were executives from the corporate and financial worlds—declared in 1968, if reliance on existing government subsidy programs and fuller participation in them by the private sector should prove unwarranted, "we would then foresee the necessity for massive federal intervention with the federal government becoming the nation's houser of last resort."

9. The Future and the Crisis

At this point in a book such as this, it is common for the author to express optimism that, however great the failures of the past, and however vast and complex the difficulties of the present, there is nevertheless hope for the future because the American people have what it takes to wipe out past failures and overcome present difficulties. The President's Committee on Urban Housing presented a typical example of such optimism when, after examining the massive extent of the nation's housing problems, it declared, "The committee believes that our nation possesses not only the financial and total resources but also the determination and ingenuity to respond to its housing challenges once the problems are fully understood and the national commitment is clearly made."

Certainly one wants to share such confidence. After all, this is America, and, as I was taught in school, when problems have loomed, Americans have always risen to the occasion. But in the early 1970's it is difficult to nurture such confidence. More and more, the kind of reaffirmation of faith expressed by the Kaiser committee sounds like a coach's pregame pep talk to a college football squad that has been drubbed in every outing so far, not because it lacks the muscle or speed for game-winning plays but because most of the players simply don't give a damn about winning to begin with, and are so rent with dissension that there is no spirit for teamwork in any case.

In short, there is no question that the United States possesses "the financial and total resources" to provide a decent home and a suitable living environment for every American family. There is certainly no question that it has the "ingenuity" to do so. But there is grave doubt, at least in my mind, that it has the *determination of spirit* to do so. For in the end the housing ills of present-day America are largely ills of the national spirit, and all the resources and ingenuity in the world cannot effect a cure for housing—if, indeed, they can even be sufficiently applied—while this illness of spirit persists. And it is persisting, ever more strongly, in the virus of indifference combined with the cancer of racial hostility and fear.

Indifference to the plight of the miserably housed predominates among comfortable Americans. "The plight of the urban poor, the anger of the rebellious, and the bankruptcy of the municipal treasury have not yet hurt or even seriously inconvenienced the vast majority of Americans," the sociologist Herbert Gans has observed. Jason Nathan, New York City's former housing and development administrator, declared in late 1969, shortly after a hurricane had smashed its way into the headlines:

> When a Hurricane Camille strikes and leaves 4,000 or 5,000 families without homes, the nation's attention is galvanized. The federal government responds with crisis aid, declarations of emergency are issued, the National Guard is thrown into action. The calamity calls forth emergency responses of all sorts. Yet in our cities a thousand times that number of families are ill-housed, virtually homeless. But because they are the victims of a slow, creeping process rather than a sudden catastrophe, we as a nation are neither excited nor galvanized into action, even though the emergency, the crisis, the disaster is more real than ten Camilles.

Except for the omission of the plight of rural slum dwellers—just as fully neglected, if not more so, because the slums of the countryside have been quieter than those of the cities—these statements sum up the predominant attitude of America's majority today.

As a result of this attitude, there is a widespread reluctance in Middle America to spend the money that must be spent, and to invest the national resources that must be invested, if a truly full-scale assault is to be mounted against the squalor that blights the nation's great cities and its countryside. Part of this reluctance is certainly understandable. A sizable portion of America's middle class, and especially its lower middle class, is caught in a vicious squeeze between spiraling inflation and soaring taxes, which most emphatically do take a heavy toll of the paycheck brought home from factory and office. But programs to feed the poverty-stricken and provide decent shelter for the miserably housed are not responsible for this squeeze, for these programs are, and always have been, but a minuscule part of national expenditures. The villains, if we are to think in terms of villains, are elsewhere—in the budget-bloated Pentagon; in the headquarters of the wealthy agricultural enterprises, which become even wealthier on public bonuses received for keeping their tracts cropless; in the ranks of the lobbyists for such extravagant ventures as a supersonic airplane that, had Congress not finally come to its senses in 1971, already nearly a billion dollars too late, would have soaked up additional billions of public funds so that a small minority of Americans could get to foreign cities a few hours sooner.

But part of the reluctance to spend meaningfully for such needs as low-rent housing and slum clearance extends beyond the squeeze of inflation and taxes. Many middle-class and affluent Americans simply regard such spending as an undeserved handout.

There is more than a little irony in this attitude. Although their members are usually the last to acknowledge it, America's middle and affluent classes have themselves, over all, been the beneficiaries of a vast amount of subsidies from the public treasury, which have played an incalculable role in developing and strengthening much of Middle American society. What, after all, but public subsidies built the roads and highways that made possible the post-World War II suburban explosion—kindled also, as we have seen, by the federal government's mortgage-backing policies? And what, if not a subsidy, are we to call the very sizable income tax deduction that homeowners are permitted for their mortgage interest and property tax payments—a subsidy whose main beneficiaries are the middle class and the well-to-do, and which, again, has been a major factor in the development of suburbia?

Once, in a moment of especially keen frustration, George Romney threw out the thought that "maybe we ought to repeal part of the right to deduct the interest rate from the income tax return to bring home to middle-income and affluent families that they are getting a housing subsidy. Maybe that [money] ought to be earmarked to meet the problems of the slums." (Romney's public relations man hastened to explain that "he just tossed this out as an idea—it is not an administration position.")

Maybe indeed, but not likely. For the predominant thoughts of middle-class and affluent America today are reflected in the predominant thinking of public officials at all levels. And, whatever the sense of urgency felt by some office-holders over such shortcomings of American life as slums and miserable housing, this sense still remains the exception rather than the rule. One need not be a left-wing malcontent to perceive this. Louis Barba, then president of the very Middle-America-respectable National Association of Home Builders, observed as 1970 was drawing to a close: "The nation's involvement in the achievement of the housing goals established by the Congress in 1968 is less than total. . . . Establishment of these goals by the Congress and the acceptance of them by two administrations is insufficiently felt at all levels of government."

And, of course, whether the Nixon Administration has *really* accepted these goals as being of topmost priority is itself uncertain, inasmuch as the commitment of its housing agency under George Romney and the commitment of its White House brain trust are not necessarily identical.

Complicating all of these elements is the race issue. Perhaps one of the most tragic contributions of the poison of racial antagonism and fear is its distorting effect on the perception of what a truly adequate campaign to wipe out the nation's housing deficiencies would signify. For many middle-class white Americans, slum-clearance and low-cost-housing programs are largely programs for blacks, and any expansion of these programs means giving "them" more. But, as we have seen, there are more whites in substandard housing than blacks, and more whites unable to afford decent housing on their own than blacks, and any program truly mounted to provide a decent home and a suitable living environment for every American family cannot possibly be referred to with justification as a "black" program.

But so the matter is perceived among a large segment of Middle America, and so it will continue to be perceived for a long time to come. And this fact, if no other, makes it difficult to hope for a national effort vast enough not only to make a reality of the goals of the 1968 Housing Act, but also to wipe out the much greater deficits in American housing that these goals, as we have seen, severely understate.

One would like to be proved wrong in this discouragement. But from the vantage point of the early 1970's, the vision of an America acting to provide a decent home and a suitable living environment for all its citizens, or even making significant strides toward redeeming this already two-decades-old pledge, seems at times as realistic as the hope of a palace-studded Camelot suddenly arising out of the squalor and decay of Brownsville in Brooklyn.

Which is where this study in national failure began more than 230 pages ago.

Reference Notes

Chapter 1: Introduction to the Crisis

16 *two major governmental reports: Building the American City: Report of the National Commission on Urban Problems to the Congress and to the President of the United States* (Douglas Report), and *A Decent Home: The Report of the President's Committee on Urban Housing* (including staff studies) (Kaiser report). All references are to the editions published by the U.S. Government Printing Office.

20 *subnormal by any decent standard:* Edith Elmer Wood, *Recent Trends in American Housing* (New York, 1931), p. 9.

Chapter 2: Local Government and the Crisis

25 *One government-sponsored study:* Dick Netzer, *Impact of the Property Tax: Effect on Housing, Urban Land Use, Local Government Finance: Prepared for the Consideration of the National Commission on Urban Problems,* Research Report No. 1, (Washington, 1968), pp. 9, 11, 14, 16, 17.

25 *One researcher: ibid.,* pp. 22, 25. Emphasis added.

29 *3,800 were in effect:* Douglas report, p. 256.

30 *"many codes were either written:* Kaiser report, p. 178.

30 *fifty-two largest cities:* Douglas report, pp. 258, 260.

32 *highly informative survey: ibid.,* p. 262.

41 *some 5.7 million suburbanites:* Mollie Orshansky, "Counting the Poor: Before and After Federal Income-Support Programs," cited in Douglas report, pp. 50, 51.

41 *"suburban slum-ghetto":* from a study by Urban America, Inc., and the Urban Coalition, quoted in *The New York Times,* Feb. 28, 1969, p. 20.
42 *only 20 per cent of the poor:* Orshansky, *loc. cit.*
42 *nonwhites were forming:* Kaiser report, p. 40: Douglas report, p. 43.
47 *Of the nearly 10,000:* Douglas report, pp. 208-9, Tables 1 and 2.
48 *" In many suburban jurisdictions: ibid.,* p. 215.
49 *In the words of the President's Committee:* Kaiser report, p. 140.
49 *Department of Labor:* quoted in *American Builder,* November, 1968, p. 47.
53 *According to one observer:* Jerry M. Flint, *The New York Times,* July 29, 1970, p. 27.
53 *Romney's statement . . . to a Senate committee:* cited in *The New York Times,* August 27, 1970, p. 29.
55 *one journalistic observer:* John Herbers, *The New York Times,* December 4, 1969, p. 49.
55 *President Nixon finally spoke: The New York Times,* December 11, 1970, p. 32, and February 18, 1971, p. 14.
56 *the American Jewish Committee noted:* Judith Magidson Herman, *Housing for the Other America: A Fifty-State Strategy* (Report of the American Jewish Committee, New York, 1969), p. 7.

Chapter 3: WASHINGTON AND THE CRISIS—I

61 *"woefully inadequate scale:* Kaiser report, p. 11.
61 *need of 11 million units:* Douglas report, pp. 73–74.
62 *"government action . . . has destroyed: ibid.,* p. 67. Emphasis added.
63 *scholar of the American housing scene:* Wood, *Recent Trends in American Housing,* pp. 12–19.
64 *"definitely subnormal: ibid.,* p. 9.
65 *Massachusetts Homestead Commission:* quoted in Edith Elmer Wood, *The Housing of the Unskilled Wage Earner* (New York, 1919), p. 19.
68 *Nolan, a Washington political commentator: The Reporter,* December 28, 1967, pp. 16–21.
70 *"until 1948 . . . the covenants.":* Douglas report, pp. 100–101.
72 *According to the President's Committee:* Kaiser report, p. 98.
74 *Department of Housing and Urban Development reported:* Douglas report, p. 131.
81 *land costs are high: ibid.,* p. 123.
82 *Albert Walsh . . . of the New York Housing Authority:* quoted in *Journal of Housing,* No. 2, 1969, p. 65.
83 *To quote the Douglas Commission:* Douglas report, p. 116.
85 *figures cited by the National Commission: ibid.,* p. 100, 104.

Chapter 4: WASHINGTON AND THE CRISIS—II

88 *Douglas commission noted in presenting these figures:* Douglas report, p. 163.

90 *In the fifty-one largest cities: ibid.,* p. 85.

90 *study . . . by Harry Reynolds, Jr.:* cited in *The New York Times,* January 10, 1965, Section 8, pp. 1, 6.

90– *Chester Hartman . . . wrote:* cited in *The New York Times,* January
91 10, 1965, Section 8, p. 6.

91 *Over all, the National Commission:* Douglas report, pp. 90, 167.

97 *As the President's Committee:* Kaiser report, p. 17.

98 *"Complexities and bottlenecks:* Douglas report, p. 148.

100 *"to mollify congressional pressures:* Kaiser report, p. 64.

101 *"testimony before our commission:* Douglas report, pp. 150–151.

104 *"just another . . . pork barrel:* Ruth Cheney, "Model Cities: Magic Pork Barrel," *New York Advocate,* December, 1968, p. 5.

105 *words of one economist:* Edwin P. Reubens, Letter to the Editor ("Model Cities in Peril"), *The New York Times,* April 20, 1969, Section 4, p. 13.

109 *Only 621 of the houses:* Byron Fielding, "Home Ownership for Low-Income Families May Be on the Way as Result of New Federal Aids," *The Journal of Housing,* No. 6, 1969, p. 282.

110 *difference in rents that can result:* Kaiser report, p. 63.

112– *In the 1966 fiscal year:* National Science Foundation figures, quoted in
13 Kaiser report, p. 195.

113 *But, as the President's Committee: ibid.,* p. 197.

116 *"The 1967 report:* Eugene Gulledge, in *Journal of Homebuilding,* August, 1969, p. 2.

120 *as the National Commission . . . summed up:* Douglas report, p. 403.

120 *"In the case of slum properties:* Richard Slitor, *The Federal Income Tax in Relation to Housing: Prepared for the Consideration of the National Commission on Urban Problems,* Research Report No. 5 (Washington, 1968), pp. 105–6.

121 *One estimate: ibid.,* p. 27. Slitor was citing an estimate by Richard Goode in *The Individual Income Tax* (Washington, 1965), p. 122.

125 *Among these questions:* Alexander A. Kolben, *Enforcing Open Houseing: An Evaluation of Recent Legislation and Decisions* (New York, 1969), pp. 10–12.

127 *the President's Committee . . . reported:* Kaiser report, p. 9. Emphasis in original.

Chapter 5: THE STATES AND THE CRISIS

132 *National Commission . . . stated:* Douglas report, p. 191.

137 *"first modern housing law":* Frank Grad, *Legal Remedies for Housing Code Violations: Prepared for the Consideration of the National Commission on Urban Problems,* Research Report No. 14 (Washington, 1968), p. 40.

142 *"state government has moved into the mainstream:* James L. Martin, assistant director of the Washington offices of the Council of State Governments and the National Governors' Conference, *The Book of the States, 1970-71* (Lexington, Ky.) p. 449.

145 *"This singular event: Journal of Housing,* No. 2, 1969, p. 74.

Chapter 6: BUSINESS AND LABOR AND THE CRISIS

152 *HUD reported:* in *HUD Challenge,* March–April, 1970, p. 6.
152 *President's Committee . . . found:* Kaiser report, p. 10.
156 *one government survey noted:* Douglas report, p. 433.
158 *As President's Committee . . . put it:* Kaiser report, p. 182.
159 *percentage breakdown: ibid.,* p. 118.
161 *Thus, the National Commission:* Douglas report, p. 182.
161 *"two-year jump:* in *HUD Challenge,* July–August, 1970, p. 6.
164 *basically the same conclusion:* Douglas report, p. 474; Kaiser report, p. 169.
165 *"While there are honest differences:* Douglas report, p. 467.
166 *Institute for Public Administration:* quoted in *City,* November–December, 1968, p. 35.
171 *according to one critic:* Ada Louise Huxtable, in *The New York Times,* February 28, 1970, Section 2, p. 1.
172 *words of Robert Borg:* writing in *The New York Times,* November 30, 1969, Section 8, p. 1.
172 *another expert put it:* Guy G. Rothenstein, "Slice High-Rise Costs Through Systems Building, Says Expert," *Apartment Construction News,* May, 1969, p. 102.
174 *"Evaluating the cost savings:* Douglas report, p. 445.
174 *"It is not wholly evident:* Kaiser report, pp. 212–13.
174 *comments . . . by Gunnar Myrdal:* from *The Journal of Housing,* quoted in *ibid.,* p. 212.
175 *"most Soviet housing:* Kaiser report, p. 213.
179 *"the crux of the housing problem:* Wood, *Recent Trends in American Housing,* p. 1.
179 *President's Committee . . . concluded:* Kaiser report, p. 3.

Chapter 7: IGNORANCE AND THE CRISIS

185 *The National Commission . . . complained:* Douglas report, p. 68.
185 *"No one who has:* Frank Kristof, *Urban Housing Needs Through the 1980's: An Analysis and Projection: Prepared for the Consideration of the National Commission on Urban Problems,* Research Report No. 10 (Washington, 1968), p. 88.
185 *"with no particular experience:* United States Bureau of the Census, *Measuring the Quality of Housing: An Appraisal of Census Statistics and Methods,* Working Paper No. 25 (Washington, 1967), p. 24.
186 *"For most units: ibid.,* p. 23.
186 *The bureau made the following points: ibid.,* pp. 5, 11, 19.
187 *the three categories:* from the enumerator instruction booklet on rating housing used by the Census Bureau in 1960.
189 *"measured only the physical condition:* Bureau of the Census, *Measuring the Quality of Housing,* p. 1.
190 *"significantly less reliable: ibid.,* pp. 31–34.
191 *The commission concluded:* Douglas report, pp. 68, 301–2.
191 *"This, too:* Ben J. Wattenberg, in collaboration with Richard M. Scammon (Director, U.S. Bureau of the Census, 1961–65), *This U.S.A.: An*

Unexpected Family Portrait of 194,067,296 Americans Drawn from the Census (Garden City, N.Y., 1965), p. 242.

191 *"use of the:* Bureau of the Census, *Measuring the Quality of Housing,* p. 5.

192 *"tempest in a teapot":* Kristof, *Urban Housing Needs,* p. 90.

192 *"the single most important:* Bureau of the Census, *Measuring the Quality of Housing,* p. 13.

193 *Census Bureau warns: ibid.,* p. 6.

194 *President's Committee . . . has projected:* Kaiser report, pp. 8, 39–40, 43–44.

195 *definition . . . was "fairly restricted: ibid.,* p. 100.

195 *National Commission . . . estimate:* Douglas report, pp. 73–74.

198 *A joint report:* cited in *The New York Times,* February 3, 1970, p. 15.

198 *By way of illustration:* Kaiser report, pp. 8, 42.

198 *"The over-all quality:* Frank G. Mittelbach, "Understanding of Mexican-Americans Is Important to City Rebuilding, Particularly in Southwest," *Journal of Housing,* June, 1969, p. 296.

199 *betterment group Urban America said:* "Housing Mexican-Americans," *City Chronicle,* July, 1969, back page.

199 *On the Blackfoot reservation:* Steven V. Roberts, *The New York Times,* May 6, 1969, p. 49.

200 *Oglala Sioux preserve:* Robert G. Sherrill, "The Lagoon of Excrement," *The Nation,* November 10, 1969, pp. 500–503.

200 *A Consultant to the President's Committee:* Kaiser report, p. 41.

200 *extensive body of literature:* see, for example, *Housing-Health Relationships: An Annotated Bibliography,* Council of Planning Librarians, Exchange Bibliography 82 (Monticello, Illinois, May, 1969).

201 *"essential space requirements: Planning the Home for Occupancy* (Chicago: Public Administration Service, 1950), p. 36.

203 *President's Committee . . . summed up:* Kaiser report, p. 45.

Chapter 8: THE EXPERTS AND THE CRISIS

207 *adherents of this position: American Builder,* November, 1968, p. 41.

211 *"Philosophically and socially:* Eugene Morris, in *Real Estate Reporter,* June 30, 1969.

219 *President's Committee . . . recommended:* Kaiser report, p. 14.

219 *National Commission . . . concluded:* Douglas report, p. 59.

221 *The commission noted: ibid.,* pp. 404–5.

225 *"Local government is characteristically:* Arthur Schlesinger, Jr., in *The New York Times,* January 30, 1971, p. 27.

227 *As the President's Committee . . . declared:* Kaiser report, p. 5.

Chapter 9: THE FUTURE AND THE CRISIS

228 *President's Committee . . . presented:* Kaiser report, p. 5.

229 *"The plight of the urban poor:* Herbert Gans, writing in *The New York Times Magazine,* August 3, 1969.

231 *"The nation's involvement:* Louis Barba, in *Journal of Homebuilding,* December, 1970, p. 6.

Bibliography

This does not purport to be an inclusive, or even a representative, listing of the works dealing with housing in America. Rather, it is a list of the books, government reports, and periodicals used in writing this book, along with some additional ones that would be of interest to those seeking an understanding of the state of American housing.

Books and Government Reports

ABRAMS, CHARLES. *Forbidden Neighbors.* New York: Harper & Bros., 1955.

———. *Man's Struggle for Shelter in an Urbanizing World.* Cambridge, Mass.: The MIT Press, 1964.

American Public Health Association, Committee on the Hygiene of Housing. *Basic Principles of Healthful Housing,* 2d ed. New York, 1961.

———. *Planning the Home for Occupancy.* Chicago, 1950.

BANFIELD, EDWARD C., and MORTON GRODZINS. *Government and Housing in Metropolitan Areas.* New York: McGraw-Hill, 1958.

CANTY, DONALD, ed. *The New City.* New York: Praeger Publishers, 1969.

DOUGLAS, PAUL, *et al. Building the American City: Report of National Commission on Urban Problems to the Congress and to the President of the United States.* Washington, D.C.: Government Printing Office, 1968.

DRURY, MARGARET J. *Mobile Homes: The Unrecognized Revolution in American Housing.* Ithaca, N.Y.: Department of Housing and Design, New York State College of Home Economics, Cornell University, 1967.

FALTERMAYER, EDWARD K. *Redoing America: A Nationwide Report on How to Make Our Cities and Suburbs Livable.* New York: Harper & Row, 1968.

FISHER, ROBERT MOORE. *20 Years of Public Housing.* New York: Harper & Bros., 1959.

FORD, JAMES, *et al. Slums and Housing.* Cambridge, Mass.: Harvard University Press, 1936.

FRIEDMAN, LAWRENCE *M. Government and Slum Housing:A Century of Frustration.* Chicago: Rand McNally & Co., 1968.

GENUNG, GEORGE R., JR. *Taxes, Housing and Urban Renewal.* Washington, D.C.: National Association of Housing and Redevelopment Officials, 1969.

GLAZER, NATHAN, and DAVIS MCENTIRE, eds. *Studies in Housing and Minority Groups.* Berkeley and Los Angeles: University of California Press, 1960.

HELPER, ROSE. *Racial Policies and Practices of Real Estate Brokers.* Minneapolis: University of Minnesota Press, 1969.

HUNTER, DAVID R. *The Slums: Challenge and Response.* New York: The Free Press, 1964.

KAISER, EDGAR, *et al. A Decent Home: The Report of the President's Committee on Urban Housing.* Washington, D.C.: Government Printing Office, 1969.

KEITH, NATHANIEL. *Housing America's Low- and Moderate-Income Families: Prepared for the Consideration of the National Commission on Urban Problems,* Research Report No. 7. Washington, D.C.: Government Printing Office, 1968.

KOLBEN, ALEXANDER *A. Enforcing Open Housing: An Evaluation of Recent Legislation and Decisions.* New York: The New York Urban League, 1969.

KRISTOF, FRANK S. *Urban Housing Needs Through the 1980's: An Analysis and Projection: Prepared for the Consideration of the National Commission on Urban Problems,* Research Report No. 10. Washington, D.C.: Government Printing Office, 1968.

LINDBLOOM, CARL G., and MORTON FARRAH. *The Citizen's Guide to Urban Renewal.* West Trenton, N.J.: Chandler-Davis Publishing Company, 1968.

MERMIN, ALVIN A. *Relocating Families: The New Haven Experience, 1956–1966.* Washington, D.C.: National Association of Housing and Redevelopment Officials, 1970.

NICHOLSON, JOHN, *et al.*, eds. *Housing a Nation.* Washington, D.C.: Congressional Quarterly Service, 1966.

NIXON, RICHARD M. *Message From the President of the United States Transmitting the Second Annual Report on National Housing Goals.* Washington, D.C.: Government Printing Office, 1970.

OSBORN, FREDERIC J., and ARNOLD WHITTICK. *The New Towns: The Answer to Megalopolis.* Cambridge, Mass.: The MIT Press, 1970.

RIIS, JACOB. *How the Other Half Lives: Studies Among the Tenements of New York.* New York: Charles Scribner's Sons, 1891.

SLITOR, RICHARD E. *The Federal Income Tax in Relation to Housing: Prepared for the Consideration of the National Commission on*

Urban Problems, Research Report No. 5. Washington, D.C.: Government Printing Office, 1968.

SPIEGEL, HANS B. C., ed. *Citizen Participation in Urban Renewal,* Volume I: *Concepts and Issues.* Washington, D.C.: NTL Institute for Applied Behavioral Science, 1968.

STARR, ROGER. *The Living End.* New York: Coward-McCann, 1966.

STERNLEIB, GEORGE. *The Tenement Landlord.* New Brunswick, N.J.: Rutgers University Press, 1969.

U.S. Bureau of the Census. *Measuring the Quality of Housing: An Appraisal of Census Statistics and Methods,* Working Paper No. 25. Washington, D.C.: Government Printing Office, 1967.

Urban Coalition. *Guide to Federal Low- and Moderate-Income Housing and Community Development Programs.* Washington, D.C., 1968.

WEAVER, ROBERT. *Dilemmas of Urban America.* Cambridge, Mass.: Harvard University Press, 1965.

WENDT, PAUL F. *Housing Policy—The Search for Solutions.* Berkeley and Los Angeles: University of California Press, 1962.

WHEATON, WILLIAM, *et al. Urban Housing.* New York: The Free Press, 1966.

WOOD, EDITH ELMER. *The Housing of the Unskilled Wage Earner.* New York: The Macmillan Company, 1919.

———. *Recent Trends in American Housing.* New York: The Macmillan Company, 1931.

PERIODICALS

American Builder (Brookfield, Wisconsin, monthly—through 1968).

Apartment Construction News (New York, monthly).

Architectual Forum (New York, monthly).

Architectual Record (New York, monthly).

City (Washington, D.C., bimonthly—publication of The National Urban Coalition).

HUD Challenge (Washington, D.C., monthly—official magazine of the U.S. Department of Housing and Urban Development).

Journal of Homebuilding (Washington, D.C., monthly—publication of the National Association of Home Builders of the United States).

Journal of Housing (Washington, D.C., monthly—publication of the National Association of Housing and Redevelopment Officials).

National Civic Review (New York, monthly—publication of the National Municipal League).

Nation's Cities (Washington, D.C., monthly—publication of the National League of Cities).

Real Estate Forum (New York, monthly).

Index

Some other books published by Penguin are described on the following pages.

Benjamin DeMott

SURVIVING THE 70'S

A survival manual for the 1970's by one of America's top social critics. In these pages Benjamin DeMott considers the liberated woman, the college dropout, the "ecological summons," the new sexuality, and various other patterns of thought and action that characterize the contemporary scene. He asks: "How can a human being cope with the tilts of assumption and belief now occurring regularly in all corners of the culture? . . . What kinds of order can a mind work out for itself?" In answering such questions, *Surviving the 70's* looks not only at the mixed nature of experience today but also at the opportunities that lie beyond.

Leonard Downie, Jr.

JUSTICE DENIED
The Case for Reform of the Courts

An indictment of the American court system. This broadly informed, thoroughly documented report shows that speedy trial does not exist—except in assembly-line travesties; that court fees shut many poor people out entirely; and that the courts' interpretation of the law often gives those with economic power privileges not enjoyed by debtors, tenants, or consumers. Leonard Downie, Jr., traveled thousands of miles and visited scores of courtrooms in his search for the truth about the failings of the courts and about the possibilities of reform. His book is essential reading for all who want to see justice done in America. As an investigative reporter for the *Washington Post*, Leonard Downie, Jr., wrote a series of articles now credited with having led to important court reforms.

Harry W. Richardson

URBAN ECONOMICS

A look at the problems of how to locate urban resources efficiently and to maintain the quality of life in the cities. The author believes such questions to be among the most serious facing society for the rest of this century. In these pages he carefully examines key economic issues within the single city, including location decisions, urban rent and land values, urban growth, transportation, fiscal problems, urban renewal, the environment, and planning. Throughout, he stresses the theoretical principles of urban economics and goes on to underline them with pertinent empirical observations. Harry W. Richardson is Director of the Center for Research in the Social Sciences at the University of Kent.